ADVANCE PRAISE

"Why and how people select their intimate partners is a historical mystery. Even more mysterious is why, when the relationship fails, intimate partners select an almost identical partner and replay the same drama, especially when it involves emotional and physical abuse. In his first book on the subject, Ross illuminated the universal attractive force of lovers. In this second one, he opens the dark side of romantic attraction to the light of analysis and offers the tragic narcissist/codependent lovers a well-lighted path to understanding and healthy relating."

—Harville Hendrix, PhD, and Helen LaKelly Hunt, PhD, are the authors of several *New York Times* best-selling books, including *Getting the Love You Want* and *Receiving Love.*

"Ross Rosenberg's newest book will treat the reader to an invaluable body of knowledge and experience, one that thoughtfully expresses key conceptual and personal insights, along with a treasure trove of useful tools and tips. Ross generously contributes a well-crafted and relevant resource for healing from the aftermath of dealing with one of the most challenging personality types in relationships; demonstrating a means for transforming painful lifelong patterns into meaningfully healthy ones."

—Wendy T. Behary is the best-selling author of *Disarming the Narcissist,* founder and clinical director of the Cognitive Therapy Center, and a faculty member at the Cognitive Therapy Center and Schema Therapy Institute of New York.

"Thank goodness for Ross Rosenberg. In this new edition of his popular book, *The Human Magnet Syndrome,* he has identified a previously unnamed factor that makes a significant portion of the population vulnerable to entering into potentially damaging relationships. Ross not only identifies and names the Human Magnet Syndrome, he also describes it in a personal, colorful, engaging way, sharing much of his own personal story to bring it to life.

A master of the metaphor, Ross not only redefines codependency, he also explains it in ways that are meaningful and useful to readers. Each chapter ends with insightful questions to help the reader think about him or herself, their childhood and current life.

Ross does not blame narcissistic people, or paint the codependent person as a victim. Instead, he describes the complicated "dance" between them, and explains that each needs the other for completeness.

The first edition of *The Human Magnet Syndrome* has been in the waiting room of my psychotherapy practice for years. I can't wait to offer the new edition to my clients, friends and colleagues as a resource for understanding and healing."

—**Jonice Webb, PhD,** is a licensed psychologist, blogger, and best-selling author of two books, *Running on Empty No More: Transform your Relationships* and *Running on Empty: Overcome Your Childhood Emotional Neglect.*

"Ross is a highly skilled psychotherapist who clearly understands the codependent and narcissistic dynamic. When I was first diagnosed with codependency, I was incredibly confused and all I wanted to understand was how my childhood had helped create the attraction I felt towards narcissistic others. *The Human Magnet Syndrome* was one of those pieces of work that helped my mind clearly comprehend how my childhood experiences had conditioned me to believe I was not enough and laid the groundwork for becoming a codependent person. His latest piece of work is even more concise, informative, and comprehensive. If you are struggling with codependency and, like me, would like to understand how your past has created your current experiences, this book will be of great value to you. If you are a mental health professional who wishes to understand the clients you serve in a whole new way, this book will serve as a great resource. Congratulations, Ross, on your current labor of love."

—**Lisa A. Romano** is a YouTube™ self-help sensation, Certified Life Coach, and best-selling author of six books, including the best-selling *The Road Back to Me.*

"Thanks to Ross Rosenberg's latest Human Magnet Syndrome work, more and more people can discover how childhood attachment trauma is responsible for an adult's alienation from self, others and the world. Ross is an absolute pioneer in the field and many people will find in his work a much longed-for understanding of their unanswered question: why do I keep holding on to this relationship that is hurting me so much? And even more importantly, Ross shows how to start healing from these old wounds, so we can create healthier bonds in which giving and taking are more in balance. A must read for any therapist, counselor, health care professional or anyone caught in the prison of a toxic relationship."

—**Ingeborg Bosch** is a best-selling author and internationally renowned trainer, psychotherapist, and consultant; creator of the Past Reality Integration (PRI) psychotherapy method; and best-selling author of five books, including her latest, *Our Love.*

THE
HUMAN MAGNET
SYNDROME

THE
HUMAN
Magnet
SYNDROME

THE CODEPENDENT
NARCISSIST TRAP

ROSS ROSENBERG
M.Ed., LCPC, CADC, CSAT

NEW YORK

LONDON • NASHVILLE • MELBOURNE • VANCOUVER

THE HUMAN MAGNET SYNDROME

The Codependent Narcissist Trap

© 2019 Ross Rosenberg

Published in New York, New York, by Morgan James Publishing. Morgan James is a trademark of Morgan James, LLC. www.MorganJamesPublishing.com

The Morgan James Speakers Group can bring authors to your live event. For more information or to book an event visit The Morgan James Speakers Group at www.TheMorganJamesSpeakersGroup.com.

The Codependency Cure, Self-Love Recovery, Self-Love Deficit Disorder, and Self-Love Recovery Institute are registered trademarks of Ross Rosenberg at 3325 Arlington Heights Rd., Ste 400B, Arlington Heights, IL 60004.

Ross Rosenberg's educational and personal development products are available at Self-Love Recovery Institute. www.SelfLoveRecovery.com

To protect their privacy, some of the names of people, places, and institutions have been changed.

ISBN 9781683508670 paperback
ISBN 9780683508687 e-book
Library of Congress Control Number: 2017918364

Cover and Interior Design by:
Marisa Jackson

Development and Content Editing:
Corrine Casanova

Copy Editing:
Karla Crawford and
Korrel Crawford Rosenberg

In an effort to support local communities, raise awareness and funds, Morgan James Publishing donates a percentage of all book sales for the life of each book to Habitat for Humanity Peninsula and Greater Williamsburg.

Get involved today! Visit
www.MorganJamesBuilds.com

DEDICATION

I dedicate this book to my wife, Korrel Crawford Rosenberg, the partner of my dreams. Korrel has loved me more fiercely than anyone has ever loved me in my life—and has done so without wavering one bit. Her love has emboldened me to fearlessly discover who I really am, to keep learning from my mistakes, and to evolve into the person I believe I was always meant to be. By supporting me and allowing me to chase my dreams, she has ultimately sacrificed some of her own. For this and more, I will always be indebted to her. Because of her, I can claim to know true and lasting love and what it is like to be married to a best friend, companion, and lover. Korrel, my love, I could not be more grateful for you.

I also dedicate this book to my only child, Benjamin Rosenberg, whose very existence has imbued me with a sense of wonder, calm, and understanding of perfection. His fiery, independent spirit and self-confidence have taught me that a parent's problems do not have to be their child's curse. Ben's purity of heart, unconditional love of others, and inspiring ideals remind me that being a good father is not measured entirely by what you do or how you do it, but who your child becomes on their own.

This is dedicated to my sister-in-law, Karla Crawford, whose love, respect, and care I cherish. Getting to know her, learning of her own passions and struggles, and witnessing her fight for survival reminds me of the preciousness of this fleeting life and the mandate to live it with an unwavering sense of purpose, awe, and appreciation.

I once again dedicate this to my deceased mother, Mikki Rosenberg. Her spirit of unconditional love and compassion forever lives in my heart and is instilled in every page of this book.

Lastly, I dedicate all my work to anyone desperately trying to end their emotional suffocation, while courageously traveling the twisted and often dangerous path towards Self-Love Abundance (the ultimate codependency recovery goal). My success would mean nothing if it were not for you. You have allowed me to fulfill my teenage dream of making a difference in this world. We are in this together, and I am grateful to you for joining me in my attempt to eradicate codependency (Self-Love Deficit Disorder™), one person at a time.

ACKNOWLEDGMENTS

I owe a great deal of my success to my wife, Korrel Crawford Rosenberg. She has sacrificed herself for years, spending many nights and weekends alone, without complaint, because she believed in and supported my dream, unconditionally. She is always there to bounce ideas off of (many of which ended up in some form in this book), make me laugh when I need a pick-me-up and give me that extra shot of determination with her unwavering love. We live life passionately and to the max—something I don't know if I could do without her. She is, without a doubt, my *soulmate*.

When I first approached my sister-in-law, Karla Crawford, about working together in February 2017, anyone who knew us instantly thought we'd lost our damn minds. The epitome of a brother-sister relationship, we do not always see eye to eye, and neither are afraid to tell the other our opinion. However, we took the plunge and she is now my Director of Operations, my right hand, my sanity keeper and a trusted friend. Whether it be dropping everything on a Saturday to edit a chapter to help me meet a deadline, being all-in at an impromptu brainstorming session or building up my confidence by telling me how great this book is (and she really believes it!), she has become an integral part of both my business and personal life.

My son, Benjamin. What can I say about him? He has turned into the young man I could have only dreamed of, always very supportive and willing to provide his 20-something opinion and feedback. A kind soul with a gentle personality, we've had many great discussions and, even though he no longer lives at home, I feel we have been able to bond in a way that we hadn't before. He has developed into a man I am so proud of.

Linda Crawford, my mother-in-law, always intuitively knows when I need to hear how proud my mom would be if she were alive and how equally proud she is as "my second mom."

Karen Kaplan, fellow-author, and advocate for self-love and healing, is one of my closest friends and confidants. When we met 12 years ago, neither of us imagined we would both write a book about childhood trauma and the importance of healing its wounds. Her book, *Descendants of Rajgród: Learning to Forgive*, was a catalyst for my personal growth and emotional healing.

My good friend, Dave Siegel, changed my world when he introduced me to YouTube. Thanks to him, I have become part of a global community who shares my excitement about Self-Love (codependency) Recovery. He wrote, produced, played and sang the Human Magnet theme song, which is probably one the most thoughtful gifts anyone has ever given me. I am grateful for our friendship.

Melody Beattie, a pioneer in this genre who was kind enough to read (and like!) and endorse my first book, gave me the credibility that I, as a new author, needed. With her sage advice and direction throughout the years, great strides have been made to make the public much more aware of an issue that is critical to our society's future.

My first book publisher, PESI, gave me, a relative unknown, support and guidance along with an opportunity to present my material to a national audience. Their suggestion and willingness to publish my first book opened a door to me that, on my own, would have been much more difficult to accomplish.

I am grateful to Jonice Webb, author of the Running on Empty series, whose friendship and wise advice has been a beacon of light for me. There are few talented authors I know who are just as nice as a person as they are good in their profession. She is the real thing!

Corrine Casanova, sensitive and sincere, has been instrumental in the development and content editing of the revisions to my work. Her guidance in the publishing world, and helping me navigate the twists and turns, made me feel like someone absolutely had my back.

Marisa Jackson put her heart and soul into the design of this book. Her attention to detail, creativity, passion and intensity shows through loud and clear in her work. She is an extremely patient and talented lady, and I am very fortunate to have found her.

I am grateful to my publicist, Christine King (TMG International), whose infectious optimism and excitement for this book makes me believe even the biggest dreams are possible.

Finally, I extend my appreciation to David Hancock and his team at Morgan James Publishing. It has been an absolute pleasure partnering with a company with such amazing integrity and work ethic.

TABLE OF CONTENTS

FOREWORD

The larger patterns at work in our lives can often seem mysterious, purposeless, and even incoherent at times, if not completely undetectable. But given enough time, a magnificent logic often appears in them. The story of how I came to write the foreword for this book is an excellent example of that.

All the way back in 1990, I published my first book, titled *Iron Man Family Outing: Poems about Transition into a More Conscious Manhood*. I had high hopes for the book, but it suffered a series of setbacks at the hands of a disinterested and unscrupulous publisher. Within six months, it was clear to me that I was stuck with 1,500 physical copies of a book for which there seemed to be no interest whatsoever.

Heartbroken and discouraged, I stowed the books away in my closet in the unopened original cartons. I stopped writing for publication, believing there was no interest and no place in the world for what I had to share.

Seventeen years later, I woke up one morning with an idea: What if I gave those books away to people who might have some use for them? But to whom? I decided to search the web for anyone who worked with men, anyone who worked with survivors of childhood abuse, neglect, and trauma, or anyone else who might be interested in the sort of book I'd written. I was determined to get my books in the hands of those who might put them to good use in helping other men heal, which had been my original intent in writing it, and I didn't care if I had to give every last copy away to do it.

Using the results of my searches, I compiled a list of names and addresses and sent a short letter to each person describing my book and offering to provide a complimentary copy for their use. Initially, I sent actual physical letters in actual physical envelopes. I did so for about six months before switching to email. I had neither a website nor any public presence at that time. I was a complete unknown trying to give away a 17-year-old poetry book no one had ever heard of.

Ross Rosenberg was a recipient of one of my letters. I don't recall exactly what I saw in his information that told me "This might be a person who'd be interested in receiving my book," but whatever it was, I was correct. He responded with interest and I sent him a copy. And that is how we met.

In the less than ten years since I met Ross, he has transformed himself from a staff counselor at a practice in Buffalo Grove, Illinois, into an internationally recognized expert on narcissism, codependency, trauma, and sex addiction. He is a best-selling author. He has founded his own counseling center, as well as a training/seminar and professional certification company. He also has a YouTube channel that is hugely popular. In short, he has emerged as a global influencer and thought leader in the very brief time since I first made his acquaintance by sending him a letter offering him a free book in January 2008.

There's a point in sharing all of this, and here it is: We live in a world of wounded people. Many of them don't even know they're wounded or in what ways, or how those wounds influence their thoughts, perceptions, behavior, their very lives. Many of those people also carry the seed within them to heal not only their own wounds, but also to contribute to the healing of the wounds in others as well. Ross is one such person. So am I.

Ross has often told me that reading my book helped open the way for him to write his own book. This book. A most unexpected result of my sending him that letter, to be sure, but one that speaks to the apparently unintentional and often inscrutable magic of those larger patterns I mentioned at the outset.

I thought my work was worthless for almost two decades, but I was wrong. It just wasn't time for it yet. When it came time, I had the great good fortune to cross paths with someone else who was waiting at the threshold for his moment to bust right out and bloom.

You'll never know what benefit might emerge from the good work that can come of healing your own wounds. Sometimes it comes in the form of something, or someone, quite extraordinary that you'd never expect.

Ross, and his work, are quite extraordinary by every definition I have. Enjoy this book, take everything you can from it, apply it as best you can, and move your own healing out into the world in all the ways that are waiting inside you to be engaged.

Rick Belden
Poet/Author/Artist/Men's Coach
Austin, TX

INTRODUCTION

Everything has gone so fast—so very fast! Just six years ago, a prominent U.S. training company, PESI, expressed an interest in my professional training, "Codependents and Narcissists: Understanding the Attraction." Their interest in my original content was flattering, if not downright exciting! Training other psychotherapists, as well as the general public, on material developed from my own codependency recovery discoveries and professional work on the topic, was a dream come true.

As with anything desirable, there was a catch: I would have to present PESI's home-spun pop-psychology training entitled, "Surviving Emotional Manipulators." Despite their belief that it was related to my work, I did not want to associate myself with a program that was based on the non-descript "emotional manipulator" term. It was clear to me that it was chosen more for its marketing and advertising appeal than its clinical merit. As a psychotherapy purist, I struggled with the offer as my ethics compel me to not sugar coat or misrepresent the truth. Even with the company's assurances that it would draw in sizable registrants, I would not agree to be their talking head and sellout my ethics, even for a once in lifetime career advancement opportunity. Moreover, I felt it would be humiliating to put my own brand-new codependent-narcissist training on the back burner to represent something I didn't believe in.

The other disappointing expectation was the requirement to travel at least once a month—giving three back-to-back full-day seminars. Making the decision even

1

more complicated was the fact that I was just six months into a new counseling center I had created/opened in Arlington Heights, Illinois, Clinical Care Consultants,[1] and I was providing psychotherapy services to 30 clients a week.

The intersection of this ethical dilemma and professional opportunity was a frustrating place to be. Thanks to a moment of inspiration and some creative thinking, I convinced PESI to allow me to use my codependent-narcissist training while swapping out my "pathological narcissism" concept for their "emotional manipulation" term. And just like that, our problem was solved: I would present my material without limitations, and they could keep their catchy title. It was a satisfying compromise for both sides!

In the middle of my highly successful 26-state/60-city USA tour, PESI offered me another once in a lifetime opportunity: a book contract. They believed the training could be easily converted into a sure-fire best seller. Regardless of my excitement and appreciation, I was once again facing off over their "emotional manipulator" term. Although I had broadened its meaning to represent actual diagnostic terms, I was against it appearing on the book's cover. The best I could do was agree to use it in the manuscript as I did in the training. Even this requirement wasn't ideal, as I was harboring resentment over its use in the training.

Despite having a signed contract that relinquished my rights to determine the book's title,[2] I maintained my position. Because it was a matter of personal and clinical integrity, I refused to change my stance. As with other dilemmas in my life, I sought my wife's advice. Relieved that she supported my decision to break the contract, despite the potential ramifications, I held firm. The prospect of a lawsuit and the possibility I would not be offered a publishing deal again created a lot of anxiety.

My problems are often worked out as I sleep. History has shown that when I am upset or conflicted about a personal or professional challenge, it is quite common for me to awake the next morning with a clear solution. The morning following the discussion with my wife, in a half-awake state, I heard myself say "*The Human Magnet Syndrome.*" It was a eureka moment that felt heaven sent. Not only was the publisher delighted by this title, but we were able to put aside the tensions surrounding our disagreement and resume our shared excitement.

---

1   Clinical Care Consultants now has two offices in Illinois: one in Arlington Heights and the other in Inverness. More about the company can be found at www.ClinicalCareConsultants.com.

2   A rookie mistake, to be sure. My attorney and I both missed the importance of that clause.

Now is the time to finally rid my work of the ubiquitous emotional manipulator terminology. Pathological Narcissism, my original and more accurate term, has resumed its rightful place in my Human Magnet Syndrome work. It is also the time to broaden my Human Magnet Syndrome and Continuum of Self theories.

All of this represents the culmination of the last five years of thinking about and making discoveries about the Human Magnet Syndrome topics. While this book holds substantial value for helping both professionals and the general reader, it will appeal most to those who want to know more about the Human Magnet Syndrome and how it might impact their life. It is a universal phenomenon transcending culture, ethnicity, political persuasion, language, and many other real and artificial dividing distinctions. For this reason, I couldn't be prouder that it has been translated into Spanish, French, and soon, Czech.

This book will help you understand and accept the painful truth about why you have remained loyal to people who profess their love for you, but who, at the same time, hurt you—over and over again. It will guide you and hopefully help you recognize why you keep falling prey to the same empty promises that never come to fruition, and why your own *happily ever after* is nothing more than a revolving, disappointing delusion. You will also be compelled to admit the unthinkable: you are as much a victim of, as you are at fault for, your dysfunctional relationships.

Since knowledge is power and reading this will teach you what you need to know, expect to feel inspired and excited. This book will become an indispensable resource as you begin to learn why you keep falling in love with someone who, in the beginning, seems virtually perfect and, in an instant, becomes your lover, best friend, and confidant—your soulmate. It will equally help you understand why these *soulmates* eventually take off their masks to reveal their harmful, and sometimes malignant and narcissistic, true selves.

SAME PERSON BUT WITH A DIFFERENT FACE

I have firsthand knowledge of being a codependent participant in the Human Magnet Syndrome. In retrospect, my dysfunctional relationship pattern should have been clear, especially after two failed marriages and countless relationships with harmful narcissists. However, I needed to hit the proverbial rock bottom, which I did in 2003. That's when I had no other choice but to stop riding the insane and alluring relationship roller coaster.

A friend changed my life with one comment, "Every woman you fall in love with is actually the same person but with a different face." This was the wake-up call, the ice-cold shower, which finally opened my eyes. Until I recognized this was my issue and sought treatment for it, I was destined to be involved with the same harmful and disappointing narcissistic women, while never experiencing the love, respect, and care I yearned for.

This deceptively simple but profoundly life-changing message rocked my world. For the first time, I considered that it wasn't bad luck after all but, perhaps, there was something wrong with me. Giving up my victim mentality was a hard pill to swallow. This was when the famous recovery quote, "Insanity is doing the same thing over and over again and expecting different results," finally made sense. I was ready to take responsibility for my actions, reach way down deep, embrace my fears, seize control of my future, and finally stop my relational suicide patterns. I was ready to stop being insane!

I won't lie; it has been a difficult path. Breaking a cycle embedded in the deepest recesses of my psyche took time and a great deal of discomfort and effort. It required me to believe the impossible: despite my shortcomings, I am perfect just the way I am. I couldn't expect others to understand this until I first embraced it myself. Boiling up from a cauldron of fear, shame, and loneliness arose my commitment to stop running away from my pain and the desire to put in the work to resolve it.

I am confident that my 17-year-old self would have laughed at the suggestion that I might grow up and write a book connected to the same issues I first began to understand in 1978. More than that, I would have completely disbelieved the idea that I would write a book that would sell over 50,000 copies, be published in four languages, and be responsible for changing thousands of lives. Moreover, I would not have been able to grasp having a YouTube channel that would amass more than 7 million video views and 75,000 subscribers. *Hey 17-year-old self, we did it! Your idea of wanting to change the world wasn't all that crazy after all!*

INTRODUCING THE HUMAN MAGNET SYNDROME

Since the dawn of civilization, people have been magnetically and irresistibly drawn together into romantic relationships not so much by what they see, feel, and think, but by more invisible forces. When people with healthy emotional backgrounds meet, the irresistible *love force* can create a sustainable, reciprocal, and stable relationship. People in this camp can rightfully boast about their remarkable love-at-first-sight experience and how the spark has endured. However, our stories become quite different when we are raised by abusive, neglectful, or absent parents. For example, when codependents and narcissists meet and become enveloped in a seductive dreamlike state, their relationship often unfolds into a "seesaw" of love, pain, hope, and disappointment.

For people like me whose parents deprived them of unconditional love during their childhood, especially the first five or six years of their life, they will likely be drawn to a narcissistic romantic partner by a magnet-like force from which it will seem impossible to break free. This magnetic force, or what I refer to as the Human Magnet Syndrome, has the raw power to bring codependents and narcissists together in a perfect storm of love and dysfunction. The magnetic power of this dysfunctional love keeps these seemingly opposite lovers together despite their shared misery and fervent hopes of changing each other. For the codependent and narcissistic lovers, the dream of perfect and everlasting love will sadly never come to fruition.

When I was a teenager, my dad unwittingly gave me unforgettable relationship advice. He said, "the *soulmate* of your dreams is going to become the *cellmate* of your nightmares." Although he meant it as a joke, it represented my dad's cynical views on love and relationships. Like other narcissists and codependents, my mom and dad's relationship had a love-at-first-sight foundation. He proposed to my 18-year-old mother after dating for only six months. As perfect as their love seemed, it was nothing more than a fantasy that couldn't be sustained. Like other codependents and narcissists, their "perfect love-cloud" would devolve into a desert sandstorm that would permanently cement their dysfunctional relationship. But only one of them would be encumbered by the "ball and chain" that accompanied the cellmate experience; that would be my codependent mother.

Little did I know I would have firsthand experience with my dad's soulmate/cellmate pronouncement. It seemed each time I fell in love with a woman, it felt natural and perfect. And each time, this "perfect" soulmate would transform into a completely unrecognizable narcissist. As a cellmate I wouldn't—I couldn't—escape the dysfunctional drama; I kept thinking that, with enough patience and hope, my lover could turn back into my original recognizable soulmate. History would prove I was chasing a dream that could never come true. Still, I am grateful for the struggles and emotional pain I experienced. Without that pain, and my need to end it, my Human Magnet Syndrome work would have never been created.

Through a great deal of challenging and difficult personal work, I eventually figured out why I habitually gravitated toward harmful romantic partners. It ultimately came down to how my narcissistic father and codependent mother raised me. I was not alone. I realized other children who were brought up by a pathologically narcissistic parent had similar issues. I also saw how adult relationship patterns, whether healthy or dysfunctional, are affected by the type of parenting a child receives. I learned codependency and pathological narcissism are directly connected to the psychological scarring caused by attachment trauma. Sadly, children of pathologically narcissistic parents are destined to become either codependent or pathologically narcissistic.

I chose this book's title, *The Human Magnet Syndrome*, because it succinctly captures the attraction dynamic of dysfunctional love. When it comes to romantic relationships, we all are indeed human magnets. All of us are compelled to fall in love with a specific personality type that is dichotomously opposite from our own. Like metal magnets, human magnets are attracted to each other when their opposite personalities, or "magnetic relationship poles," are perfectly matched. The bond created by perfectly matched "human magnets" is infinitely powerful, binding two lovers together despite negative consequences or shared unhappiness.

In a relationship between a codependent and a pathological narcissist, this magnetic force will likely create a long-term dysfunctional relationship. Conversely, with healthy romantic partners, the Human Magnet Syndrome results in relationships that are empowering, affirming, and mutually satisfying.

We all have the human desire to be understood, to love and to be loved. This compels us to find a romantic companion. A human *love drive* motivates us to seek a companion who we hope will understand our struggles, validate our pain, affirm our dreams, and, most of all, co-create an explosion of emotional and sexual excitement. We can't help it; we are naturally inclined to look for someone who will spark our deepest romantic desires.

If this book has just one purpose, it would be to give hope to others who, like myself, yearned for "true love" but, instead, kept finding "true dysfunction." Its intent is to become an essential resource to those who crave freedom from their traumatic and emotionally burdensome pasts, as well as to the clinicians who treat them. Perhaps my greatest ambition for writing this book is that it may inspire readers to extricate themselves from their own destructive relationships, while also motivating them to develop a capacity to find and sustain a healthy and mutually satisfying loving romantic relationship.

This book has been written with the intention of helping all who want to understand the Human Magnet Syndrome and its impact on themselves and others. With that in mind, I have ensured that a portion of my most recent work on codependency, Self-Love Deficit Disorder™ (SLDD) and Self-Love Recovery™ (SLR), is introduced in Chapter Twelve. Expect this information and more to be included in my forthcoming book, *The Codependency Cure:™ Recovering from Self-Love Deficit Disorder.*™ [3] If you are looking for additional resources to deepen your knowledge or resolve any questions you may have, my suggestion would be to review my Self-Love Recovery related educational and personal development products and services that are available at my Self-Love Recovery Institute's website. [4]

Shouldn't we all choose to look honestly and courageously at ourselves and seek to understand our entrenched, unconscious motives? Shouldn't we also strive to heal deeply imbedded psychological wounds that, without resolution, will likely block us from ever finding our soulmate? The answer is a resounding YES! Without the resolute willpower and bravery to change our relational path, we will needlessly suffer the plight of unrealized goals, aspirations, and dreams. Let's take that fearless leap together as I share how to discover healthy, affirming, and mutually romantic love while breaking free from destructive and dysfunctional relationship patterns.

---

3   I estimate the book will be published in the middle of 2019.
4   www.SelfLoveRecovery.com

Chapter One

PASSING OF THE DYSFUNCTIONAL BATON

A s much as we would like to, we cannot avoid certain indisputable facts of life: we have to pay taxes, we will get older, we will most likely gain a few pounds, and we will always be connected to our childhood. Sigmund Freud was right; we are, indeed, creatures of our past and affected more by our formative years than by recent events and circumstances. Although genes play a significant role in determining our adult selves, how we were cared for as children is integrally connected to our adult mental health and the quality of our adult relationships. Whether we embrace our unique childhood history, or we try to mute, forget, or even deny it, there is no way of refuting its impact on our lives.

You may have had a childhood that was absent of major trauma, abuse, deprivation, or neglect. As one of the fortunate ones, you would have had parents who made mistakes but who also unconditionally loved and cared for you. Just by being yourself, despite your imperfections, you would have proved to your parents that all babies are perfect, and the gift of life is sacred. Your healthy-but-imperfect parents would have been intrinsically motivated to foster your personal and emotional growth, not because they had to but because they believed you deserved it.

The only requirement to receive your parents' unconditional love and nurturing was to simply be your genuine self. With such nurturing and protection, you would be the next to join your family's multigenerational pattern of emotionally healthy children who would later become a balanced and emotionally healthy adult. If you chose to have children, you would perpetuate the positive parenting "karma" by raising your own emotionally healthy offspring. Unfortunately, this was not my experience.

BECOMING A TROPHY CHILD

The child of psychologically unhealthy parents would also participate in a similar multigenerational pattern, but one that was perpetually dysfunctional. If one of your parents was a pathological narcissist, you would have been born into this world with specific expectations determined by that parent. If you could figure out what these expectations were, and could deliver on them, you would have been able to motivate your narcissistic parent to nurture and love you. If you kept in sync with your parents' narcissistic fantasies, you would be the grateful recipient of their conditional love and attention.

By molding yourself into their "trophy child," you might have found a way to be hurt less, but it would come at an unimaginable cost. Although your "trophy-ness" might save you from the darker and more menacing side of your narcissistic parent, it would deprive you of emotional freedom, safety, and happiness. Relaxing and enjoying the wonders of childhood would never be yours. Your comfort in sacrificing and being invisible would eventually coalesce into adult codependency. This, in turn, would compel you to replay your childhood trauma with the people with whom you chose to be intimate.

However, if you were unable to be your parents' "trophy," you would trigger their feelings of shame, anger, and insecurity, which, in turn, would be punishingly projected onto you. As the "bad seed," who is unable or not allowed to make their parent feel better about themselves (relieve their toxic shame), you would likely be penalized through deprivation, neglect, and/or abuse. The nightmarish quality of your childhood would require you to find the biggest psychological boulder under which you would permanently hide your agonizing memories. Your lonely, deprived, and/or abusive childhood would lay the foundation for a potentially permanent mental health disorder. This would compel you to selfishly hurt others and experience limited or conditional empathy or remorse. Just like the parent who emotionally disfigured the beautiful child you naturally were, you will instinctively replicate the same harmful patterns with those who love you.

THE BATON METAPHORS

Simply put, each generation in my family groomed the next to participate in a dysfunctional family relay team. Not only did the parents of each generation pass on their zeal and enthusiasm for relay races, they were highly influential about which of two possible team roles each child would eventually adopt. The baton was either passed on to the child who could make the narcissistic parent feel good about themselves or to the child who could never make his narcissistic parent happy, becoming a grave disappointment.

Despite my mother's dysfunctional loyalty to helping my dad win every race, she never experienced the joy of crossing the finish line with a win. Even when she lay prostrate on the ground, exhausted and unable to move, she convinced herself that my dad's win was also hers. Though her experiences were joyless and demeaning, she never thought to quit the team. Like any other dysfunctional family relay team, my siblings and I received the proverbial batons that had been passed from my parents' generation to our own. Only the very strong and committed are able to break patterns like this. Without courage, and lots of psychotherapy, the probability that our family's relay race will end with this generation is highly unlikely.

FOUR GENERATIONS OF DYSFUNCTION

To better understand the forces that are responsible for my childhood attachment trauma, the ultimate cause of my codependency, I am sharing selected historical elements about four generations of my family. Instead of taking a "blame my parents" approach to explain why I became a codependent adult, I am choosing to be more sympathetic and empathetic to some family members against whom I once held great resentment and anger. The intent of this chapter is not to hurt, malign, or discredit any one person. Rather, it's to illustrate the multi- and transgenerational forces behind the development of codependency and narcissism in my family, while focusing on how we are all victims, despite some seeming more like perpetrators.

Please accept the disclaimer that the historical information I will share is limited in scope, potentially incomplete, and often generalized. My goal is to highlight relevant psychological features of each family member for the sole purpose of illustrating the transgenerational nature of codependency and narcissism. Despite my attempts to be accurate and neutral, I concede the conclusions I have reached may very well have been impacted by my own personal "lens." In writing this chapter, I carefully considered the value of sharing the material versus the relational consequences. With a heavy heart, I offer you the following explanation for why I became a codependent adult.

I am the second oldest child, born to Earl Rosenberg and Muriel (Mikki) Rosenberg, both of whom are deceased (2015 and 2008, respectively). My parents were only children, not by choice but by dysfunctional or medical circumstance. They had four children in the span of 10 years: Ellen, born in 1959; me, born in 1961; Steven, born in 1963; and David, born in 1969. According to my parents, the only planned child was David. My mother would later disclose that she pushed my father for the fourth child because of feeling lonely and in need of a purpose.

In my opinion, my father had most, if not all, of the symptoms of narcissistic personality disorder (NPD). Conversely, and unsurprisingly, my mother was a textbook codependent, as described in most books on the subject, including this one.

MY FATHER'S MATERNAL GRANDPARENTS—IDA AND RUBY

Spurred on by persecutions and ethnic cleansing of Jews in Eastern Europe in the late nineteenth century, both of my great-grandparents immigrated from Russia in the later part of the 1890s. Although both were Jewish and met each other in Russia, Ida was of Prussian (Germanic) background and Ruby was Russian. According to my dad, Ida was mean, bitter, and controlling, like a dictator. She had little time for other's opinions, and ran her household with an iron fist. Ruby was the softer, more loving and nurturing one.

Ida's grandiosity and entitlement, coupled with her family's fear of her, put her in an unchallenged position to raise a grandson for whom she harbored harsh judgment and bitter resentment. Ruby and Molly (Ida and Ruby's daughter) wouldn't dare challenge her, for the consequences were always far worse than they anticipated. Ruby, the codependent in the relationship, was the soft, forgiving, and accepting father (and grandfather), who always recognized the good in his children and my dad (his grandson). His generosity, according to my dad, was his downfall. Because of his apparent naiveté during the onset of the Great Depression, the loans he gave to his friends and associates were not repaid, causing his family to lose their substantial wealth. Ida never forgave Ruby for what seemed to her as weakness, gullibility, and fear of confrontation. Ida's propensity for not forgiving people who crossed her left an indelible mark on the three generations that lived with her tyrannical ways.

MAX AND MOLLY: MY FATHER'S PARENTS

Due to the lack of interaction, little is known about Max, except that he was born in Romania and joined the Army in the early 1920s. He escaped (AWOL) to illegally immigrate to the U.S. My dad described him as a handsome, charming, and likable professional gambler and con man, who could "charm the pants off any woman." This is evident, as Max was married nine times before he died at age 90. Max boasted to my dad that he was banned from Las Vegas casinos after being caught counting cards. His father's vocation was to separate people from their hard-earned cash. It is highly likely that Max was a sociopath, which means he would have easily been diagnosed with an Antisocial Personality Disorder (APD).

I don't know much about Grandma Molly's childhood, other than she was the oldest of six children, equally divided by boys and girls, and was raised by her ultra-strict and uncompromisingly narcissistic mother. As a grandmother, she was gentle, meek, and sensitive . . . a codependent like her father. Because Molly was a private person, perhaps beleaguered by shame, she disclosed virtually no information to me about her childhood (and I asked!).

Prior to meeting Max, Molly did not have much experience with dating. Most of her decisions, including her choice of men, were strictly controlled by her mother. When Molly met the very handsome and charming Max Rosenberg, she was smitten, as most women were. I suppose the relationship developed very quickly, as would be expected when a lonely, controlled, and powerless young codependent meets the suave and debonair man of her dreams. It was the Human Magnet Syndrome, circa 1929. My dad told me he believed his father was interested in and eventually married his mother because she came from a wealthy family who owned a great deal of real estate.

Ida was openly judgmental and quite hostile to Max, who my dad said she "saw right through." Like other pathological narcissists, she was able to quickly identify others who were psychologically like herself. Despite Ida's attempts to stop Molly from dating Max, the two star-crossed lovers eloped six months after meeting. Approximately three months later, my father was conceived. Six months after my dad's birth, Molly filed for divorce because Max was abusive and subsequently abandoned the family. Molly told my father that Max had no interest in holding down a real job to support his new family. While the conditions that preceded the divorce are a mystery, Max's absence from my dad's life was not. My dad had to wait until he was a teenager to meet his father for the first time, and only met him four additional times as an adult.

As a young, divorced woman with a newborn child, Molly quickly entered the work force, where she worked up to six days a week. She had no other choice but to depend on her mean and unnurturing mother for childcare. Although Ida begrudgingly accepted her "parenting" role, she never hesitated to express her resentment and bitterness to anyone who was within earshot.

MY FATHER'S ATTACHMENT TRAUMA

As difficult and downright mean as Ida was to most people, she was much more so to my father, who she often referred to as "the devil's child." As far as Ida was concerned, her grandson was permanently and irrevocably "damaged goods," simply because he carried the same DNA as his father. She was unable to see my dad beyond her hatred for Max and her resentment for having to care for his child.

According to my dad, Ida hated him because he was biologically related to his father, and, worse, looked like him. He recalled her constantly swearing in German to express her thoughts about both him and the father he had never met. Apparently, no one in the family would stop Ida's maltreatment of my dad, as she was too powerful and frightening. A week before my dad died, I asked him to talk about the abuse he endured. He told me that, to that very day, he had recurrent "horrible" intrusive memories of Ida's abuse of him. He even shed a tear, which was quite a display for my normally emotionless father.

Some of my dad's fondest childhood memories were attributed to the kindness and love he received from his grandfather, Ruby, and his three uncles, who loved him very much. Despite Ruby's powerlessness to protect his grandson, my dad remembers him as the nicest person he ever knew. Sadly, and unfortunately, his mother's, uncles' and grandfather's kind and loving ways were no match for the trauma caused by his terribly abusive grandmother.

Although he was unable to spend as much time with his mother as he would have liked, he recalled having an exceptionally close relationship with her. He idolized Molly, who he adored until the day she died. He always considered her his best friend. In fact, my dad once told me a story of when he was in the hospital getting his tonsils removed. The doctor came out to the waiting room and asked Molly if she had my dad's doll, as he was crying and pleading for "his Molly." Although the stories of my dad's extraordinarily close relationship with Molly are warm and fuzzy on the outside, they bear a striking resemblance to what is often referred to as a severely enmeshed or emotionally incestuous parent-child relationship. This had a bearing on his attachment trauma also.

In addition to being abused by his grandmother, Ida, my dad also suffered from social anxiety and moderate depression. His biological and environmental handicaps, especially his profound verbal and emotional abuse, culminated in severe emotional, personal, and relational deficits as an adult. The love and tenderness available to him from his mother, uncles, and grandfather were no match for the attachment trauma that shaped his adult narcissistic personality disorder.

As a child and teenager, my father found refuge in academic pursuits and with his tight-knit group of friends. At age 18, he escaped the tyranny of his grandmother and the limited opportunities available to him and his family by enlisting in the Army. My dad described his four years in post-World-War-II Germany as being fun, as he had the freedom for the first time to learn about himself, life, and the world around him. Like his own father, he was quite the charming lady's man. I remember several occasions when my dad boasted about his romantic conquests with the "gullible, needy, and dirt-poor" German women.

Four years after his discharge from the Army, my father graduated from the University of Illinois with a bachelor's degree in engineering. Like his Army stories, he often bragged about having several non-Jewish girlfriends who he never intended to marry. Once he decided to settle down, he actively began searching for a Jewish wife. Aside from her religion, she had to be young and attractive. When he elected to marry my mom, he ended a long-term relationship he was having with an older, non-Jewish woman. Not only was he quite cold and unempathetic in his description of the break up, he also smiled when telling the story.

In the mid-to-late 1950s, the best place for Jewish singles to meet was at synagogue-sponsored dances. The first time my dad met my mom, he coldly rejected her because she was only 16 years old. My mom painfully recalled his rejection and smooth transition into hitting on her 18-year-old girlfriend. Two years later, at the same dance, they met a second time. Once my dad established that she was of legal age, he transitioned into his charming mode. According to my mom, she was deeply infatuated with my dad because he was older and seemingly more mature, charismatic, and handsome. But what she liked the most was that he was Jewish, had a degree in Engineering from the University of Illinois, a job, a car, and the capability to afford his own home. My mother was easy and quite agreeable prey.

My dad helplessly fell for my mother because of her striking beauty, her naiveté, and her willingness to admire him (put him on a pedestal). My mother would allow him to play out his good-husband, good-father, and hardworking-provider fantasy. Conversely, my dad would give my mom her adoring-and-dutiful-wife, mother, and homemaker fantasy. Not only did they find emotional refuge in each other, both were given access to a realistic "boy-meets-girl, happily-ever-after" storyline, even though it was only temporary. Neither really knew how lonely their spouse was, nor how much each of them needed the marriage, despite attempts to escape from it. Unbeknownst to them, their unique family history and respective childhood attachment traumas had created a perfect love match.

My father was plagued by social anxiety and clinical depression throughout his life. At 55, he was officially diagnosed with Major Depression, which was when his first of 10 subsequent inpatient hospital admissions occurred. I would later learn that, as early as 40 years old, he began abusing prescription medication to escape his psychological pain. By the time he was 65, his emergent drug addiction required inpatient treatment. His drug of choice was stimulants. Later in life, he developed a full-blown addiction to both stimulants and narcotics, which landed him in an inpatient drug addiction treatment program. Whether for his Major Depression or addiction, my dad longed for the safety, security, and escape of his inpatient residential stays. It was in these facilities he could escape his problems, be worry free, all while being cared for and coddled. It was an odd pattern that none of the family could comprehend.

CHUCK AND LIL: MY MOTHER'S PARENTS

My mother's codependency, like my father's NPD, can be explained by her childhood attachment trauma. Her codependency baton was passed to her by her parents, codependent father, Charles (Chuck), and narcissistic mother, Lillian (Lil), both of whom were recipients of their own respective batons.

Around 1885, Chuck's father, Max, at age 16, was kidnapped by Russian "patriots," who forcibly conscripted him into the Army. Thanks to various political connections and bribery, his family secured his return, but only after he had served at least one grueling year of servitude away from his family. In the late 1890s, Max and his wife, Dora, were exiled from their Russian homeland because of the Russian expulsion of Jews (pogroms). As husband and wife, the two would eventually arrive in Ottawa, Ontario, penniless, where they would raise a family of eight boys.

My grandfather, Chuck, was the second oldest of his eight siblings, whose ages spanned nearly 25 years. His father was a strict disciplinarian who believed in the adage, "spare the rod, spoil the child." By today's standards, his method of discipline would easily be considered severely abusive. Max seemed more concerned about chasing his dreams, attempting to capitalize on various get-rich-quick schemes, than keeping a steady job. His unfulfilled wanderlust contributed to his family living in poverty. The family's size, coupled with their financial struggles, required each of the eight boys to work the local Ottawa street corners hawking newspapers.

In a recorded interview, my grandfather spoke of the stressful, demanding, and difficult nature of his childhood:

Once every summer, all eight boys would have to have all of their hair clipped off for health's sake. We couldn't dare say no, because if we did, we would get the back of his hand. And that's the way we thought it should be. And that's why we are upstanding fathers, grandfathers, and citizens, thanks to my parents.

As soon as I was able to add two and two, I was out peddling newspapers. Before school started I was running out to pick up the papers so I would be the first one on the street. Before Hebrew school, I ran out again to sell the afternoon edition, so I wouldn't miss anything. After, I would run out again and sell more papers. I would do that until 7 or 8 o'clock at night. And then I would shine shoes for my uncle at Union Station in between selling newspapers. I would then come home to do my homework. I never knew what childhood meant; I had to help make money for the family and care for the growing [number of] children, and that continued on until I left Ottawa for Chicago at age 16½ [shortly after his father died].

Consistent with the times and the Russian Jewish culture in which Dora grew up, she had little power over, or influence in, major family decisions. Notwithstanding, she put all her energy into caring for her husband and eight children. Grandpa Chuck affectionately described his mother as a tireless advocate for her children—she devoted her life to making them better men. All her boys loved and revered her.

Dora and her children suffered greatly because of Max's lust for job opportunities that he hoped could move his family from poverty to comfortable living, but never did. The biggest blow to the family was Max's early death, which left the family without a sustainable income. This financial crisis compelled 16-year-old Chuck to quit high school and join his oldest brother in Chicago, where he could earn money to support his Canada-based family. Despite the odds that were stacked against her, Dora was able to cobble together whatever resources were available to raise her children. The boys adored her and considered her their personal hero.

MY MOTHER'S NARCISSISTIC MOTHER—LILLIAN

I know very little about my maternal grandmother, Lillian's, childhood other than she was the oldest of six siblings. Her father, Sam, and mother Etta, were Lithuanian Jews, who were born in New York City. Sam was a successful butcher and meat packer and Etta, a homemaker. Sam died from a heart attack when Lil was 28. I remember hearing stories of Grandma Lil's mother being unemotional, cold, and demanding. I naturally assume, as I do with most of my clients who are either codependent or pathologically narcissistic, that one of their parents was a codependent and the other a narcissist. Apparently in this situation, Etta was the dominant personality that was primarily responsible for Lil's trauma.

Each time Lil fell, my frail grandfather, who was seven years her senior, would be expected to lift her overweight frame off the ground. She tended to shun her walker because she didn't want to look old. Her denial about getting old was evident in her insistence that she had blonde hair when, in fact, it was snow-white.

By the time Lil was 78 and Chuck was 85, he was physically and emotionally worn out. It was heart-breaking to witness the grandmother I loved dearly harm my defenseless grandfather. Once, about a year before he died, he very uncharacteristically shared his desperation about Lil's relentless needs and expectations. He said if something wasn't done quickly, Lil's treatment of him "would kill him." Such a desperate plea was disturbing because of the position it put me in, and the fact that Grandpa Chuck was normally a deeply private man who rarely shared any negative feelings about anyone. I was simply too young, inexperienced, and codependent myself to provide him with any helpful advice or a solution.

Six months later, on the evening of my birthday, Chuck enraged Lil by complaining about her increasing selfishness. That night, Chuck suffered a fatal stroke. Until she became incapacitated from Alzheimer's disease, Lil would give anyone who would listen her sage advice: never go to bed mad at your loved one because if you do and they should die, you will feel guilty for the rest of your life. True to her narcissism, she made her husband's stroke all about her.

MY MOTHER'S ATTACHMENT TRAUMA

Chuck was a self-sacrificing, devoted, and hardworking codependent husband and father. Although he dearly loved my mother, the absence of nurturing in his childhood and his own attachment trauma all but guaranteed that, by the time he was a parent, he would be incapable of displaying or communicating any discernable affection for her. As an adult, I can remember numerous times when I hugged Grandpa Chuck and his body would be stiff as a board. Despite the reflexive forward thrust of his arm for a manly and non-demonstrative handshake, he would begrudgingly return my affectionate overture, clearly uncomfortable with the physical contact.

I do not know much about my mother's relationship with her mother, other than the obvious emotional distance between them, and Grandma Lil's inability to be emotionally sensitive or empathetic with her. Having a demanding and entitled narcissistic mother and an invisible, subservient, "salt of the earth" codependent father clearly sowed the seeds for her attachment trauma. Like her father, she would become a selfless codependent, avoiding emotional closeness while relishing opportunities to help others in need. She would also emulate her father by becoming an invisible person.

Because of my mother's shame-infused, almost secretive, nature, her emotional self remained unknown to everyone in her life. Sadly, this was convenient for her mother, husband, and children, who were manipulated into showing more interest in and favor for their father than her. From the bits and pieces of real emotions and sad stories my mother shared with me, I can say with confidence that she was a very lonely child and teenager who lived in an austerely strict home that was absent of affection and unconditional positive regard.

I assume the reason she agreed to marry my dad at age 18 was impacted by having little-to-no self-esteem, confidence, or belief in being inherently lovable. The time in my mother's life when she dreamed of escaping her lonely and unhappy existence coincided with the period when my father began his search for a trophy wife to bear him children. Insecurities and low self-esteem made her the perfect codependent bait for my controlling and manipulative narcissistic dad. Six months later, after an intense courtship, they married. One year later, my sister, Ellen, was born.

THE FAMILY THAT COULDN'T TAKE AWAY THE PAIN

Because of my mother's deeply-rooted insecurities, addictions (gambling and food), and long-buried emotional secrets, I surmise she rarely experienced a full sense of happiness or emotional freedom. Like other codependents, she placed all her childhood hopes and dreams into the person she decided to marry. Unfortunately for my mother, her "pot of gold at the end of the rainbow" was my pathologically narcissistic father. She would never find a person who would quell the burden of shame, self-loathing and loneliness she secretly carried inside her.

Hence, my parent's first child, Ellen, was born to an emotionally-stunted, terribly insecure, lonely 19-year-old codependent mother and a pathologically narcissistic, self-absorbed, 29-year-old father. My father knew exactly what he wanted for his first-born child, and it wasn't a daughter. When the doctors told him of his daughter's birth, he reacted with open disbelief and disappointment. The first time he saw her, he insisted on removing her diaper in the hope of proving the doctors wrong. I firmly believe that the shock of being married to a narcissist, the pain of pregnancy and giving birth, her husband's open disappointment over not having a son, and the harsh realities of being the parent of a newborn pushed my mother further into her darkly private world of loneliness and shame. One-and-a-half years later, to my dad's great delight, his next child, me, possessed a penis.

My father's desire to be the type of father he always wished for was no match for the dysfunctional, unconscious forces created by his childhood attachment trauma.

As an adult, especially as a husband and father, he could never rise above his primal instinct to make everything all about him, while conditionally doling out meek rations of attention, praise, and "love" to those he professed to care about. At the end of the day, his wife and children were nothing more than objects for which he had an intermittent fondness and connection. He simply did not know how to, and was not intrinsically interested in, emotionally bonding with anybody, including his wife and children.

My mother's secret world of shame, low self-esteem, and utter powerlessness translated into her not knowing how to connect with her children, even though she genuinely wanted to. I could easily write a whole chapter, if not more, detailing the many wonderful moments in my life when my mom was there for me when I needed her most. Despite these precious memories, I have few detailing emotional nurturance and closeness. Like her father, she was a dedicated and dependable caretaker, who lacked the capacity for warmth and tenderness.

The most obvious illustration of my mother's codependency was when she was dying of cancer. Even as her days on earth dwindled away, she stayed focused on everyone else's needs and ignored her own. Despite her pain and suffering, and the knowledge that her days were numbered, she focused minimally on getting her own emotional and personal life in order. Rather, she seemed to be on a mission to prepare my chronically helpless and dependent father for a life without her. I will never forget coming to visit her in the hospital, where she was placed because of her chemotherapy-induced malnutrition and dehydration. She had multiple books of carpet samples on her lap with her food pushed to the side. When I asked her to put them down and eat—let dad or someone else worry about the house—she shot me an annoyed, "you don't know what you are talking about" glance. She told me emphatically that she wouldn't leave "your father" in a rundown house. Knowing she needed to do this, I begrudgingly obliged her codependent pursuit of the perfect medium-length, stain-resistant, and beautifully-colored shag carpet that would make my dad "happy."

Whenever I or my siblings asked her how she was feeling, my mom deflected the question and would ask us if we were visiting "our father" and taking care of him. She also asked about her beloved dogs, as she knew my dad would likely not take good care of them. If someone asked her whether she wanted anything, she would adamantly insist they bring nothing. If she couldn't convince that person otherwise, she insisted on a fruit basket, as she knew the nurses or hospital staff would like it. She once confided in me her belief that, if she gave the nurses little gifts, they would take better care of her.

The saddest example I can recall is when my fiancée, Korrel, and I asked her for her permission to arrange a small marriage ceremony in her hospital room. Knowing she would not live long enough to see our December wedding, we wanted to share our special moment with her. Not surprisingly, she adamantly refused, stating it would be "selfish" to take our special day away from us. Nothing we could say would sway her decision.

My mother's cancer also brought out the worst side my father's pathological narcissism. He often refused to visit her at the hospital, as it made him depressed and uncomfortable. It was even impossible for him to sit with her and offer her comfort as she was dying at home. When he talked to his children about her imminent death, the subject matter was almost always about his fear of the future and the loneliness he was dreading. He even joined an Internet dating site before she died so he could find a good woman to take care of him.

THE GHOST OF MY DAD'S FAMILY FEUD

Little is known of Grandma Molly's relationship with her siblings. I grew up knowing she had not talked to her two sisters since the passing of their mother. According to my dad, one of her sisters cashed in their mother's $200 life insurance policy and didn't share it with the others. One of her sisters took the side of this sister, and the others accused her of stealing the money. It wasn't until my grandmother was 88 years old and dying of cancer that all her siblings were together in one room. That room happened to be her hospital room, where she would die five days later.

Molly's family dysfunction had a significant impact on my family, especially me and my siblings. Not only were we deprived of first cousins, aunts, and uncles by having two parents who were only children, we would grow up not knowing any of my dad's relatives. Adding insult to injury, my siblings also had almost no relationship with the cousins on my mother's side, as most lived in Canada. Hence, my Dad's family's feud was instrumental in putting my nuclear family on its own family relationship island.

My immediate family was visited by my dad's "family feud ghost," appearing when my mother was dying of cancer. A month before she died, she began distributing her valuables to each of her children. Just before sharing her final wishes with me, her cancer spread to her brain, rendering her unable to communicate. When I informed my dad which pieces she had previously promised me, he vehemently denied any such promise had been made and refused to give me anything. I would later find out he had been scheming with my siblings to distribute the jewelry, deliberately excluding me.

My protests fell on deaf ears, as my dad and siblings had formed a tightly-knit coalition that kept me from getting any of my mother's heirlooms. Not only did they lie about their involvement with my father, they also hid the gifts he had already given to them. Adding insult to injury, they tried to gaslight me into believing I was deprived of my mother's gifts because of the anger I expressed to everyone. Not only did this create a seismic shift in our relationships, it caused me great emotional pain.

This despicable "family feud ghost" reappeared once again when my dad was dying, a time when family relationships were already fractured and seemingly beyond repair. During his slow deterioration, each sibling lobbied for their desired valuables. Once again, he made covert deals with each child to not disclose the details to anyone, especially me. Naturally, I was incensed and felt even more abandoned and hurt.

When I confronted my father and siblings, the family immediately rallied to combat my protests. No one was honest about the duplicitous nature of my father's actions. Moreover, they defended their own actions by repeating my dad's inaccurate narrative about me being a "bad son" whose temper and hurtful treatment of him was responsible for his decisions. Unbeknownst to anyone, this "bad Ross pill" had been sneakily administered to each of them since they were children.

The irony of my family's alliance to keep me from getting any of my father and mother's valuables was I was the one from whom they always sought help and comfort. Whether it was a crisis or a computer glitch, they would call me—their most reliable, available, and willing-to-help-them child.

THE STRAW THAT BROKE THE CAMEL'S BACK

The proverbial straw that broke the camel's back was when my dad bequeathed his most prized and valuable piece of jewelry to one of his grandsons. This was yet another "deal" resulting from one of my father's meticulously coordinated secrets. It wasn't that he did not deserve such a gift, as he is a wonderful young man, but that the accidental disclosure of it came on the heels of my learning about a secret pact my dad made with each of his three other children to exclude me from getting any of his or my mother's valuables.

This incident was the tipping point for me: when I would calmly, without feeling abandoned or emotionally wounded, relinquish my life-long, unrequited desire for an honest, fair, and accountable family. Deciding to end the never-ending cycle of expectations and disappointment, I compelled myself to accept the facts about my family: having an honest and supportive relationship was not possible, and it would never happen. This is when I realized that my expectations and reactions to them were as much a part of the problem as anything they did or did not do to, or for, me. Wanting something from those who neither had it to give me, nor would if they could and were motivated to do so, was an epiphany that changed my life. By accepting my family's antagonistic relationship "dance," and not jostling for the command of it, I lost the desire to "dance."

These realizations allowed me to accept my family's sad, but true, reality. They also helped me wrap my arms around the difficult, but important, fact that it was better for me to not have family relationships than to pursue relationships that predictably disappointed and hurt me. Paradoxically, I now feel more relaxed, present, and empathetic when I am in the presence of my family. "Acceptance, tolerance, and boundaries" would become my silent, but potent, mental-health-saving mantra. And that is how I was able to bid farewell to my "family feud ghost."

MY LONELY CHILDHOOD

I was an extremely lonely child who was taunted and harassed by most of my peers. My sensitivity, insecurity, and fear of being bullied made me the easiest of targets. Not only was I considered one of the most unpopular kids in my class, I was invisible to most, including my teachers. I endured eight humiliating years of my childhood being called "Booger" and being treated as an outcast. I spent my entire childhood, including most of my teen years, starving for acceptance and friendships. I often felt like some of my friends had to play or hang out with me in secret; letting others know of their association with "Booger" would have had disastrous consequences for their own social standing. In total, my childhood was a very dark and lonely time during which I only knew what was wrong with me rather than any inherently positive qualities I had.

As early as I can remember, I yearned and often fought for my dad's attention. For the first 12 years of my life, I was "the apple of his eye." As his favorite child, I received more affection and attention from him than did the rest of the family, but it was hard-won and never enough to impact the other darker and more insidious psychological forces grinding me down in other aspects of my life. My favorite-child status could not save me from the chronic unhappiness, self-loathing, and loneliness I had inside.

The only time I felt lovable and important was when my father gave me attention. All of his children fought for the morsels of affection and attention he would parsimoniously dole out. My reactions to his conditional love fluctuated from ecstatic happiness when I got it to profound shame when I didn't. For most of my childhood, I was trapped on a metaphorical "hamster wheel," where I furiously ran toward what I most wanted and needed, but always was worn out before ever arriving at my elusive destination.

Like the rest of my family, my early psychological problems worked to my father's benefit. My insecurities, lack of friends and self-esteem, and complete dependence on being his "favorite" child kept me in constant search of his validation and attention. This, in turn, guaranteed predictable and constant fuel for his perpetually depleted, narcissistic "gas tank." Aside from lacking a genuine interest in me as a person and how I felt, he rarely showed interest in any of my activities. To get him to do something I enjoyed, like playing catch, I had to beg and plead while molding my personality to accommodate his. I intuitively knew that, if I did voice my burgeoning anger and resentment, I would fall from grace and be replaced by my younger brother, who was poised and ready to be his next ego-emboldening "narcissistic appendage."

At approximately age 13, thanks to puberty, my role as "daddy's perfect son" came to a crashing end. The disappearance of his resplendent "perfect father" image—and the abrupt termination of his attention and interest—left me seething in rage, feeling abandoned, and caught up in a confusing battle of power and control. My sensitive and reactive nature, and my belief in justice and honesty, caused me to angrily confront my father about his unfair and controlling treatment of me. No different from other pathological narcissists, he took great offense to my actions and punished me for my brazen attempts to make him feel bad. Falling from favorite to least favorite child would gravely impact my already-suffering mental health, as well as my future chance for being a happy, secure, and self-loving adult.

Quickly, and seemingly overnight, my feelings of awe and appreciation for my dad transmuted into resentment and disdain. Openly and unabashedly questioning his authority and methods of punishment fanned the flames that would quickly engulf our relationship. In normal or moderately healthy families, a teenager's challenge of his father's authority and accusations of unfairness are grist for the mill. However, for a pathological narcissist like my dad, it destroyed a boy's dream that he was good enough to be adored by his father.

REPLACED BY ANOTHER SOURCE OF NARCISSISTIC SUPPLY

My dad regularly set up his children to compete for his attention and praise. He proactively created controversy and conflict so that some, if not all, would be angry or resentful toward the other. Worse, he regularly disseminated negative and often inaccurate information about any one of us so he could foment anger, distrust, and resentment among family members. Even more disturbing was the joy he apparently experienced from watching the conflict unfold.

When I "fell from grace," my sister, Ellen, was not an ideal replacement, as she had given up on getting my dad's positive attention during her toddler years. She was either invisible to him or locked into her negative attention-seeking cycle. The "heir apparent" was the third-born child, my younger brother (the fourth child wasn't born yet). This child, the former outsider, seized the opportunity to adorn himself in the "favorite child" costume, while being groomed to fulfill my dad's need for attention and narcissistic supply. It was an ideal transition for him, for up to that moment in his life, he was forgotten, unimportant, and completely unseen by my father. Without ever realizing it, my dad's third-born child was molded into someone who would not only make my father feel good about himself, but who would also become alienated from the rest of his sibling group and mother.

To cement his new ally, my father poisoned his mind with a false narrative about us—his sister, brother, and mother. My brother unknowingly became a puppet whose "strings" were carefully manipulated so he would be my father's lieutenant, mini-judge, and informant. This child, who was barely 11 years old, blindly drank the "Kool-Aid" given to him because it made him feel special and important, experiences of which he had been formerly deprived.

His being programmed to turn on me fueled my anger and rage, which resulted in me becoming the bully. Any of my acting out—my angry tirades at my dad, bullying my brother, abusing drugs—would serve as proof to my brother that my dad's negative pronouncements about me were true. I was indeed trapped: the more my dad set my brother up to judge, dislike, and inform on me, the more I retaliated against him. My father's appalling treatment of his children not only permanently damaged the relationship between us, but it deprived my younger brother of any bonding opportunities with his mother.

By the time my youngest brother was born, both of my parents were nearly on the verge of complete emotional bankruptcy. As my father remained lost in his own narcissistic world, my mother began a frantic search for identity and meaning, which motivated her to start her own business and convert to Christianity. Our father further poisoned our minds against our mother by implanting an "our mother abandoned us" and "our mother humiliated us" narrative. The increased "dosage" of "mind poison" turned our pliable and vulnerable minds against the only parent who could have provided any form of nurturing. My dad's incessant gaslighting[5] was a despicable act that would be directly responsible in the passing of the baton to yet another generation.

Despite my mother convincing my dad to have their fourth baby so she would have someone to need and want her, neither she nor my dad had much emotional or personal time left in their life for the child. Born eight years after me, my youngest brother found himself growing up in a substantially different family environment than the rest of us. Not only did his two oldest siblings (my sister and me) move out of the house by the time he was ten, the only sibling left, his brother, who was six years older than him, had been fed a belief that he had parent-like rights and responsibilities to teach his brother "right from wrong." This brother was given carte blanche to use a destructive form of juvenile policing to make sure his brother kept in step with his rules. The "baby" of the family was subjected to a form of harmful emotional and relational neglect that would have life-altering implications.

MY DAD, THE GASLIGHTER AND PUPPET MASTER

My dad, the Grand Puppet Master, managed to engineer the destruction of his family's internal relationships in the midst of "gaslighting" his eldest son. Gaslighting is defined as causing a person to doubt their sanity through psychological manip-

5 Discussed in Chapter Eleven

ulation. (I will share more about the harm of gaslighting in Chapters Eight and Eleven). I sometimes ask myself if my father truly enjoyed getting me to "play the fool" so he could prove his gaslit narrative to the family and, most unfortunately, to me. At the end of the day, the only thing that ever mattered to him was enjoying a constant and steady supply of attention while avoiding any accountability for the harm he caused.

My father admitted five days before he died that the gaslit narrative he had craftily implanted in all his children's minds about me was wrong; this was when I received the greatest compliment he had ever paid me. While I was caring for him in home-based hospice, he told my sister, "Hey, I was wrong about Rossy, he really is a good man and a great son." Strangely, my sister thought I should be happy with such a "compliment." I allowed myself 10 minutes to feel bad and then shrugged it off as nothing new. It is a shame it took him until he was only days away from death before he suggested to his other children that his oldest son was a good guy.

MY MOM, THE NICEST PERSON I NEVER KNEW

No one ever had to fight for my mom's love or attention. She simply didn't expect it. Being so emotionally disconnected and self-loathing, my mother had the perfect personality for my father. She was a longtime victim of his attempts to poison our minds about her inadequacies and problems. To consolidate and maintain his powerful and revered position in the family, he needed to turn us into his ally and our mother's foe. He would constantly encourage us to degrade our mother by criticizing her body image and weight problems; my dad or one of his children would often call her "fatso" or "Mikki Moose." An even more disturbing example of disempowerment and triangulation was when my dad asked each of his children which parent they would want to live with should they get a divorce. Since all the children were gaslit to seek the elusive love and attention from my dad, and to not value or appreciate our mother, we all naturally and openly chose him. I was the only one who stated a preference for my mom, which was more of a sympathy vote than a real preference (I was gaslit, too). She wasn't my actual choice, but I felt sorry for her.

My mother's distorted sense of loyalty, pervasive insecurities, and fear of being alone—in essence, her codependency—kept her from divorcing my father. Even after my dad disclosed two extramarital affairs, she stood by his side. Unbeknownst to my mother, my dad actually had numerous affairs with other women. I will always wonder what she would have done if she knew what my dad told me a few days before he died. He shared that he had many more affairs than he had originally admitted to, including with one of her closest friends.

Adding insult to injury, my mother's dutiful care for my dad's severe clinical depression (for over 15 years) kept her mired in a caretaking role for a person who, because of his narcissism and depression, behaved like an obstinate 7-year-old child. The last 10 years of her life had to be the most difficult. She was completely overwhelmed by my dad's exhausting dependence on her for companionship, as he had very few friends. During this time, he became hooked on prescription drugs and behaved like any other dishonest, manipulative, and irrational drug addict. The sacrifices and emotional costs of her codependency had to be on a par with her father Chuck's experience with her mother, Lil.

Cloaked in invisibility, she tried hard to be an exceptional parent. Despite her generosity with her time and attempts to give us everything we needed, we never really knew her, nor did she know us. Because of her own attachment trauma, the resulting codependency, and an Anxiety and Attention Deficit Disorder, I was never aware of her deeply hidden emotional and personal struggles. Like her father, she was stoic and private about her personal suffering.

My mother was an extraordinarily generous woman, accepting and forgiving of all her children, especially me. Considering we both were very similar, we shared a special bond. Every so often, she would let me know how proud she was of my various life achievements. I remember a few conversations when she confided how she related mostly to me because I followed the same dreams she had had, but didn't pursue. Like other codependents, her deep and overwhelming self-love deficit and her fear of failure became the roadblock that prevented her from fulfilling her goals. And, as a codependent, she wouldn't dare blame her personal "failures" on anyone other than herself.

Due to my dad's triangulation and poisoning of our minds, my mother was more connected to her friends than she was to her own children. Starving for people to need and love her, she worked hard to be any lucky person's friend. Everyone loved my mom. All her friends admired her for her love, caring, and sacrifices. Like her own codependent father, Chuck, she would "give the shirt off her back" to make another person happy. It is a sad fact that everyone, except her children and husband, adored my mom. Her children might have, had they not been experiencing the countervailing forces of their narcissistic father. As paradoxical as this might sound, *my mother was the nicest person I never knew.*

Her quickly spreading terminal cancer pushed us to have conversations about difficult and frightening emotional topics we should have had sooner but were unable and too afraid to initiate. The interaction of our codependency kept a mother and her son from ever having a proper relationship. If it wasn't for my father's selfish and intentionally divisive actions, I would have been able to know my mom, and she, me. To this day, I carry regret, sorrow, and some level of blame for this sad fact. This is precisely why I dedicated my first book to her.

MY 17-YEAR-OLD BREAKING POINT

My loneliness, insecurity, and susceptibility to falling prey to the harmful actions of others followed me into my teen years. By age 14, the intense bullying, name calling, and shaming had worsened. The combination of normal adolescent angst and the neglect and emotional harm at home made me descend into a deep abyss of shame and depression. I would eventually discover the numbing qualities of marijuana and, later, harder drugs, which I used regularly by age 15. By the middle of 11th grade, at age 17, I was self-medicating my sadness, anger, and loneliness with dangerous levels of drugs. After a three-month suspension for drug dealing and possession, I descended into a major near-suicidal drug binge. After discovering the large quantities of stimulants I was using and selling, my parents placed me in a 90-day inpatient psychiatric program for teens.

Until that point, I had no insight into my self-destructive ways and the dangerousness of my drug abuse. When I was initially hospitalized, and all the way up until the end of the third week, I was adamant about my reason for using drugs: to have fun and feel good. I tried my best to convince people that having fun and feeling good was no reason to be hospitalized. But treatment providers would have no part of the fable I made up. They kept the pressure on me to be honest about the reasons why I constantly needed to be high and was slowly killing myself.

By the fourth week of treatment, following a slew of confrontational and highly anger-provoking individual and group therapy sessions, I opened to the idea that I could actually be running away from something. I will always remember the moment when Dr. Schwartz, my psychiatrist, and Dr. Yapelli, my psychotherapist, burst into our group therapy and told my peers I was a pathological liar and was completely pulling the wool over their eyes. They warned the group to not believe a word I said or to let up on me until I came clean. Following their proclamations, they abruptly left. I was left seething in anger at their lies and unfair manipulation of my peers. This was an especially huge blow, as I always considered myself an honest person.

It was then something started to bubble up inside of me, something that would result in a startling emotional realization: I was a horribly sad, lonely boy who was starving for acceptance and love. Triggered by this realization, the dam of suppressed (unconscious) emotional pain broke wide open. I would finally admit to how much anguish I felt and why I would do just about anything to escape it. I cried harder than I ever had, and for the first time felt a sense of inner peace and happiness. This experience prompted me to write the following poem, which expressed the pain and suffering that had dogged me my whole life. My poem, "Loneliness," served as a window into the world of my tortured emotional self.

LONELINESS
Ross Rosenberg (1978)

Loneliness is a feeling,
which is so hard to accept.
It will gnaw at you for a lifetime.
No matter how hard you try to forget.
The pain it causes is unbearable.
Only if you knew of this pain
and how it hurts.
You hope someone will understand,
but no one does.

All I ask for is one mere favor.
Just a friend, someone who cares,
someone who loves.
Someone who will give me strength.
And how I need this.
Many times my dreams are shattered.
But I swear, if they are ever fulfilled,
You will see me with an outstretched hand.

I am ready now to experience something

I have craved for so long.
If it takes a fight to get over this dreadful feeling,
I am ready,
I am waiting.

Just let me get knocked down,
You will see me get right back up.
And yet I will still fight.
Fierce and determined I will have to be.

You might even see me bruised and injured.
But I will never give up.

Here I am.
Just maybe,
Just maybe if I shed enough tears,
I might look and notice.
Just maybe there will be someone at my side.
Someone who really cares,
Someone who understands.

How excited I get at this thought.
A dream it may sound to be,
But if it is, I beg of you,
Please do not wake me up!

MY GROUND ZERO

I consider that particular group therapy session as "ground zero" of my codependency recovery. At this moment in time, I could finally sift through the emotionally fractured nature of my life, express my feelings about it, and not need drugs to hide from the resulting pain. Perhaps my biggest breakthrough was the realization of my deep-seated anger toward my father and the need to break free from his harmful control over me. It would take another 25 years until I could completely deconstruct the true nature of my attachment trauma for which he was mostly responsible. But still, it was a crucial first step!

As much as I have pointed out my parents' limitations, I am forever indebted to them for getting me the help I needed; it undoubtedly saved my life. It also had a profoundly positive impact on our relationship. Because of them, I could take the very important first step toward facing my emotional demons and seeking a path of healing and positive mental health. Without them, I would not have been able to face the still-broken family in which I lived and be able to execute a practical plan to individuate from my parent's dysfunction. (One year later I joined the U.S. Army). Additionally, and maybe most importantly, the hospital treatment experience led me to discover my talent for helping others. This would culminate into a promise I made myself and have kept: to become a psychotherapist who could help others who experienced the same emotional suffering I did.

WHY THIS CHAPTER?

For anyone to grasp the magnitude of their own codependency (or narcissism), they must thoroughly examine the attachment experiences of past generations: parents, grandparents, and even great-grandparents. Parents who subject their children to abuse resulting in attachment trauma are ultimately responsible for their children's codependency and/or pathological narcissism. Although the lion's share of the blame lies with the narcissistic parent, the codependent parent also shares responsibility. It is an unfair assessment to reduce this complicated problem to a "good" versus "bad" parent dilemma. Both parents are on the same dysfunctional track team. Both prime their children to pass the baton off to the next generation.

I am hopeful that, by sharing my family experience, you will have a better frame of reference and understanding of the forces that shaped your own codependency. By understanding the circuitous but predictable direction in which codependency (and narcissism) travels, we will have better insight into it and be able to fully recover from it.

Reflections

- What role did your great-grandparents have on your codependency?

- How was your parents' childhood attachment trauma related to their parenting of you?

- Does a multigenerational explanation of your own codependency change the way you feel toward your parents?

Chapter Two

THE EXCITING BUT TERRIBLE TANGO

THE METAPHOR THAT CHANGES LIVES

At 17 years old, I discovered a penchant for writing poems. My early poems helped me uncover deeply buried or rarely expressed feelings that, despite their invisibility, were creating havoc in my life. Early on, I learned that the act of writing, sharing, and reflecting on my poetry helped me unravel the twisted knots of my psychological suffering. The use of descriptive and emotionally evocative words and phrases seemed magical to me, as they helped me express my thoughts and feelings that, until writing them down, I didn't know even existed. In addition to its "medicinal" impact on my hurting heart, poetry helped me secure affirmation from others; something for which I was starving. Up until that point in my life, I was unaware (never told) of any particular talent that I had.

My predilection to use poetry as a conduit for emotional healing and growth naturally transformed my professional use of descriptive and emotionally suggestive symbolic language. Early on in my career, I gravitated toward forms of psychotherapy that uncovered trauma through a prescriptive use of metaphors and allegory. These techniques were predictably effective in helping my clients access (remember) repressed or suppressed traumatic memories. Moreover, the use of such symbolic language and storytelling was instrumental in the integration and/or resolution of the trauma.

My knack for reducing complicated psychological phenomena into simple, but expressive, symbolic words and phrases also had educational value. This was especially the case for my clients deeply steeped in denial, whether it was about their addiction, destructive habits, or trauma history. I would learn that a well-articulated and specifically-placed metaphor could move a person from an adamant position of denial to a free-flowing expression of emotions about what they previously wouldn't think or feel. Furthermore, the use of a metaphor could transform a difficult-to-comprehend or complicated psychological construct into something that was emotionally palatable and understandable.

Although I cannot remember exactly when I first used the metaphor "dance" to illustrate the codependent-narcissistic relationship and "dancers" to represent the codependent and narcissist, I am quite certain it was born out of my personal psychotherapy work. I estimate the metaphor discovery occurred in 2005, a time when I was preoccupied with an epiphany I experienced in psychotherapy: I was much less anxious or paradoxically comfortable with narcissistic women than those who were codependent. The healthier I became, the more acutely aware I became of my gut reactions (comfort and discomfort) with different types of women. In no time, I was using this new-found discovery with my codependent psychotherapy clients.

The use of the "dance" metaphor and the subsequent explanation of how and why codependent and narcissistic romantic partners are attracted to each other (and dysfunctionally compatible) quickly became a necessary component of early-stage codependency treatment. These discussions single-handedly helped my clients have a logical explanation for their life history of relationship problems.

Perhaps the more important discovery was they were not hapless victims falling prey to bad luck. Since it's very difficult to take personal responsibility for problems that are perpetuated by choice and poor judgment, these discussions were monumentally important. Avoiding feelings of embarrassment, guilt, or shame might make a person feel better in the short run, but it comes at a cost.

By recognizing that they were unfortunate victims *and* willing participants, they were more apt to dig deep into the darker, more remote unconscious forces that kept them repeating the same distressing, but often exciting, dance. The realization of complicity had a paradoxical effect on them. Instead of feeling anger, shame or even more self-hatred, they felt optimistic. Having an explanation for their suffering, and being with a therapist who knew how to solve it, gave them hope—some for the very first time.

It is not an overstatement that the role of my "dance" and "dancing" metaphors in uncovering the mysteries of codependency and narcissism was life-changing. This simplistic, but profound, discovery created a domino effect of subsequent discoveries, epiphanies, and numerous "aha moments." As the ideas expanded and built on each other, my codependency treatment "tool bag" became increasingly more complete.

With an accumulation of positive psychotherapy outcomes, I began to fantasize about sharing my discoveries with the world. Then, in 2012, I was given an opportunity to provide a local professional training on this subject, which I entitled, "Codependents and Narcissists: Understanding the Attraction." It took another year before a PESI training manager would stumble upon this work and offer me a training position. The rest is, as they say, history.

My dance metaphor proposed that codependents are passive, accommodating, and welcoming (to narcissists) "followers" (dancers) who feel natural and comfortable dancing with controlling "leaders" (dancers). Conversely, it explains why narcissist "dancers" feel natural and comfortable when taking charge of the dance. The "dancing partnership" explains the accepted comfort and intuitive actions (and reactions) of both, as well as their love of the dysfunctional dancing experience.

Dictionaries define dance as "rhythmical and sequential steps, gestures, or bodily motions that match the speed and rhythm of a piece of music." My metaphor is virtually the same: sequential steps, gestures, and romantic behaviors that match the speed and rhythm of each partner's personality and relationship expectations. The behavior of codependents and pathological narcissists supports the idea of a dance-like phenomenon, which ultimately creates a lasting dysfunctional relationship or dancing partnership. Dance partners with oppositely matched dysfunctional personalities often find themselves in a dramatic, roller-coaster-like pathological relationship that continues despite one side's unhappiness or desire for the dance to stop.

DANCING WITH THE STARS

If you watch *Dancing with the Stars*, you know what it takes to win the coveted Mirror Ball Trophy. As with any successful dancing collaboration, each partner is experienced with, and acutely attuned to, their partner's dance style and idiosyncratic moves. To be successful on the dance floor, or to thoroughly enjoy the dance, the two partners need to be compatible on as many levels as possible, while knowing each other deeply and completely.

Codependents dance well with narcissists because their pathological personalities or "dance styles" fit together, like a hand in a glove. Almost instantly, they dance magnificently together because they are able to instinctively anticipate each other's moves. The choreography is effortless, as it feels like they have always danced together. Not only does each dancer instinctively and reflexively know his or her role and stick to it, they do it like they have practiced it all their life. Dysfunctional compatibility is the engine that drives these dancers to the dancing championship finals.

Codependents are drawn to pathological narcissists because they feel comfortable and familiar with a person who knows how to direct, control, and lead. The narcissistic dancer is simply the yin to their yang. Their giving, sacrificial, and passive codependence matches up perfectly with their partners entitled, demanding, and self-centered nature. Just because the codependent is the more passive of the two, does not mean they lack dancing mojo. Their dysfunctional agility and ability to predict their dancer partner's moves just by the subtlest of cues, makes her equally important to the illusionary grand prize both are feverishly seeking.

Codependents expertly and adeptly predict and anticipate their pathologically narcissistic partner's every step, while still experiencing the dance as a passive, but positive, experience. Pathological narcissist dancers enjoy dancing with codependents because they are allowed to feel strong, secure, and in control. Dancing with their malleable partner is thrilling, as they direct the whole experience, while believing they are the only star on the dance floor.

Perhaps my best early explanation for the metaphorical dance experience was my essay, "Codependency: Don't Dance!," which I wrote in 2007. Like my other essays and poems, it was written after an inspiring breakthrough session with one of my codependent clients. It is not a joke when I say the essay virtually wrote itself, as the ideas had already been "percolating" in my mind for several years. I consider it the beginning moment my Human Magnet Syndrome ideas took on a written form. The following is my beloved essay in its original form:

Codependency: Don't Dance!

The "codependency dance" requires two people: the pleaser/fixer and the taker/controller. This inherently dysfunctional dance requires two opposite but distinctly balanced partners: a codependent and a narcissist. Codependents, who are giving, sacrificing, and consumed with the needs and desires of others, do not know how to emotionally disconnect or avoid romantic relationships with individuals who are narcissistic—selfish, self-centered, controlling, and harmful. Codependents habitually find themselves on a "dance floor" attracted to "dance partners" who perfectly match up to their uniquely passive, submissive, and acquiescent dance style.

As natural followers of their relationship dance, codependents are passive and accommodating dance partners. Codependents find narcissistic dance partners deeply appealing. They are perpetually attracted to their narcissistic partner's charm, boldness, confidence, and domineering personality. When codependents and narcissists pair up, the dancing experience sizzles with excitement—at least in the beginning. After several "songs," the enthralling dance experience predictably transforms into drama, conflict, and feelings of neglect and being trapped. Even with the chaos and discord, neither one dares end the partnership.

When a codependent and narcissist come together in a relationship, their dance unfolds flawlessly: the narcissistic partner maintains the lead and the codependent follows. Their roles seem natural because they have been practicing them their whole lives; the codependent reflexively gives up their power and, since the narcissist thrives on control and power, the dance is perfectly coordinated. No one gets their toes stepped on.

Typically, codependents give of themselves much more than their partners give back. As "generous" but bitter dance partners, they seem to be stuck on the dance floor, always waiting for the "next song," at which time they naïvely hope their narcissistic partner will finally understand their needs. Codependents confuse caretaking and sacrifice with loyalty and love. Although they are proud of their unwavering dedication to the person they love, they end up feeling unappreciated and used. Codependents yearn to be loved, but because of their choice of dance partner, find their dreams unrealized. With the heartbreak of unfulfilled dreams, codependents silently and bitterly swallow their unhappiness.

Codependents are essentially stuck in a pattern of giving and sacrificing, without the possibility of ever receiving the same from their partner. They pretend to enjoy the dance, but secretly harbor feelings of anger, bitterness, and sadness for not taking a more active role in their dance experience. They are convinced they will never find a dance partner who will love them for who they are, as opposed to what they can do for them. Their low self-esteem and pessimism manifests as a form of learned helplessness that ultimately keeps them on the dance floor with their narcissistic partner.

The narcissist dancer, like the codependent, is attracted to a partner who feels perfect to them: someone who lets them lead the dance, while making them feel powerful, competent, and appreciated. In other words, the narcissist feels most comfortable with a dancing companion who matches up with their self-absorbed and boldly selfish dance style. Narcissist dancers are able to maintain the direction of the dance because they always find partners who lack self-worth and confidence and have low self-esteem. With such a well-matched companion, they can control both the dancer and the dance.

Although all codependent dancers desire harmony and balance, they consistently sabotage themselves by choosing a partner who they are initially attracted to, but will ultimately resent. When given a chance to stop dancing with their narcissistic partner and comfortably sit the dance out until someone healthy comes along, they typically choose to continue their dysfunctional dance. They cannot leave their narcissistic partner because their lack of self-esteem and self-respect makes them feel like they can do no better. Being alone is the equivalent of feeling lonely, and loneliness is too painful to bear.

Without self-esteem or feelings of personal power, the codependent is incapable of choosing mutually giving and unconditionally loving partners. Their choice of a narcissistic dance partner is connected to their unconscious motivation to find a person who is familiar—someone reminiscent of their powerless and, perhaps, traumatic childhood. Sadly, codependents are children of parents who also flawlessly danced the dysfunctional codependent/narcissistic dance. Their fear of being alone, compulsion to control and fix at any cost, and comfort in their role as the martyr who is endlessly loving, devoted, and patient is an extension of their yearning to be loved, respected, and cared for as a child.

Although codependents dream of dancing with an unconditionally loving and affirming partner, they submit to their dysfunctional destiny. Until they decide to heal the psychological wounds that ultimately compel them to dance with their narcissistic dance partners, they will be destined to maintain the steady beat and rhythm of their dysfunctional dance.

Through psychotherapy, and perhaps a 12-Step recovery program, codependents can begin to recognize their dream to dance the grand dance of love, reciprocity, and mutuality is indeed possible. Through therapy and a change of lifestyle, they can build (repair) their tattered self-esteem. The journey of healing and transformation will bring them feelings of personal power and efficacy that will foster a desire to finally dance with someone who is willing and capable of sharing the lead, communicating their movements, and pursuing a mutual loving rhythmic dance.

Reflections

- What is your dancing role?

- What are the forces that keep you dancing when you do not want to?

Chapter Three

CODEPENDENTS, NARCISSISTS, *AND THEIR* OPPOSITE LOVE

Disclaimer: In this chapter, almost everything you think you know about codependency will be challenged, redefined, and hopefully replaced.

The way the world defines codependency is simply incorrect, excessively simplistic, and has not kept pace with advancements in the medical and psychiatric fields. That is why, in my experience, codependency treatment rarely works. To put this into perspective, ask yourself the following questions:

- Of all the codependent people you know who have sought professional help, what percentage have been able to terminate relationships with the harmful, narcissistic people who claim to love, respect, and care for them?
- Of these "success cases," how many returned to the same narcissistic partner, like a well-meaning and sincere recovering alcoholic who slips back into drinking binges?
- Of the stronger and healthier people, how many of them fell in love with another person who, at the beginning of the relationship, seemed "normal" and healthy, but was really a narcissist in hiding?

- For the handful of leftover "success stories," how many credit their "success" to slamming and locking the emotional "door" that leads them to romantic and sexual feelings?

If you are not steeped in denial, and have good counting skills, I believe you will be left with a very small number of people who have had successful long-term results with their codependency-specific treatment. Early in my psychotherapy career, I concluded that codependency treatment was largely ineffective. My experience is that most reach a feel-good state in psychotherapy, stop attending therapy and then return to, or remain in the relationship responsible for, their relapse. This observation is supported by my work with codependent clientele, as well as my own treatment-resistant codependency.

After more than a decade of my own psychotherapy and research, I have determined that once-weekly individual psychotherapy simply does not provide long-term relief for codependency's troubling and treatment-resistant symptoms. Despite thousands of therapists claiming to be specialists in codependency, it seems few, if any, really understand it—its origin and its treatment.

My intent is not to malign the valuable contributions of the researchers, writers, theorists, and psychotherapists who helped advance the understanding of codependency. Rather, my desire is to move beyond the current body of knowledge, suppositions, and hypotheses, and develop compelling and irrefutable information about it, so we can create a conclusively effective treatment for it.

How can we treat a problem if we don't really know what it is? Such a question should not be taken lightly, as history is replete with ineffective treatment methods assigned to poorly understood medical and mental health disorders. Worse, many procedures were used without question, despite the patient receiving no benefit from them. In some cases, the patient never had the disorder for which they were being treated, and/or the method never had been proven to work. Therefore, it is incumbent on the mental health field to know exactly what codependency is, while simultaneously validating the value and efficacy of its treatment.

Cases in point: bloodletting (medical) and prefrontal lobotomies (mental). Both are striking examples of how blind faith in flawed or absent science has hurt many more people than it purported to help.

Bloodletting, the removal of blood from the body, was used for over 3,000 years for nearly every ailment known to man (Davis and Appel, 1979). Those who administered it were priests, doctors, barbers, and even amateurs. It was so widespread in 1830s France that six million leeches were used for the procedure in a country of 35 million people (Greenstone, 2010). By the 1870s, the procedure had become so popular that many ill patients had to be convinced not to be bled (Cardiology Today, 2008). Retrospective medical data analysis showed the procedure was harmful to a majority of patients, many of whom died from it (Colović, 2016).

Prefrontal lobotomies were ineffectively used to remedy various mental illnesses and behavior problems. The procedure basically consisted of severing the part of the brain that connected the prefrontal cortex to its underlying structures. Between 1940 and 1950, nearly 40,000 patients in the U.S. received this "miracle cure" for their supposed mental illness. It was also used on the criminally insane, political dissidents, angry and oppositional children, and husbands' wives who complained too much. It's supposed "miraculous" value garnered Doctor Antonio Moniz a 1949 Nobel prize in Medicine.

Not only did this procedure rarely work, it left most of its victims with pervasive permanent brain damage. By the 1970s, it was outlawed in most countries, deemed inhumane and a violation of basic civil liberties.

For any medical or mental health method to be viable, the problem it is meant to resolve or cure must be clearly understood and backed up by research, scientific data, and repeated successful clinical trials. AIDS is a perfect example. The current effective treatment would never have been discovered if scientists and researchers hadn't work so diligently to identify the disease and its origin. Thanks to a legion of heroes, HIV (Human Immunodeficiency Virus) was identified as the cause of AIDS, and a medication for it followed shortly thereafter. *To be clear, in no way am I equating codependency to AIDS.* My point is to demonstrate the importance of understanding a ubiquitous and treatment-resistant problem, prior to creating a treatment strategy or protocol for it.

TAKING ON THE CODEPENDENCY TREATMENT FIELD

It takes an outside-the-box and pioneering spirit to challenge established and widely accepted scientific conclusions. Debunking false results or unchallenged and ineffective mental health treatment comes with risk, as many have a vested interest in defending it. Some researchers or famed practitioners would rather attack a person's credibility or skill level than accept a valid conclusion and admit they were misled or just plain wrong.

I wrote both of my *The Human Magnet Syndrome* books based on my long-held belief that *the problem* of codependency is misunderstood and *the treatment* is largely unsuccessful. Unlike other mental health disorders, there is a dearth of specific diagnostic criteria (list of symptoms) for codependency, which results in difficulty making an accurate diagnosis. As a consequence, the medical, psychiatric, psychological, and mental health communities have had no choice but to use a broad definition and description for the problem experienced as "codependency," which lacked an agreed upon theoretical foundation and the manner in which it is applied in clinical settings.

With a fire lit beneath me, I committed myself to a journey of discovery, which would result in no stone being left unturned. I was hell-bent on identifying the invisible dysfunctional forces behind the self-destructive psychological condition known as codependency. More important than understanding the "whats" and "whys" of the problem, I knew I had to find a lasting solution for it. My eagerness to put an end to the anguish caused by codependency culminated in the creation of my first two books. Without further ado, let me offer more information about what I believe codependency is and why it requires magnetic-like relational forces to exist.

THE HUMAN MAGNET SYNDROME THESIS

Due to unconscious, trauma-based psychological forces, codependents and pathological narcissists are almost always attracted to each other. The resulting relationship is mostly breakup resistant. Narcissists benefit the most from this situation.

CODEPENDENCY

Codependency is both a relationship and an individual condition[6] that can only be resolved by the codependent.[7] Many codependents are attracted to, and main-

---

6 Codependency cannot be called a "disorder" because it is not listed as such in the *Diagnostic and Statistical Manual of Mental Disorders V* or the *International Statistical Classification of Diseases and Related Health Problems 10.*

7 Marriage/couple's therapy cannot solve codependency. In fact, it is almost always "stacked against" the codependent, clearly favoring the narcissist.

tain long-term breakup-resistant relationships with, pathological narcissists. Most codependents are selfless and deferential to the needs and desires of others over themselves. They are *pathologically* caring, responsible, and sacrificing people whose altruism and good deeds are rarely reciprocated.

While some codependents are resigned to their seemingly permanent relationship role, others actively, albeit unsuccessfully, attempt to change it. These people become preoccupied with opportunities to avoid, change, and/or control their narcissistic partners. Despite the inequities in their relationships, and the consequent suffering, they do not end the partnerships. Codependency is not just limited to romantic couplings, as it manifests itself in varying degrees in most other significant relationships.

PATHOLOGICAL NARCISSISM

Although pathological narcissism is not a new term, I use it in this book to represent a person with one of four disorders. Pathological narcissists are people who fit the diagnostic criteria for either Narcissistic, Borderline, or Antisocial (Sociopathy) Personality Disorders, and/or active addicts. Despite the many differences between these four disorders, they all share core narcissistic personality, thinking, and emotional and interpersonal characteristics.

To varying degrees, all pathological narcissists are selfish, self-consumed, demanding, entitled, and controlling. They are exploitative people who rarely or selectively reciprocate any form of generosity. Pathological narcissists are only empathetic or sensitive to others when doing so results in a tangible reward for themselves and/or when it makes them feel valued, important, and appreciated. Because narcissists are deeply impacted by their personal shame and loneliness, but consciously unaware of it, they do not end their relationships. Positive treatment results are rare for narcissists.

Although active addicts are included as one of the four pathological narcissism disorders, their narcissism may only be addiction specific. In other words, when sober and in recovery, their true personality type will surface. This can be any possibility reflected on the continuum of pathologically selfless to pathologically selfish personality types.

OPPOSITE ATTRACTION—THE CODEPENDENT

Codependents instinctively react to the pathological narcissist's (narcissistic) traits in a positive manner, finding them intensely desirable and strangely familiar. They are reflexively drawn to opposite (narcissistic) individuals who match up with their submissive, giving, and sacrificing natures. Codependents appreciate the pathological narcissist because they are enamored with their positive and charming personality traits, over-the-top confidence, an articulate understanding of themselves, assertive or aggressive nature, and alluring sex appeal. Not only are codependents beguiled by the quirky, arrogant, and self-aggrandizing personality, they also feel strangely emotionally balanced by it.

Since codependents take great pride in their instinctive propensity for compassion, empathy, patience, and sacrifice, they naturally seek partners who value, need, and are seeking those qualities. Since they feel completely at ease and comfortable in their altruistic relationship role, they are unsurprisingly captivated by people who respond favorably to it. Where an emotionally healthy person would be uncomfortable and possibly annoyed by their altruism, narcissists are enamored with it. As such, being in this "role" allows them to develop pseudo self-esteem, which requires the dysfunctional role of a selfish partner. Because feeling needed is mistaken for being loved, they experience a wealth of distorted "love" in relationships with narcissists.

On a conscious level, the codependent and narcissist experience the other as their soulmate. However, far from their conscious awareness are deeper and darker feelings of dysfunctional familiarity. These unconscious feelings of familiarity compel both people to repeat the Catch-22 relationship pattern of their childhood—needing to be loved by a person who is characteristically unable to love them or anyone else. More specifically, they will be compelled to repeat a version of their childhood relationship with their pathologically narcissist parent.

The psychological forces that bring codependents and narcissists together in long-term and often intractable relationships are unconscious, reflexive, and repetitive. When they consciously experience each other as desirable, the magnetic-like, unconscious attraction forces are almost impossible to resist. The chemistry is profoundly intense, almost trance-like. The experience of safety and bliss is short-lived because the narcissists will eventually expose their previously withheld or secretive selfish and self-centered tendencies. When the "love-cloud" of infatuation lifts, the relationship becomes inflexibly dysfunctional and seemingly permanent.

The codependent-narcissist relationship matchup is considered mutual and reciprocal. This is not because of the similar levels of generosity exchanged, but because both are relieved of their significant psychological burden of shame, loneliness, and self-loathing they have been carrying around their entire lives. Because neither partner can tolerate being alone, or the subsequent feelings of loneliness, and both get their dysfunctional needs met through the alliance, the bond is replete with apparent dysfunctional benefits. To illustrate, the care-needing narcissist gets to play out their grandiose fantasies of importance with a partner who is keen on making them a reality. The caregiving codependent is relieved of their life-long pessimism, anxiety, and fear about their fundamental inadequacies and the consequent possibility of being forever alone and unloved.

Codependents fall prey to the pathological narcissist's assertive, strong, and commanding persona because they are perceived as positive traits they consciously prefer and by which they are spellbound. The intense experience of enmeshed infatuation renders the codependent unable to recognize their latest "soulmate" as a wolf in sheep's clothing, hiding their narcissistically harmful and more despicable traits. Although they do not intentionally seek narcissistic romantic partners, they unfortunately find themselves perpetually in their company.

OPPOSITE ATTRACTION—THE PATHOLOGICAL NARCISSIST

Like their codependent partners, pathological narcissists are naturally attracted to people who are compatible with their unique, but dysfunctional, personality type. They instantly feel comfortable, familiar, and safe with a potential lover who consciously appeals to them and makes them feel attractive and desirable. These narcissists are especially interested in those who respond favorably to edgy, gritty, seductive bad boy or girl looks, overt sexual innuendos, and a backstory of being a victim of adversity and unfair treatment.

The pathological narcissist's natural and instinctive propensity for selfishness, self-centeredness, entitlement, and appreciation draws them towards partners who will put them on a pedestal where their needs remain more important than anyone else's. Since they take great pride in nearly everything they do and relish opportunities to brag about themselves, they naturally gravitate to people who are awed by their ever-expanding list of accomplishments and qualities. A lover who allows them to stay in the "most important person role" fortifies their pseudo self-esteem, which is often one comment or criticism away from being challenged or shattered. When their lover makes them feel important, revered, and in control, they mistake that for true and complete love. Narcissists unconsciously prefer codependent partners because they do not push them off their pedestal of self-perceived importance and near-perfection.

Pathological narcissists are in unfamiliar relationship territory when surrounded by others who are either similarly narcissistic or psychologically healthy with good self-esteem. Such people make them feel judged, misunderstood, awkward, and easily agitated. When these narcissists meet an attractive codependent, they respond to their core caretaking and sacrificing personality traits as being angelic, perfect, and intensely arousing. The codependent's natural caretaking proclivity for being sensitive, empathic, and patient fits perfectly with the narcissist's constant need to be cared for, understood, and appreciated.

The codependent's spontaneous abandonment of power and control in the relationship is the ultimate sacrifice and sets the groundwork for the narcissist's intense *soulmate* experience. Lost in their own new and perfect love experience, their life-long fantasy of being loved, cared for, and respected finally comes to fruition. The codependent is the perfect choice for romantic partner, especially because their sacrifice of self serves to further cover the narcissist's deeply hidden (unconscious) reservoir of shame, self-hatred, and loneliness. In addition, they experience emotional freedom when they do not have to worry about upsetting someone because of their off-putting narcissistic personality traits, which they deny having.

Please note: not all opposite personalities are compatible in a relationship. When opposite and different personality traits are not balanced, the individuals are not likely to form a friendship. If they do, it will predictably be unstable or short-lived. Without the compatibility of balanced opposite personality traits, the relationship will generally not be experienced as mutually beneficial and rewarding. In other words, without a payoff for their differences, the romantic or personal association will undoubtedly not last. These are the friendships that typically end with conflict, or the relationship just fades away.

THE INVERSE ATTRACTION DYNAMIC

The natural attraction to opposite personality traits is an *inverse process*. The Merriam-Webster dictionary defines inverse as "opposite in order, nature or effect."

The inverse attraction dynamic is based on proportionally opposite or dichotomous personality traits. Friends who are opposite but compatible are inversely attracted to each other because their differences correspond to, or match with, each other. A proportionally balanced inverse attraction is paradoxical in nature, as it requires perfectly matched dissimilarities. For example, a compulsive clean-freak may be attracted to a disorganized and messy person. Although both might be annoyed by the other's perceived shortcomings, they adapt because of the inherent benefits of their compatibly different personality traits.

As much as compatible extreme opposites are attracted to each other, so are compatible mild opposites. For the mild opposite bond to be successful, there needs to be a balance in the inverse or diametrically opposite personality traits. To illustrate, a mildly shy and socially awkward person and a moderately extroverted and socially confident individual may likely form a mutually satisfying friendship. In this "odd but natural" friendship, the differences may result in occasional mild feelings of discomfort or conflict, but both will ultimately feel safe, comfortable, and cared for within the relationship. The shy-gregarious combination will enhance the relationship as long as both individuals benefit from it. Such a friendship is likely to survive the test of time.

Examples of personality traits that are dichotomously opposite, but potentially compatible, include:

- Thinking versus feeling
- Introverted versus extroverted
- Private versus public
- Career-oriented versus home-oriented
- Tidy versus messy
- Generous versus thrifty

DYSFUNCTIONAL OPPOSITES: JOHN DILLINGER AND BILLIE FRECHETTE

History is replete with romantic couples who were irresistibly attracted to each other, not so much by what they saw, felt, and thought, but because of an imperceptible —albeit overwhelming—magnetic-like attraction force. Anthony and Cleopatra (codependent-narcissist), John and Jacqueline Kennedy (narcissist-codependent), and Elvis and Priscilla Presley (narcissist-codependent) are just three of a countless number of famous couples whose relationships were driven by a magnetic-like love force. Love at first sight between completely opposite personality types is a common theme in movies, novels, and songs, replete with the naïve woman (codependent) falling for the edgy and aggressive (pathological narcissist) "bad boy." One such example is John Dillinger, the notorious American bank robber, and his caretaking girlfriend, Billie Frechette.

Dillinger was considered a ruthless and cold-hearted psychopath who was quite successful at robbing banks, escaping jail, and finding himself on the front page of most newspapers. Fascinated with the public's interest in his criminal version of a rags-to-riches story, he relished any opportunity to see his name in print. A handsome, daring, and audacious public figure, he captured the interest of millions of people in the U.S. Dillinger rose to infamy because of his unique, bigger-than-life persona, the mystique of his criminal activity, and the fact that he stole money from banks. During that time, the public mistrusted banks because of their front-row-center role in causing the Great Depression. Dillinger's celebrity status was almost guaranteed; he had an affinity for periodically giving gifts of stolen loot to poor and disenfranchised people in areas where the banks he robbed were located. But make no mistake, his acts of altruism were motivated by the need to craft a grandiose and entitled "Robin Hood" narrative.

Billie Frechette, Dillinger's accomplice, had a long history of falling in love with criminals. Her history involved a long line of relationships with narcissists for whom she had become a sacrificing caregiver and mother figure. Before she met Dillinger, and all the way up to the time she was arrested, Frechette had a knack for being the beautiful, but invisible, companion who would sacrifice almost anything to take care of her man. Unlike Bonnie Parker, Clyde Barrow's lover and accomplice, her role as the doting girlfriend in the shadows made her very happy.

Like other codependents, Frechette was entranced by her pathological narcissist's toughness, independence, and over-the-top confidence. Dillinger's aggression, bravado, and all-consuming feelings of importance and superiority were completely opposite to her passive, deferential, caretaking, and accommodating personality traits. This perfectly inverse match set the stage for the moment in time when she met and fell instantly in love with Dillinger. It carried through until the day Dillinger's life came to an end just like he would have wanted it: a spectacle befitting a movie script.

OPPOSITE RELATIONSHIPS RESIST BREAKUP

The codependent-narcissist relationship is naturally resistant to
ther can tolerate being alone. The absence of an emotional ancho
rooted feelings of inadequacy and shame, which predictably triggers intense bouts
of loneliness. Being alone brings them closer to their lonely emotional core, the
part of them that has long been separated from their consciousness. Since being
alone makes them feel isolated, and loneliness is an unbearable emotion, the relationship remains intact despite shared unhappiness and negative consequences
(mostly for the codependent).

The mechanics responsible for the resistance of the codependent/narcissist relationship to breakups is specifically addressed in Chapter Five. Basically, these dysfunctional relationships are stable because both partners are often unwilling and/
or incapable of ending the relationship. The codependent defies logic by remaining
with their damaged partner. Despite the harm they endure, both obvious and subtle, they either actively choose to stay with the narcissist or are incapable of leaving
them. The same can be said for the narcissist. Despite their direct and indirect pronouncements of dislike for their codependent partner, when push comes to shove,
they will backpedal on most threats to leave the relationship.

Despite one or both partner's proclamations of wanting to end the relationship,
they are reluctant to pull the trigger. Both use a variety of psychological maneu-
vers to prevent or sabotage each other's termination plans. All forms of emotional
manipulation are fair game when it comes to tripping up the escaping partner. A
complete and comprehensive list of such sabotaging actions (or inactions) is beyond
the scope of this chapter, but the common forms of such emotional manipulation
are: (1) guilt; (2) insincere promises to change or participate in couple's and/or
individual therapy; (3) threats of harm to the partner and/or their loved ones; (4)
frightening but insincere suicidal threats; and (5) triangulation and/or poisoning
of their children's minds. Most narcissists who are facing "the boot" will do almost
anything to stall or buy time. They try to regain a foothold on the codependent's
demonstration of power, control, and resolve. Any last-ditch efforts or promises to
change or stop may be genuine, but are impossible and do not elicit permanent
results. This is because pathological narcissists lack the psychological resources, ability, and insight to stay focused on what is wrong with themselves.

If the codependent-pathological narcissist couple were to break up, one or
both would be likely to use threats, guilt, and/or some form of overt or covert

manipulation as a tactic to reconnect. Insincere promises to change, reminders of good deeds, threats to relapse on a drug they are addicted to, or threats of emotional or physical harm to self or others are some of the many manipulative ploys used to reconnect. A common manipulative maneuver is triangulation, or using a third party, to facilitate reconciliation.

Breakups are often short-lived, as both the codependent and pathological narcissist will be pulled back together by a magnetic-like dysfunctional love force. If they manage to decisively part ways, it is likely both will unconsciously and unknowingly repeat their dysfunctional attraction pattern with their next romantic partner. This person will be someone who feels exciting and different at first, but ultimately has the same dysfunctional self-orientation as the previous partner. Thus, another dysfunctional relationship dance begins with a new partner but, sadly, the dance will be to the same old music.

CODEPENDENCY ADDICTION

A primary explanation for why codependents often lack the emotional fortitude and resolve to permanently break up with their harmful narcissistic partners is what I refer to as "codependency addiction." Like addicts who are chemically dependent, codependents compulsively seek the company of a romantic partner to numb or medicate the intense emotional pain that has followed them throughout their life. When codependents first meet the oppositely aligned narcissist, they experience limerence—the wallop of intense pleasure and euphoria—that immediately numbs their lifelong battle with core shame and loneliness. Codependents are prone to this addiction, as it is their drug of choice.

Even though the "high" is indescribably pleasurable in the beginning, it can never be maintained. After prolonged exposure to this "drug," tolerance develops. From this point on, more of the drug is needed to deliver the same high. This parallels the timeline during which the codependent's euphoria rapidly decreases and their relationship with the narcissist begins to shift towards one of conflict, dismay, and disappointment. Like other drug addictions, there is a transition when the drug is no longer taken for the sheer experience of euphoria, but to take away the pain that occurs when it wears off.

Despite mounting consequences and losses, the "addicted" codependent dares not stop taking the drug, as to do so would trigger its primary withdrawal symptom—

pathological loneliness. Most codependents describe this as the most pain
emotions. The intense distress it causes, like other withdrawal symptoms, crea
irrational desires to reconnect with the narcissist, their primary drug of choice.
Despite the broken promises to themselves and to others, as well as the loss, harm,
and abuse endured, they willingly go back to what they knew was intolerable. If
the relationship is irreconcilable or too risky to return to, the codependent unconsciously seeks other potential "drug sources." Therefore, for a codependent, addiction needs to be addressed; if it isn't, the likelihood of relapse, or continuation, is
extremely likely.

HEALTHY OPPOSITES: JASON AND FRANKIE

This vignette is an actual client story for which the names and identifying information have been changed. Jason and Frankie are almost the complete opposite
of each other in personality, profession, and how they interact with others. For the
18 years that preceded the counseling referral, Jason and Frankie had been happily
married, both feeling appreciated and supported by one another. Jason was referred
to me by his wife, Frankie, who was angry at his predilection to isolate himself in a
bubble when he had important work-related projects that demanded his attention.
When immersed in his bubble, he was unaware he was neglecting the needs of his
family and believed he was fulfilling his responsibility as the primary breadwinner.
Unfortunately, his wife and two teenage children had become increasingly annoyed
and frustrated with his psychological absence.

Jason, a 40-year-old accountant, and Frankie, a 39-year-old nurse practitioner,
met when they were in college and married two years after the last one graduated.
Jason is the quintessential numbers guy. He can spend hours, if not days, going
over the specifics of most anything to find out what is missing—or, for that matter,
what is not. He is hyper-focused, serious about whatever he does, and won't stop
any task, important or not, until it is adequately completed. Besides being friendly,
kind, and secure in himself, he's shy, socially awkward, and anxious when he meets
new people.

Because Jason gets lost in his own projects and his perception of their importance, he needs someone to snap him out of his self-absorbed trances. Jason frequently tells Frankie of his love and appreciation for her contributions to the family. He is especially grateful to his wife when she pops his periodic selfish bubble.

re-emergence from his bubble-land, he tries to personally
ect with Frankie and his children.

others she was born to take care of people. Her career as a
only allows her to take care of, heal, and nurture her patients,
lf helps the physicians for whom she works. She is a person
who ge... es often, lives in the moment, and relishes moments of personal
connection. Being a naturally nurturing person, she enjoys both the big and little
moments when she can take care of Jason and their two children. Although she can
get lost in the emotional world of others, she knows when to extract herself when
her emotional tank nears empty.

When Frankie met Jason, she thought his nerdy, socially unaware, focused, and
get-the-job-done ways were endearing. She enjoyed being his personal compass,
steering him in the right direction and alerting him when he obliviously put himself in harm's way. She also appreciated how his focus and drive moved him quickly
up the ladder in his firm, which allowed her to stay home with the children when
they were very young. As the kids got older, and her work as the homemaker took
less time, she became increasingly impatient and annoyed with Jason's selfishness.

Frankie and Jason have always been perfectly inverse partners whose mental
health, solid marriage, and compatibility allowed their yin-and-yang personalities
to sync well. Eventually, Jason's self-focus, career ambitions, and episodes of losing
himself in the project du jour became a lightning rod for marital conflict. Since he is
not a pathological narcissist, he was earnest and motivated in our counseling sessions
to "right the marital ship." Because he applied the same work ethic and focus to our
counseling work, he righted the ship in a matter of eight sessions (a rarity for me).
Their relationship consisted of healthy opposites, neither of whom was a codependent or a pathological narcissist.

SIMILAR ATTRACTION IS ALSO AT WORK

As demonstrated by the Human Magnet Syndrome related explanations and theories, most romantic and many platonic relationships are created and maintained by
unconscious factors. Despite the power of the unconscious mind and its complicity in the formation of codependent/narcissist relationships, conscious preferences
are also at work. For anyone who uses Internet-based dating sites or apps, romantic interest is exponentiated when each partner has common interests, values, and

desires. Research has confirmed what might seem obvious: we are attracted to those who are like us. This could be because of physical appearance, compatible attitude, peer group associations, political affiliation, social and cultural interests, hobbies, or work preferences (Lydon, Jamieson, and Zanna, 1988). It is common to be steadfast and even stubborn about our *must-have* relationship preferences.

According to Susan Perry (2003), author of *Loving in Flow: How the Happiest Couples Get and Stay That Way*, "People tend to look for almost a clone of themselves . . . they are very specific—too specific." Perry believes people take their own inventory and compare it against possible mates. I believe our conscious preferences play a specific role in the forming of a romantic relationship. Conscious thought and decision-making patterns account for the first phase of romance when we actively seek a mate or are open to the possibility of meeting a potential love interest.

ONLINE DATING WEBSITES HAVE IT ALL WRONG

Unfortunately, all the effort in writing one's personal biography, choosing the best photographs, and fitting oneself into the most descriptive and representative personality and lifestyle categories is all for naught; it simply doesn't matter. Adding insult to injury, it is futile to rely on the careful reading and interpreting of a potential love interest's profile by scanning every pixel of their photograph with a magnifying glass looking for potential clues or red flags. Simply speaking, dating chemistry is not based on your prospective match's body type, musical interests, favorite movies, political leanings, education, religion, or other criteria. It is based on the Human Magnet Syndrome!

When a caretaking woman feels chemistry bliss over the narcissistic romantic hopeful, it is not because of any similarities they share—not at all. It is because of the activation of unconscious psychological attraction mechanisms that recognize a perfect "dancing partner" who makes her heart skip a beat or two. His boldness, charisma, self-confidence, and charm create the illusion he is the man about whom she has always dreamed. Little does she know that she, a codependent, has yet again picked another in a long list of narcissists.

Human Magnet Syndrome chemistry, of course, goes both ways. Mr. Perfect's unconscious chemistry machinery has also been stimulated. His heart is aflutter over this perfect angel who listens to and cries for him. She validates all the unfair treatment he has received from his ex-spouses or partners who demand more money than they deserve, the IRS who is stealing his hard-earned money, and the long line of jobs that didn't work out because his bosses were "threatened" by his "superior intellect and management skills."

The multi-billion-dollar Internet dating industry doesn't realize it, but they are selling the Human Magnet Syndrome. As discussed throughout this book, when two romantic hopefuls meet, whether by chance or through the careful selection process, they will instantly feel comfortable, familiar, and safe with each other if one is more of a caretaker (codependent) and the other is a care-needer (pathological narcissist). *It is almost always this way.* Just ask some friends, think about your own family, or analyze your own dating history.

The folks at the helm of the big Internet dating companies either don't know about the Human Magnet Syndrome, or shy away from negative and complicated "blame your parents" psychological explanations. I am sure the perfect match or soulmate promise sells more subscriptions than the matching of similarly lonely and unhappy personality types—codependents and narcissists alike. It is difficult to imagine such companies embracing the Human Magnet Syndrome explanation over the multi-million-dollar research and development, marketing, and advertising campaigns that rest on the promise of finding a soulmate because of their scientific, relationship-matching algorithm.

The Human Magnet Syndrome explains why a smoldering, sexy man with six-pack abs who loves sky diving and skinny dipping, and the drop-dead gorgeous woman who sports a perfect set of lips and long legs, and who also loves jumping out of a plane and swimming in her "birthday suit," just might not be a good match.[8] If these seemingly well-matched romantic hopefuls have a similar self-orientation, then Mr. Smoldering will never connect with Ms. Gorgeous. Or, if entranced by lust, the lack of chemistry will surely be the bucket of cold water that tears them apart.

Everything in my life, both personally and professionally, confirms the causal connection between the Human Magnet Syndrome and romantic chemistry. Not only is it a universal phenomenon everyone has a story or two about, but it is also predictable in how it works, and who it impacts. Simply stated, romantic chemistry IS the Human Magnet Syndrome. Such a bold pronouncement is supported by

---

8 This, of course, applies to same sex match-ups, too.

everyone with whom I share my clinical work, personal dating and relationship experiences, as well as the thousands of testaments by clients, readers, social network connections, and YouTube video subscribers.

Reflections

- What are some opposite relationships you have observed or know of?

- Which opposite role do you most identify with, and why?

Chapter Four

WHY WE CONTINUE TO FAIL "CHEMISTRY" AND "MATH"

The relationship template is an unconsciously driven blueprint that guides all people, healthy or not, in their choice of romantic partners. It informs and guides relational behavior, identification with roles, and thought and emotional patterns. It also represents the unconscious processes responsible for well-matched "opposite personality types" in conjunction with the comfort and ease of the dance partnership. When these psychological and relational processes are combined, the love-struck partners believe (and feel) they have finally arrived at a personal and relational sanctuary, where loneliness and core shame are no longer nipping at their heels.

According to most developmental- and psychodynamic-oriented mental health professionals, people tend to duplicate their childhood parent-child experiences in their adult relationships. Suffice it to say, childhood attachment creates an instruction manual for all future relationships. It is the guide of conscious and unconscious interpersonal preferences, otherwise known as *relationship instincts*. It teaches people the various "rules" for their relationships.

The relationship template unconsciously compels a person to gravitate toward an attractive and seemingly safe person. In psychodynamic terms, the emotional energy of their once-traumatized child-self, who is repressed or blocked from memory, directs the attraction and early courtship process. The "trauma child" clearly communicates to her adult self through what people refer to as "intuition," or "gut feelings," and by reflexive somatic (body) responses. An example of a positive somatic messages would be "butterflies" in the stomach. Nausea or back tension could be experienced on the negative path.

When in the company of a romantic interest with a matched relationship template, people instinctively experience a calm and intuitive feeling of familiarity and safety. Ironically for the codependent, this creates a mistaken assumption that these feelings will translate to the feeling of security. Sadly, nothing could be further from the truth. Hence, a person's attraction patterns are driven, almost exclusively, by a person's relationship template—the heart and soul of the Human Magnet Syndrome.

RELATIONAL CHEMISTRY

When two romantically interested people have instant feelings of connection and comfort, they are experiencing relational chemistry. Chemistry is a reflexive and automatic phenomenon; that is, it is simultaneously and mutually experienced by oppositely compatible people. People often refer to this reaction as feeling "sparks" or love at first sight. The chemistry provokes a shared emotional experience of hope, excitement, and anticipation. It is not unusual for these bonded people to throw caution to the wind and move moderately-to-rapidly forward into a courtship process. This is when strong sexual impulses occur, or what I call *the urge to merge*.

Chemistry cannot happen without the opposite matching of the codependent and narcissist dancers. It doesn't matter if they met through a carefully coordinated and vetted process or by happenstance. Whether brought together through a blind date, Internet dating service or app, or Aunt Yente (matchmaker from *Fiddler on the Roof*), the chemistry reaction will determine if the date ends with a perfunctory handshake and the insincere suggestion to *just be friends*, or a mutually dreamy experience that has no boundaries and begs to never end.

Although unconscious forces are the primary cause of chemistry, conscious choice and preferences play a significant role in how lasting romantic relationships form. Simply put, the conscious mind gets the person *to* the dance, while the unconscious mind *gets them to dance* (and not stop!).

I have created three categories of chemistry, each representing different configurations of personality couplings:

- **Positive Chemistry:** the perfect matching of personality types, which results in comfortable familiarity and feeling safe. This is where "fireworks" and intense infatuation take place. It can be the playground of both healthy and dysfunctionally matched lovers. It is exponentially more intense for dysfunctional matches like codependents and narcissists.
- **Neutral Chemistry:** when both people are more like each other, but are not unhealthy or emotionally impaired. It is a bland, almost sister-brother experience with neither excitement nor discomfort.
- **Negative Chemistry:** when two dysfunctionally similar personalities connect, such as two pathological narcissists or two codependents. This can be a very uncomfortable and even upsetting situation.

POSITIVE CHEMISTRY

Positive chemistry between emotionally balanced and healthy individuals is the "wow, I really like that person" feeling celebrated in thousands of romantic movies and love songs. People in the throes of such an encounter immediately sense comfort and familiarity, followed by a shared interest in each other. Everyone experiences optimism and motivation about a potential and gradual courtship process. Although chemistry for healthier partners can still have an impactful and powerful response, it does not come close to matching the psychological, behavioral, and biological wallop of the dysfunctional matchups.

Positive chemistry between dysfunctionally opposite personality types, like codependents and narcissists, is felt as an overwhelming surge or tidal wave of exhilaration and euphoria, which quickly overtakes baseline feelings of loneliness and insecurity. For some, it is equivalent to winning the lottery. This chemistry is the cause of one or both person's temporary blindness to warning signs and obvious red flags. For these individuals, lessons learned and promises made to never repeat their past relationship mistakes are nullified in the rush of intensely elated and blissful feelings of romantic perfection. His over-the-top alcohol consumption, coupled with the fact he has not been gainfully employed in three years, will go unnoticed or be overtaken by the more prevalent explosion of romantic interest. Her insecurity, clinginess, and constant fear of making a mistake will just be background noise drowned out by the deafening roar of the love-at-first-sight infatuation.

NEUTRAL CHEMISTRY AND ME

Neutral chemistry is the most common of all chemistry experiences. It neither packs the euphoric punch of positive chemistry nor sinks to the antagonistic and uncomfortable lows of its negative counterpart. This occurs between similar personality types who are both mentally healthy. Some people describe this type of chemistry as analogous to meeting a sibling.

Twelve years ago, when I was on an upward swing in my mental and relational health, I started using Internet dating to take my first important steps toward finding a healthy relationship. The added security features of some sites allowed me to be selectively careful and safe in my foray into unchartered territory. These sites allowed me to rationally consider biographical information, while also getting an idea of physical appearance. The ability to instant message, email, text, and talk on the phone was helpful in my efforts to analyze my choices and maintain healthy boundaries. Still, despite all the safety buffers, I realized only a face-to-face encounter could answer the question about chemistry. The following is a true story about my first conscious experience with neutral chemistry.

Kris, according to all the data included in her profile, was the most perfect match for me. According to everything I read, we were almost identical. We were both in the mental health field, she liked rock 'n' roll and classical music, preferred the Cubs over the White Sox, was Jewish but not too religious, shared my political beliefs, loved children and wanted to have one more, and had many other amazing similarities. To boot, she was absolutely gorgeous and had a smile that could light up a room.

After a dozen or so emails and twice as many instant messages, we graduated to phone calls. Two delightful three-hour phone calls later, we finally decided to meet for dinner. There was much excitement and anticipation surrounding our first date. When we met, the positive bang I had hoped for was replaced by the softer "whoosh" of neutral chemistry. Almost immediately, I experienced extreme disappointment for the lack of "bells," "fireworks," and other corny but quintessential signs of positive chemistry.

As the evening progressed, our forced and labored conversation could not move us beyond the disappointing first moments of our meeting. Even though she looked like her photographs and did not misrepresent herself in her biography, we couldn't reach a comfortable and easy conversational rhythm. I couldn't help but think I must have done something wrong or made a huge psychological miscalculation about our compatibility. I was confused and disappointed about our lack of chemistry. I was strangely relieved when we both, almost simultaneously, said, "It's late, and I need to get home to my son." She had a son the same age as mine.

Two days and a few emails later, we talked openly about the unexpected awkwardness of our date and concluded it was just a bad case of the jitters. We agreed to give it another try. A week later, we met for drinks. I enthusiastically knocked down a few beers, as I thought it would help "grease the rusty romantic machinery." Despite our gallant efforts to create a spark, the conversation continued to fall flat, and chemistry remained elusive, but I refused to give up, as I had an "ace up my sleeve" that I optimistically held onto until the end of the date.

As the date fizzled out and I walked her to her car, I moved in closer to unleash my secret weapon: a soft romantic kiss. Her laser-guided defense system triggered, she turned her face away from mine, and stepped back. This was when she delivered the fatal blow, ensuring this water-logged firecracker would never ignite. She said, "I really like you, Ross, but to be honest, you feel more like a brother than a potential boyfriend." Then she finished me off with "let's just be friends."

Even with my bruised ego, I felt strangely relieved. I was able to admit to myself that, despite sharing the same lack of chemistry, I worked harder at denying it. Still, I will be forever grateful to Kris for helping me to understand that no kiss in the world, no matter how good it might be, could overcome the power of neutral chemistry.

NEGATIVE CHEMISTRY

Negative chemistry is a very uncomfortable shared experience. It occurs with unmatched, similar personality types, such as two codependents, two pathological narcissists, or, for that matter, one healthy person with either a codependent or narcissist. These mismatched couples will encounter a range of uncomfortable feelings, including anger, repulsion, fear, anxiety, dread, or boredom.

The negative chemistry between two narcissists would play out quite dramatically and, for any onlooker, rather amusingly. Both will likely harbor feelings of disgust and resentment toward the other's narcissistic behavior, which they also exhibit but cannot see. This couple will often talk over each other or compete with gushing accounts of how wonderful they are and lamentations about how life has unfairly dealt them a bad hand. These battling narcissists will never know their judgments of each other are much more about their similarities, and the reasons behind them, rather than their differences.

The negative chemistry of a codependent duo plays out as two very nice, unassuming people patiently waiting for the other to take charge. When neither does, the ensuing anxiety makes them extremely uncomfortable. They have no experience with anyone ever listening to or expressing interest in them, offering sympathy, or wanting to share their opinions and feelings. Taking turns at apologizing for illogical reasons creates a rift, putting them on edge and possibly being the deciding factor for ending the encounter early. This drama-free pairing often ends with excuses, apologies, and great sighs of relief.

When codependents meet a prospective healthy partner, they feel like a "fish out of water." These are nerve-racking connections, as the codependent is intimidated and insecure about the other's ease and comfort at setting boundaries and expressing emotions. The person's good mental health is a reminder of what is wrong with them and how pathetic they feel. This "oil and water" experience provokes both the codependent and the healthier person to prematurely end their time together or not pursue any follow-up connections.

The negative chemistry guiding the pathological narcissist and healthy person's relationship is often quietly disturbing for both individuals. The narcissist's discomfort, inexperience, and insecurity when around a healthy person results in a slight-to-moderate muffling of his outwardly narcissistic traits. As an unconsciously insecure and shame-based personality, they will feel awkward and uncomfortable around those who have emotional or social abilities that they neither have nor can ever possess. Because of their propensity to judge, they are likely to interpret the healthy person as showing off or acting like they are superior. Ultimately, this type of matchup provokes a mutual, premature end to the encounter.

CHEMISTRY CREATES "LIMERENCE"

Our brains are responsible for the lasting excitement that follows the chemistry-bonded relationship. As much as we want to externally explain pre- and post-chemistry excitement, the real cause is our brain's overproduction of interacting hormones and neurotransmitters. To explain this emotional and biochemical process, Dorothy Tennov (1979) coined the term "limerence."

The Oxford Internet dictionary defines limerence as "the state of being infatuated or obsessed with another person, typically experienced involuntarily and characterized by a strong desire for reciprocation of one's feelings but not primarily for a sexual relationship." Although some confuse chemistry and limerence, they are different psychological and biochemical processes. Chemistry is where opposite attraction begins, and limerence is where it blows up into a fireworks display.

In the beginning of a relationship, the love-struck, or *limerent*, couple is compelled by extreme emotional, physical, and sexual urges to merge into a romantic union, which they believe will make them feel whole and complete. Although sexual attraction plays a key role in the limerence experience, by itself it does not account for the burning emotional and relational desires experienced in limerence. Sex, however, almost always "seals the deal" and exponentiates the hypnotic-like experience of limerence.

When the codependent and the pathological narcissist first meet, their shared limerence creates off-the-charts infatuation that ultimately resembles Obsessive Compulsive Disorder (OCD). When apart, neither can stop thinking about the other, nor do they feel much like eating or sleeping. Each partner is obsessed with the other and is unable to control their nonstop thoughts about the new relationship. The couple simultaneously experiences powerful body sensations that may make them feel like they are floating on air. The feeling of perfection created when they are together quickly brings them into a close and enmeshed romantic relationship.

The drug-like feelings responsible for limerence are primarily caused by the neurotransmitter dopamine. When a person experiences the "high" of new love or intense attraction, neurons are activated in the reward system of the brain, which releases a flood of dopamine. At the same time, the hormone norepinephrine is released causing an increase in blood pressure, sweaty palms, and a pounding-heart. Simultaneously, levels of the neurotransmitter serotonin are lowered or inhibited, stimulating obsessive and compulsive behaviors and thought processes.

It is part of human nature to experience tremendously powerful personal, emotional, and physical sensations in the beginning of a romantic relationship—especially if there is strong physical attraction. With highly compatible relationships, each person initially feels involuntary surges of deep and overwhelming personal, emotional, and sexual excitement. This intense romantic attraction, or limerence, creates overpowering and obsessive cravings to seek the intensely stimulating company of their new love.

According to Dorothy Tennov (1979), "Limerence . . . can be experienced as intense joy or as extreme despair, depending on whether the feelings are reciprocated. Basically, it is the state of being completely carried away by unreasoned passion or love, even to the point of addictive-type behavior." Simply defined, limerence is an overwhelming, obsessive need to have one's feelings reciprocated.

Symptoms of Limerence
Tennov (1979)

- Intrusive thinking about the limerent object (LO)
- Acute longing for the reciprocation of attention and affection
- Fluctuating mood based on the LO's actions
- Experiencing this feeling only with one person at a time
- All-consuming obsession that the LO will relieve the pain
- Preoccupation (fear) with rejection
- Incapacitating and uncomfortable shyness in the beginning of the relationship
- Intensifying limerence through adversity
- Aching "heart" (in the chest) when there are doubts
- Buoyancy ("walking on air") with reciprocation
- Intensely obsessing and demotivating one from other responsibilities (friends, family, work)
- Emphasizing positive attributes of the LO, while ignoring the negative

RELATIONSHIP MATH

Back in 1986, when I was in college, I kept a bulletin board on which I thumbtacked various quotes that had psychological and personal meaning for me. These messages were daily reminders of the beliefs and values I had, or aspired to have.

Many of the quotes remain "tacked" inside of me, as their message survived the test of time. One relied on simple math to make its point. Although I cannot remember the exact wording or even find it online, my own version replaced it.

The "relationship math" image fits with my personal and professional understanding of oppositely compatible codependent/narcissist relationships. It is the simplest explanation I have for why codependents and narcissists feel balanced by each other and why the relationship endures over time. My explanation for relationship math is this:

Codependents and pathological narcissists are psychologically underdeveloped people who need each other to feel good about themselves. Alone, they are empty, lonely people who need the company of another to escape their fundamental feelings of core shame and pervasive loneliness. The codependent is conscious of these, while the narcissist successfully runs or hides from them. Alone, both will always feel incomplete, unsatisfied, and lonely. Together, they are able to forget what is essentially wrong with and what they dislike, or even hate, about themselves. They experience a respite from the chronic loneliness and shame that has followed them their entire lives. Together, they both mistake complete enmeshment and the absence of loneliness as euphoric happiness and joy. This "½" plus "½" combination is the only mathematical formula that will work with these two self-love-starved and shame-based people, who depend on one another for any modicum of happiness. They will always need each other to feel whole. This relationship of two halves can never be a whole relationship, as both people lack the requisite self-love and individuation.

RELATIONSHIP MATH

½ + ½ (CODEPENDENT & NARCISSIST) = 1.
THIS SUM REPRESENTS A ½ RELATIONSHIP
COMPRISED OF ENMESHED AND DEPENDENT INDIVIDUALS.

1 + 1 (HEALTHY PARTNERS) = 2.
THIS SUM REPRESENTS 1 POTENTIALLY HEALTHY RELATIONSHIP
COMPRISED OF 2 HEALTHY INTERDEPENDENT PARTNERS.

1 + 1 + 1 (HEALTHY PARTNERS & THE RELATIONSHIP) = 3.
THIS SUM REPRESENTS AN ENDURING & HEALTHY RELATIONSHIP
COMPRISED OF 2 EMOTIONALLY HEALTHY PARTNERS WHO
TAKE SPECIAL CARE OF THEIR RELATIONSHIP.
ROSS ROSENBERG, 2017

The codependent-narcissist relationship is fundamentally tilted toward the needs of the narcissist; the naïve and well-meaning codependent will experience a disturbing transformation from optimism and happiness to pessimism-laced bitterness. The fall from euphoric hopefulness to the realization the narcissist *half lover* cannot and will never deliver on the promise of making them happy and whole is the "kick in the crotch" from which the codependent rarely recovers.

Recovering codependent and psychologically healthy people find the 1 + 1 = 2 equation to be more fitting of their personality type and emotional needs. This "formula" better suits their ability to run toward, rather than away from, the solution to their problems. Achieving better mental health, or not being former children of attachment-traumatizing parents, allows people to individuate and to develop self-love and self-esteem. These adult "1s" need another "1" partner—not to take away painful emotions, but to add to their baseline of contentment and optimism about life in general. Therefore, two "1s" create a relationship composed of two interdependent friends, who inherently know how to balance their self-love and other-love desires, needs, and capacities.

A CODEPENDENCY BLOOD TEST?

If codependency was considered a medical condition, much like Major Depression, Bipolar Disorder, or Schizophrenia, we would be unable to locate the *genes* responsible for it. Similarly, if it was caused by a pathogen like hepatitis B or botulism, we would never find the bacteria or virus responsible for it. However, if we adjusted our medical paradigm and concluded it is not a problem by itself, but a result of a collection of other measurable problems, an imaginary toxicology report would reveal the following:

- One-part childhood-attachment trauma
- One-part part core shame
- One-part pathological loneliness
- One-part codependency addiction
- One-part childhood gaslighting[9]
- One-part adult gaslighting

9 The impact of gaslighting on codependency will be discussed in Chapter Eleven.

The third section of my relationship math illustrates the importance of the relationship itself. Not only do healthy people promote healthy relationships, but the reverse is also true. A well-cared-for relationship is a resilient and lasting one. A healthy relationship *allows* its partners to go through trying times and come out the other side as committed to each other and in love as before the situation occurred. Hence, the importance of the 1 + 1 + 1 = 3 equation cannot be overstated. *Three is the magic number!*

WHY I FAILED "CHEMISTRY" AND "MATH"

The following is a slightly altered (for legal reasons) example of my own dysfunctional chemistry and experience with bad relationship math with a pathological narcissist who was my exact opposite.

About 30 years ago, when I was 27, I was at a personal low in my life as cutbacks eliminated my first postgraduate-school counseling job. With no job and little savings, my only choice was to move back in with my parents, who I had been independent from for nine years. Not only did I return home penniless and irrationally afraid I would never find another position, I was recovering from major spinal fusion surgery. Moving back into my childhood home felt nothing short of a complete defeat. It was natural for me to voluntarily slide into a state of depression and despair, especially since I felt like an utter failure in my nine-year journey to prove to my dad I didn't need his financial help. This event started one of the darkest chapters of my adult life.

One cold Saturday evening in December, a high school friend and I decided to go to a dance club in Chicago that was sponsoring a dating event. I remember putting in a great deal of effort to get ready that night, as I had been emotionally lost in my stinging depressive funk. I hoped for the best while battling back my pessimism and fear of rejection. Although I still felt confident about my appearance and basic personality, I was equally confident no one would be interested in a pain-ridden, unemployed psychotherapist who lived with Mommy and Daddy. The thought of relaying these details to a prospective date terrified me. However, I managed to muster up the courage, and any scraps of positive thinking I had left, to begin the evening.

Once we got to the club, I reconnected with my perennial dating-performance anxiety that was based on my self-defeating prophesies. Like clockwork, I worked very hard to establish a conversation that would ultimately be undermined by my own anxiety and insecurities. These conversations would follow this pattern: ten minutes of idle chit-chat, during which I did most of the talking. For reasons that escaped me at the time, I would disclose too much information, too quickly, about my personal life. This, in turn, would make the women uncomfortable and anxious. Like similar events of the past, the results ended up sabotaging my intentions to be the relaxed and interesting version of myself I knew existed, but was unable to demonstrate. Each conversation ended the same: one of us walked away out of sheer discomfort.

That night, after two or three floundering attempts to strike up a conversation with women I found interesting, I felt an overwhelming compulsion to go home and cry. Before my *fight-or-flight mode* fully kicked in, I caught a quick glance of a gorgeous woman who was staring at me. From across the room, my eyes locked onto her hypnotic smile. She wore a titillating tight black dress that plunged deeply in the front and back, showing plenty of skin. My earlier feelings of awkwardness and anxiety evaporated in the blazing heat of the moment. Filled with confidence and bravado, I sauntered over to her table and offered to buy her a drink. The conversation was effortless, full of intrigue, and deeply seductive. Almost immediately, our guards came down and we proceeded to share private, emotionally evocative details about ourselves. No topic seemed off limits. Time stood still as we talked about ourselves, our problems, and the difficulties in our lives.

I didn't flinch when she told me she had no higher education,[10] worked a dead-end job she hated, and was chronically short of money to pay child support for her son who lived with her ex-husband. Despite these factors, which should have been red flags, my interest in her exponentially heightened as we moved so close our bodies touched. The sexually laced conversation was gasoline thrown onto an already burning fire. To make a long story short, and to spare you the lurid details, I ended up at her small apartment that night. Until I got a job two months later, I only periodically returned to my parents' home.

Over the next three months, we lived in a fantasy of exhilarating moments that took us away from our respective reservoirs of emotional pain. Then, out of

---

10 Please do not see this as an indication of my judgment against people who do not have a college degree. It was a moment in which I broke a promise to myself, which was that my preferred type would have educational and professional ambitions and experiences similar to my own.

nowhere, she lashed out at me for something I did that was so benign, I cannot even remember what it was. The codependent in me would not, or did not want to, recognize her chronic mental health problem, which I later learned was an untreated case of Borderline Personality Disorder (BPD). The next two years of verbal, emotional, and physical abuse didn't sway my resolve to save this inherently broken relationship. Finally, with the help of a codependency therapist, I broke free from the relationship. Despite my vow to never repeat this mistake, I would fall prey again to *bad math* and *the lies of chemistry* one more time.

To this point, we know the following processes are responsible for the Human Magnet Syndrome's opposite-attraction dynamic and the following courtship and relationship formation sequences:

1. Opposite personalities attract.
2. "Positive Chemistry" is experienced.
3. For the relationship to have "legs," or the potential to move forward, the "Relationship Math" must equal "1."
4. An effortless and highly coordinated relationship "dance" begins.
5. Matching "relationship templates" instruct each person on their role expectations and behaviors.
6. Limerence takes the two "to the moon" with a jolt of narcotic-like euphoria, and "I can't sleep, eat, or stop thinking of you until we are together again," OCD-like feelings.
7. With the fading of limerence, each person's baseline (hidden) personality traits emerge.
8. The fear of loneliness, or the experience of it, compels the codependent to remain in the relationship.
9. Codependency addiction is the most powerful explanation for why codependents do not terminate a relationship fraught with loss and negative consequences. The narcissist, their "drug of choice," can keep the loneliness and core shame at bay.
10. If the codependent should terminate the relationship, they would experience the powerfully painful withdrawal symptom of pathological loneliness.
11. If the relationship does end, and the problems underlying the person's codependency are not resolved, they will likely find a similar narcissist

Reflections

- Does relational chemistry work to your benefit? Why?

- Which relationship math equation can you most relate to? Why?

- Write about one or two occasions during which you got lost in limerence.

- List reasons why codependency addiction does or does not apply to you.

Chapter Five

THE RELATIONSHIP COMPATIBILITY THEORY AND OPPOSITE ATTRACTION

E ven with the overwhelmingly positive feedback from my "Codependency: Don't Dance!" essay, I knew it needed to be developed into a broader and more complete psychological theory. This was no easy task, as I had to work backwards from my intuition and gut-level understandings, to the foundational theories that inspired them. I was not interested in making something elegantly simple and user friendly into a bloated or convoluted set of psychological explanations. Trusting my intuition, I began a mental construction of a unified theory that accounted for and explained the full-range of my Human Magnet Syndrome related discoveries.

My intent was to build a theory around clear, concise, and measurable concepts that would stand up to professional and/or scientific scrutiny. In addition, it would need to explain and predict observable relational phenomena, while tying it to individual psychological theory. I would not rest until my theory would satisfy a room filled with both highly educated and experienced clinicians, as well as people without that educational background.

From my theoretical ambitions arose a model that corralled my divergent discoveries and observations into a coherent and cohesive set of explanations. It developed "legs" when I decided to create a professional training based upon these discoveries. Like alchemy, the mixture of my ideas, explanations, and discoveries resulted in the creation of gold . . . theoretical gold.

THE CONTINUUM OF SELF THEORY (COS)

The name I originally chose in 2013 for my new theory was the Continuum of Self Theory, or COS. It explained why all people, not just codependents and narcissists, are predictably drawn to a certain type of oppositely attractive partner. It intuitively accounted for why so many people remain in deeply unhappy and dysfunctional relationships despite feeling lonely, frustrated, or resentful. Similarly, it explained why some people tend to repeat their dysfunctional relationship choices despite wanting something different.

COS became a universal theory, as it applied to all individuals, ranging from those who are psychologically unhealthy to those who are completely balanced and psychologically healthy. Moreover, it accounted for the malleable nature of mental health, as we all are inherently capable of growing and learning from our mistakes, overcoming difficult personal conditions, and, with professional help, overcoming the powerful and seemingly indelible dysfunctional forces of our unconscious mind.

THE RELATIONSHIP COMPATIBILITY THEORY (RCT)

At some point in the last five years, I renamed my beloved COS Theory to the Relationship Compatibility Theory (RCT). Influenced by my education, experience, and specialization in Family Systems Theory, the name change made sense to me, since at face value it explained relationship compatibility of oppositely balanced individuals. Like its predecessor, RCT illustrates how oppositely matched chronic caretakers, or codependents, match up to care-needers, the selfishly narcissistic individuals. Despite the descriptive and terminology modifications, the theory itself remains unchanged.

Like its predecessor, RCT represents how opposite personality types interact in a relationship and how they do or do not express their emotional, psychological, and relational needs. In more specific terms, it represents the distribution patterns of love, respect, and care (LRC) in a relationship. RCT suggests all people are consciously and unconsciously attracted to romantic partners whose LRC patterns correspond with their own.

THE OTHERS AND SELF RELATIONSHIP ORIENTATIONS

Relationship Orientations, or ROs, are the driving force behind my Relationship Compatibility Theory. There are only two ROs: one that is oriented towards the love, respect, and care needs of others, and a second that is focused on the LRC needs of self. Relationships are considered compatible if the caretaking and care-needing ROs are matched up.

ROs are divided into two opposite and inversely related categories: the Others-Relationship Orientation (ORO) and the Self-Relationship Orientation (SRO). The primary difference between them is that the former focuses more on giving LRC and the latter on taking it.

The ORO maintains a natural and reflexive focus on another's emotional, personal, and relational needs, often to the exclusion of their own. The person with an ORO struggles with expressing and obtaining LRC from others, while being generous in how much they give away. All codependents have an extreme ORO.

The SRO demonstrates a natural and reflexive focus on their own needs for emotional, personal, and relational comfort, while not understanding or ignoring the importance of reciprocity. The person with an SRO struggles with sharing or giving away LRC to others, while hoarding the same for themselves. SROs are predictably targeted on, if not obsessed with, perpetuating the unequal and selfish one-way nature of a give-and-take relationship. All pathological narcissists have an extreme SRO.

Since the ORO and SRO are "opposite" and "inversely" relating personality constructs, the opposite attraction content in Chapter Three applies to them.

As much as a severe ORO represents codependency and a severe SRO, pathological narcissism, the two are not synonymous. The primary difference is that ROs represent a range of two opposite categories, each having a gamut of potentialities, from healthy to dysfunctional. People with healthy ROs are not willing to accept or tolerate a relationship that lacks personal, emotional, or relational equity and fairness. Codependents (OROs) and pathological narcissists (SROs) have the most dysfunctional form of opposing relationship orientations.

The most dysfunctional ROs are the extreme ORO and SRO, both of which are likely to exist in the same oppositely compatible relationship. The ORO's extreme selflessness and sacrifice plays perfectly into the SRO's extreme selfish and demanding traits.

RCT'S NUTS AND BOLTS

The Relationship Compatibility Theory uses a continuum to illustrate the interaction between the ORO and SRO in a relationship. I developed it to have the following attributes:

1. Simple Design
2. Operational, specific, and quantifiable definitions
3. The use of basic arithmetic—addition and subtraction
4. Logical one-dimensional rules
5. Logical interactional rules
6. Concrete explanations for complicated psychological and relational processes
7. Represents only what it claims—does not overreach or over-generalize
8. Intuitive to both codependency treatment providers and the individuals they treat

A FLEXIBLE AND INCLUSIVE THEORY

The RCT owes its flexibility and inclusive nature to the fact that it is a product of many other important, well-established psychological theories. I could never have developed it had it not been for previously introduced theoretical frameworks like Family Systems, Psychodynamic, Attachment, Cognitive Behavioral, Addictions, 12 Steps, and several others. The theory's inclusive theoretical nature has resulted in many practical applications, including mental health and addiction treatment, education, and research fields, as well as those pertaining to the general public.

The RCT is meant to be black-and-white and very specific. The inverse ROs and their Relationship Compatibility Values (RCVs) are specifically defined to represent explicit and quantifiable information and observations. Its mathematical nature requires it to be simplistic and lends itself flawlessly to research, diagnostic, and treatment applications.

THE RELATIONSHIP COMPATIBILITY THEORY IS PARADOXICAL

As much as the Relationship Compatibility Theory (RCT) is compact, straightforward, logical, and simple, it is also a complicated theory with many possible uses. I believe its flexibility and specificity substantially broaden its potential contributions and purposes.

THE RELATIONSHIP COMPATIBILITY CONTINUUM (RCC)

The sole measurement tool for the RCT is the Relationship Compatibility Continuum (RCC). Using simple graphics and math, it explains and quantifies the unconscious and reflexive attraction between two people in a relationship. The continuum also demonstrates how and why the opposite ORO and SRO personality types experience a magnetic pull of positive chemistry. Conversely, it explains the lack of compatibility between similar ROs.

Don't be fooled by the simple design of the continuum, as it brings together every concept discussed thus far, as well as many that follow. It is an indispensable theoretical and practical tool that greatly advances the understanding of the Human-Magnet-Syndrome-driven relationship, as well as the effective and lasting treatment of codependency.

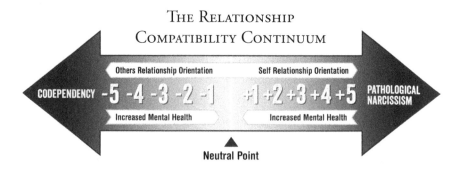

RELATIONSHIP COMPATIBILITY CONTINUUM (RCC) AND RELATIONSHIP COMPATIBILITY VALUES (RCV)

Relationship Compatibility Values (RCVs) numerically represent a person's RO, as well as their unique LRC distribution pattern. The two opposite ROs—the ORO and the SRO—are on opposite sides of the RCC.

The left, or "negative," side of the continuum contains the ORO and its five RCVs, ranging from (-5) to (-1). The SRO is on the right, or "positive," side and consists of an RCV range of (+1) to (+5). In the center of the continuum is a (0), or neutral, RCV. In this respect, there are only 11 possible RCV scores. The positive side of the continuum is not qualitatively better than the negative side. The division was made by happenstance, without any consideration of one being either "better" or "worse" than the other.

The numerically highest negative and positive RCVs represent the most dysfunctional forms of a given RO. For example, the (-5) ORO RCV represents the codependent who gives almost all their LRC to others and receives very little in return. The (+5) SRO RCV represents the pathological narcissist who takes all the LRC available and gives little to none in return.

RCV EXAMPLES

The following list matches each of the 11 Relationship Compatibility Values (RCVs) with a general personality description. These examples illustrate the wide variety of general personality possibilities, according to the RCT.

- **(-5) RCV (ORO):** A codependent who is completely absorbed with the LRC needs of others, while completely ignoring and devaluing their own. They are often powerless and unable or unwilling to seek LRC from their romantic partner and closest friends.
- **(-4) RCV (ORO):** Someone with codependent tendencies who is almost always focused on the LRC needs of others, while only intermittently seeking to have their own LRC needs fulfilled. They are able, albeit unmotivated, fearful, and/or inexperienced in seeking LRC from a romantic partner. They often choose not to ask others to fulfill their LRC needs, as they don't want to upset others or cause conflict. If asking for some semblance of LRC from their partner, they do so nervously and with distinct feelings of guilt or neediness.
- **(-3) RCV (ORO):** One who identifies with their own caring and giving nature. They are predominantly focused on the LRC needs of others, while often diminishing, delaying, or excusing away the fulfillment of

their own needs. Their identity and reputation are fused with their helping and caretaking nature. They are typically in imbalanced relationships regarding their LRC needs—giving much more than receiving. They are capable of setting boundaries in relationships, while also asking for what they need; however, they tend to feel guilty or needy when setting such boundaries or when asking for help from others.

- **(-2) RCV (ORO):** One who is involved in relationships in which their caretaking identity is valued and appreciated, but not exploited. They enjoy relationships in which they provide ample LRC, without wanting equal amounts reciprocated. They are comfortable with a partner who needs more LRC than he or she is willing to give in return. They can set boundaries and ask for what they need, though they feel slightly uncomfortable doing so when the LRC balance goes beyond their comfort level. They might experience mild feelings of guilt or neediness when asking a partner to meet their own LRC needs. As much as possible, they avoid individuals who are narcissistic, exploitative, or manipulative.

- **(-1) RCV (ORO):** Someone with a healthy balance between love, respect, and care for themselves and others. They typically seek life experiences and relationships in which they can satisfy their own LRC needs. They tend to participate in and appreciate relationships based on a reciprocal and mutual distribution of LRC. Although they derive meaning and happiness from helping and caring for others, they will not tolerate a selfish or self-centered romantic partner. They often enjoy caring for others, but do not identify as a caretaker or helper. They do not feel guilty or needy when asking for LRC from others.

- **(0) RCV:** Someone who participates in relationships where there is an equal distribution of LRC given and received. They easily ask for what they need from their partner, while being open to their LRC needs. In a LRC-balanced relationship, they easily fluctuate between being the recipient and the giver.

- **(+1) RCV (SRO):** Someone with a healthy balance of love, respect, and care for themselves and others. They tend to participate in and appreciate relationships based on a reciprocal and mutual distribution of LRC. They value personal and professional goals and ambitions, which they confidently pursue. Although they derive meaning and happiness from the pursuit of their own aspirations, they are also cognizant of the necessity to love, respect, and care for their romantic partner. They effortlessly provide LRC to their romantic partner when necessary or requested. They may identify with the role of both caretaker and helper while wanting to fulfill their own desires.

- **(+2) RCV (SRO):** One who prefers to be involved in a relationship in which their pursuit to fulfill their own hopes and dreams is encouraged and supported. In a romantic relationship, they actively seek attention, appreciation, and affirmation. Although they are go-getters and may be consumed with being in the spotlight, they are willing and able to fulfill their partner's needs. They are neither exploitative nor selfish. Oriented towards their own LRC needs, they periodically forget about the inequity of the LRC distribution in the relationship. They respond favorably and non-reactively when their partner asks for greater amounts of LRC. Although they can be comfortable in a caretaking role, they cannot maintain it.

- **(+3) RCV (SRO):** Mildly selfish and self-centered, this is someone who is predominantly focused on the LRC needs of themselves, while often diminishing, delaying, or excusing away the fulfillment of their partner's needs. Their identity and reputation are fused with their need for attention, validation, and recognition. They identify with the persona of a go-getter and a success-driven individual. They are typically drawn to relationships where there is an imbalance in the distribution of LRC needs, expecting or taking more than giving. If confronted about this inequality, they may get defensive, but will be able to make corrections. Although they may be perceived as self-consumed and self-centered, they are able to keep these qualities in check and are willing and able to love, respect, and care for their partner. They do, however, need frequent reminders.

- **(+4) RCV (SRO):** Someone who is narcissistic and preoccupied with the LRC needs of self, while rarely seeking to fulfill those of others. They come across as being entitled, self-absorbed, and self-centered as they are driven to seek LRC from others, but give very minimal amounts in return. They are comfortable with the LRC disparity, believing their needs are more important than their partner's. Although overtly narcissistic, they are still able to give nominal levels of LRC to others. If confronted about the LRC inequities, they will characteristically get angry and defensive and quickly try to justify their actions. They do not, however, experience a narcissistic injury or exhibit narcissistic rage when confronted.

- **(+5) RCV (SRO):** A pathological narcissist who is unable and unmotivated to love, respect, and care for others. They are consumed with fulfilling their own LRC needs and have no intention of reciprocating. They have great difficulty exhibiting empathy, unconditional positive regard, or love. When they do give LRC to others, it is typically with strings attached. They are not able to comprehend or accept their pathological levels of narcissism. If confronted about the LRC imbalances, they will often strike back with either direct or passive aggression.

CONTINUUM MATH AND ZERO-SUM BALANCE

The Relationship Compatibility Theory (RCT) is mathematically supported by the Relationship Compatibility Continuum (RCC). Achieved by the simple addition of each person's RCV, a relationship is considered compatible and stable with a sum of (0), which is referred to as a *zero-sum balance*. The zero-sum will always occur with the matching of inversely related and diametrically opposite personalities, as represented by exactly opposite negative and positive RCVs. In addition to relational compatibility, a zero-sum balance signifies a high potential for chemistry, the matching of relationship templates, and the coming together of opposite personality types. The rule of thumb regarding compatibility is: the lower the inverse/opposite RCV, the healthier the relationship.

The only exception to the zero-sum balance rule as it relates to positive chemistry is the hypothetical (0) and (0) matchup. This is considered hypothetical because it is unlikely to ever occur. First, the (0) RCV will rarely be more than a theoretical unit, as most people identify with either a more giving or taking RO. Second, without the chemistry action of oppositely matched personalities, this hypothetical relationship will never have the "legs" to move forward.

A relationship comprised of a (-2) and (+2) RCV matchup will be both compatible and healthy. To illustrate, a (-2) RCV ORO psychologically healthy woman, who loves being a stay-at-home mom and enjoys her several volunteer positions, is married to a psychologically healthy and stable (+2) RCV SRO man, a successful corporate executive. With the support of his wife, he works long hours to build his stature and reputation in the family business. With inversely matching lower RCVs, both feel loved and participate in a mutually and reciprocally loving relationship.

In contrast, a codependent man with an RCV of (-5) is married to a woman with a narcissistic personality disorder who has a RCV of (+5). The husband is deeply insecure, needy, and compliant. He reluctantly agrees to stay home and raise the children while his narcissistic wife, an unsuccessful salesperson, insists on being the family's sole provider. Because of his fear of enraging her, he avoids confronting her about her selfish and rigid role expectations. As a (+5) on the RCC, she will not even consider his needs unless they make her feel better about herself. If confronted about her narcissism, she reacts harshly to him. This relationship will remain intact, as neither the husband nor wife dare end the marriage; they are equally insecure and afraid of being alone.

THE RISKS OF GETTING HEALTHIER

If one partner's RCV moves in a healthier direction (closer to zero) and the other's does not follow suit, the relationship is likely to be in jeopardy. This is common when one partner goes to therapy or seeks help for an addiction, while the other partner does not, thereby ignoring their contribution to the dysfunctional relationship. Relationships with unbalanced RCVs are inherently unstable and subsequently prone to conflict and breakup.

An example of relationship instability caused by increased mental health is when a (-5) codependent woman, married to a (+5) pathological narcissist man, seeks psychotherapy. Because of her progress in therapy, it is likely her RO/RCV will change for the better, moving closer to zero. Provided her mental health improves and she chooses to remain with her pathologically narcissistic husband, the relationship will become unstable. Without the zero-sum balance, all bets are off. Conflict and irreconcilable differences are likely to result, as the wife will be compelled to seek greater levels of LRC from her husband, which he is not capable of giving.

Even with better mental health, the formerly codependent client may both consciously and unconsciously feel compelled to return to the dysfunctional relationship, thereby reversing RCV gains. This illogical compulsion is explained by codependency addiction, which is presented in Chapter Three. By continuing and maintaining her mental and relational health, and her partner not matching these gains, the lack of a zero-sum-balance will likely result in the termination of the relationship.

QUANTITATIVE AND QUALITATIVE STABILITY

Relational stability can be understood in both quantitative and qualitative terms. "Quantitative" is defined as the metric measurement and/or specific and accurate description of anything that has discernable characteristics. "Qualitative," the more ambiguous and subjective of the two, describes and/or measures discernable characteristics that are assigned a subjective value. The "quality" element of "qualitative" is confusing, as it connotes something that is positive or good. To illustrate, in the following statement, "the first time I cooked pecan pie, it was terrible!" "Terrible" is a "qualitative" term, meaning the pie really sucked! Conversely, "I could have eaten all my mother-in-law's delicious, melt-in-your-mouth pecan pie" represents the positive side of the term.

Quantitative relationship stability occurs with a zero-sum balance that is comprised of equally opposite RCVs. Such stability is independent of the psychological health of the individuals or the relationship. To illustrate, the healthy ORO/SRO (-2) and (+2) relationship is quantitatively stable, indicating a perfect balance of opposite ROs. Hence, quantitative and qualitative stability can be represented on the Relationship Compatibility Continuum.

"STABLE" RELATIONSHIPS

A "stable" relationship is defined as one that does not end despite the unhappiness, anger, dissatisfaction, resentment, and other negative states of both partners. Stable relationships are resistant to breakup because of the alignment of opposite personalities and the resulting relational balance. Relationship stability is numerically represented on the RCC as a pairing of two diametrically opposite RCVs, which, when added together, equal a zero-sum balance. The healthiest version of a stable pairing is the (-1) and (+1) couple. The unhealthiest would be the codependent (-5) and pathological narcissist (+5) pairing.

People in a stable relationship are loyal to both the relationship and the people in it. They abide by their unique set of rules guiding individual and relationship behavior. "Stable" romantic or intimate relationships require both partners to feel comfortable and secure regarding expectations and roles. Loyalty to the relationship, whether it is healthy or dysfunctional, is a key contributor to relational stability. Although harmful interactions may occur, neither partner worries about the other ending it. Regardless of discomfort, harm, or threatening events, both partners are loyal and committed to each other. This energizes the relationship and helps them overcome challenges. In this manner, a stable relationship utilizes internal and external resources to defend itself against any threat.

"UNSTABLE" RELATIONSHIPS

In intimate "unstable" relationships, partners experience discomfort, fear, and anxiety over the possibility the relationship will be harmed or ended. Partners feel unstable when one or both no longer abide by the previously agreed upon relationship rules, roles, and expectation of loyalty. Hardships, crises, or misfortune also bring on instability. Ironically, dysfunctional relationships may become unstable when something good happens to one of the partners (e.g., progress in dealing with a mental health concern or addiction, a better job, a raise, or new social opportunities). Without a return to the former healthy or unhealthy relationship status, instability will likely continue.

Relationship instability triggers a cascade of angry, uncomfortable and/or anxious feelings and thoughts in one or both people in the relationship. Such change puts pressure on the person deviating from the norm to return to their former position in the relationship or to follow the explicitly agreed upon rules. If the status quo is not returned, anxiety and fear will increase; at least until the person "breaks" and resumes the former dysfunctional role, or they break free from the relationship. It should be noted, the higher the RCV sum, the more intense the disequilibrium.

RESTORING EQUILIBRIUM

Only with a reestablishment of a zero-sum balance, independent of positive or negative mental health, can disequilibrium be neutralized and/or reversed. In other words, the Human-Magnet-Syndrome forces that compel a recovering codependent to relapse (to her former RCV of (-5)) into a relationship she terminated with her (+5) pathologically narcissistic partner, returns the relationship to its former "stable," but dysfunctional, balance.

The following scenarios illustrate how relational equilibrium and stability can be re-established:

- The healthier person in a dysfunctional partnership regresses to their former, less healthy RCV.
- The healthier person's improved mental and relational health causes their partner increased anxiety, stress, and fear. This motivates the unhealthier partner to increase their mental and relational health, which recalibrates the relationship to a zero-sum balance.
- Due to a mental health decline in the unhealthy partner, the healthier partner slides to a lower level of functioning so the zero-sum balance can be restored.
- The healthier person's growth is not reciprocated, and they consequently choose to terminate the relationship.
- The unhealthier person ends the relationship to pursue a replacement partner, thereby re-establishing a zero-sum balance.

HEALTHIER RELATIONSHIP AND RCV MATCHUPS

Romantic relationships become healthier when the equally inverse RCVs move closer to zero on the continuum. Less-severe matching RCVs result in a more matched, reciprocal relationship. This couple is no longer polarized by their RO differences. They receive an equal amount of LRC, which creates greater harmony and intimacy.

These healthier relationships are composed of partners with lower inversely matching RCVs, such as a (-1) and (+1) or (-2) and (+2) pairing. Despite the unequal distribution of LRC, both partners believe their needs are adequately met, and they can ask for what they need should an imbalance occur. Lower RCV-matched partners ask for what they need without the worry of causing resentment or feeling needy. It is not the zero balance by itself that creates a positive relationship experience, but the experience of a comfortable and mutually satisfying LRC balance.

People who fall into this category probably did not suffer childhood attachment trauma, the primary cause of both codependency and the pathologically narcissistic disorders. Alternatively, they may have received psychological treatment to remediate it. In addition to good mental health, these "healthy," oppositely connected people share moderate-to-high levels of self-esteem and self-love, can adequately communicate to resolve conflict, and can set and respect healthy boundaries. Simply speaking, this partnership is made up of two self-loving and psychologically healthy people.

Individuals in a lower RCV matched relationship are psychologically able to cross over to the other relationship orientation when necessary. Such "flexibility" is indicative of a person's ability to go against the "grain" of their personality for the sake of their partner or the relationship. An example would be the (-2) ORO, who becomes ill and needs bed rest for six months, and the (+2) SRO who will take care of the kids, clean the house, and work all day while their partner recuperates. When their health returns, so will their normal RCV configuration.

A HEALTHY ZERO-SUM RELATIONSHIP: SUSAN (-2) AND ZACH (+2)

Susan is an emotionally and psychologically healthy and balanced person, as exemplified by her RCV of (-2). Her self-orientation slants mildly to moderately toward the needs of others. Although she doesn't expect the "give-and-take ratio" to be equal, she knows her limits and has a good internal compass that directs her towards self-care. She derives happiness and fulfillment from her charitable and giving approach to life. She loves planning parties, helping friends decorate their homes, babysitting her sister's children, or simply being a compassionate listener. More than anything, Susan takes pride in how she parents her two daughters. She loves cooking their favorite meals, being a Girl Scout leader, and helping with school projects or homework. Susan is also a part-time office manager for a law firm, coordinating her boss's fast-paced, but often disorganized, schedule.

Susan is married to Zach, a talented physician whose ambition is to become the chief orthopedic surgeon of the hospital where he works. Although he is busy and often consumed with his professional obligations, he makes time to meet the personal and emotional needs of his wife and children. His family feels they get enough of Zach's attention and love. While the combination of marriage and family life are challenging, Susan and Zach are committed. They support each other's professional ambitions and have the same personal, family, and career goals.

Zach is a comparably healthy and balanced person with his mild RCV of (+2). He is ambitious and enjoys his professional status. He believes he is doing his part in the marriage and the family by working hard. Zach and Susan believe his career ambitions are going to result in greater overall comfort and happiness for the family. Although he isn't happy about his frequent time away from home, he knows it will benefit the people he loves the most: Susan and his children. Even in Zach's diminished personal and familial capacity, he does not hesitate to make Susan feel loved, respected, and cared for. When he is unable to be there for a family event because of an important professional obligation, the family supports him, even though they are disappointed. This relationship works because Zach and Susan's zero-sum relationship is balanced and mutually satisfying.

UNHEALTHY AND PROBLEMATIC SELF-ORIENTATIONS

The (5) and (4) RCV pairings constitute unhealthy and problematic relationships. Partners in these relationships either self-sabotage or are simply incapable or unwilling to do the work to achieve improved mental or relational health. This is especially the case with a personality-disordered narcissist and his or her severely codependent partner.

Couple's therapy with unhealthy (-5) and (+5) or (-4) and (+4) individuals often fail due to the pathology of both individuals. Even though the ORO wants change or progress, they are often passive, anxious, and fearful during the psychotherapy sessions.[11] Pathological SROs cannot or will not move beyond their conscious and unconscious patterns of denial, avoidance, or blame. More often than not, they tend to hijack the therapy process, which often stymies the less experienced psychotherapist. Typical of such couple's therapy sessions, the psychotherapist spends an inordinate amount of time engaging the controlling narcissist or anxiously "walking on eggshells." For this reason, I do not provide marital or couple's therapy to such individuals.

It should be mentioned that, although the (-4) and (+4) RCV pairing is considered challenging and dysfunctional, both have some capacity, albeit very minimal, to break free of their rigid and dichotomous relationship orientations.

---

11 For good reason, as many report severe consequences or punishments following couple's therapy.

THE CHALLENGING RELATIONSHIP

The (-3) and (+3) RCV pairing is considered a difficult relationship. As people with "middle-of-the-road" mental and relational health, the extent of their psychological resources tends to balance out their deficits. These people neither have a polarized or one-dimensional LRC distribution pattern, nor an abundance of reciprocal interactions. They do, however, have a mild-to-moderate ability to gain insight and exercise good judgment—the necessary psychological components of positive mental and relationship health.

The delineation between healthy and unhealthy RCV pairings is not always clear. From the vantage point of modern Western culture, a couple with a (-3) and (+3) RCV pairing may be considered unhealthy, as there is a distinct disparity with the exchange of LRC. However, from the perspective of other societies, cultures, or ethnic groups where the norm is oriented towards an acceptable discrepancy between the giving and taking of LRC, the relationship would be considered healthy. If these romantic partners are satisfied and happy with their relationship, and are not harming each other, then their somewhat polarized ROs may constitute a healthy relationship.

Even with the inequity of LRC given and received, this couple is still capable of minor levels of mutuality and reciprocity. The ORO partner can set some boundaries, as well as communicate some of their LRC needs. Complementing this, the SRO partner is capable of minimal-to-moderate levels of empathy and motivation to meet their partner's LRC needs, while also being open to some constructive feedback.

A DYSFUNCTIONAL ZERO-SUM RELATIONSHIP: SANDRA (-5) AND PAUL (+5)

Sandra is an attractive, obese 39-year-old who is the mother of a special-needs child and the wife of a man with all the primary symptoms of an NPD. She is an emotional eater, self-medicating her sadness, loneliness, and anger with food. She writes her own music, has a fine singing voice, plays the guitar masterfully, and is the choir and teen worship service director of her church. The church's congregants adore her, and she has become an icon for all she has taught. Reverend Doeman, the leader of the church and a member of its board of directors, has not given her a raise or promotion in 15 years. She has never asked for a raise, believing that if she deserves one, it will be offered to her. Recently, he demoted her to assistant music director and hired a long-time friend to take on the newly created associate pastor position, which would absorb her choir and teen director responsibilities. She was humiliated, especially because she learned about it from another staff member. When she shared her feelings with the reverend, he became quietly angry and defensive. As he always did when confronted with any wrongdoing, he manipulatively cast himself as the victim who can never make everyone happy. While defending himself, he complimented her on her competency and begged her to not be upset with him. Instead of standing her ground and confronting him, she apologized for upsetting him. Because she feels powerless, is fearful, and avoids conflict, she suppresses her anger and resentment toward the church, especially the reverend.

Sandra and Paul's son, Tyler, has been diagnosed with multiple psychiatric disorders, Generalized Anxiety Disorder, and Attention Deficit Hyperactivity Disorder. He has low self-esteem and problems with his social and academic functioning. She has never been consistent at setting limits with people, especially her family members. Consequently, her son rarely listens to her requests and refuses to help her with household chores. Feeling bad for her son's difficulties, she refrains from punishing him when he misbehaves.

Sandra met her husband, Paul, when they were both 18-year-old college freshmen. Despite nagging doubts about his selfishness and immaturity, she fell in love with him. They both enjoyed the raw excitement of their sexual relationship. She liked his playful, free-spirited, and rebellious personality. She even liked his arrogant but charming edge.

During their junior year, Sandra and Paul spontaneously got married. Although she had wanted to wait, he convinced her that by getting married he would be more motivated in college and consequently more successful in his career. Although she had many concerns about marrying him, she was convinced that no other man would be interested in her because of her obesity and lack of confidence. Her desperation to get married and have children nullified any feelings she had that he was not a suitable lifelong partner.

Sandra's alcoholic father and dependent, insecure mother had been poor role models. Because she had never been exposed to healthy and loving relationships, she believed her love for Paul was genuine. Shortly after they married, he dropped out of college. She was unaware of his failing grades, which he blamed on his professors. He was convinced they had personal vendettas against him. What he failed to understand was that his poor academic performance, combined with his arrogance and disrespectfulness, earned him a reputation as a problem student. Because he was turned down for academic probation, he was forced to drop out of college.

Paul became depressed; he was unmotivated to do most anything except drink beer and smoke marijuana. Sandra's constant requests for him to contribute financially forced him to find a job. He began working at an auto dealership, cleaning used cars and earning a dollar over minimum wage. Their relationship quickly became stressful. One year into their marriage, she became pregnant with what would be their only child. He was uninterested and seemed to distance himself from her.

Two months after their son was born, Sandra discovered that Paul was having an affair with a co-worker. She was terrified of being left behind. Because of her low self-esteem and self-loathing, she believed no other man would ever find her appealing or worthy of a long-term romantic relationship. Paul spent most of his time at a vintage auto club, where he always had an audience for his charm, tall tales, jokes, and drinking binges. Sandra stopped challenging him, as his temper flare-ups became progressively frightening. She had grown accustomed to feeling invisible and unappreciated in and outside of her marriage. When she did confront him about his infidelity, she often fell victim to his tearful emotional promises to change and pleas to not leave him.

Eventually, Sandra became numb and stopped expecting him to contribute to the family in any way except for a paycheck and medical insurance. Paul's habitual deception and infidelity shattered any hopes she had of being loved, respected, and cared for. His career never progressed past the position at the auto dealership. Twenty years later, he remains unchanged and has just been caught having his fifth affair.

Sandra's insecurities, poor self-esteem, and fear of confrontation kept her tied to a narcissistic, selfish, and dishonest husband. Known as the go-to person in her community, she helps others in need of her nurturing support. She is unable to set boundaries and feels guilty when she thinks about asking someone to do something for her. Her happy and upbeat exterior hides a cache of anger and shame.

Sandra is a classic (-5) codependent, putting everyone else's needs ahead of her own. She cares tirelessly for her child, husband, friends, and people at the church, while receiving little to nothing in return. She has not left her self-centered, emotionally abusive, and philandering husband out of fear of being alone and unable to pay the bills. Her obesity unrealistically reinforces her belief that no one could ever love her and generates feelings of powerlessness to change the nature of her one-sided relationships. Although she fantasizes about standing up to the narcissistic and intimidating people in her life, she ultimately chooses to capitulate to them. Self-medicating through her eating binges, she has gained 100 pounds since marrying Paul. Even with her doctor's warnings, she feels powerless to change her emotional eating patterns.

Paul is a typical (+5) narcissist. More specifically, he would fit the diagnostic criteria for NPD. His approach to life is focused on his own personal and emotional needs—to the exclusion and at the expense of others, especially his wife and child. He and Sandra are perfectly, if miserably, compatible, as their combined RCVs create a zero-sum relationship. Together, their ROs are perfectly, inversely compatible.

This perfectly matched opposite relationship will likely remain stable as Sandra's poor self-esteem and insecurity fuels the feelings of powerlessness that prevent her from changing the circumstances in her life, which would include divorcing Paul. Additionally, in a distorted manner, she maintains the belief that she still loves him. He wouldn't dream of leaving her, as he has the "perfect" wife who will do everything for him, including not holding him accountable for his selfish and narcissistic shortcomings. He also relies on her to take care of Tyler, the house, pay the bills, and maintain their social group. This marriage is considered stable, as they are locked into it and neither is motivated, nor psychologically capable, of leaving the other.

Two years after Sandra started therapy with me, she lost 75 pounds, divorced Paul, quit her church job, got hired by an employer who empowers her and rewards her contributions, severed the relationships with her narcissistic friends, and created healthier relationships with the rest of her friends and family. She also turned a corner with her son as she became more confident, consistent, and less fearful in her parenting approach. Because of her strides in psychotherapy, her RCV changed from a (-5) to a (-2), placing her on the healthy side of the RCC. She is now dating Bill, whose RCV is a (+2). Together, they are happy, mutually loving, respectful, and caring.

NEITHER FIXED NOR PERMANENT

As illustrated with Sandra, a person's RCV is not a permanent representation of their relational and mental health. Discounting the pathological narcissist who has a personality disorder, a person's RCV is neither fixed nor permanent.[12] An RCV typically ebbs and flows throughout one's lifetime. A few possible explanations for the RCV fluctuations, or RO switch, could include: normal developmental or maturation processes, religious or spiritual experiences, psychological or mental health services, change in life experiences, major health concerns, or age-related transitions such as a mid-life crisis. We are not indelibly stamped with a specific personality type or characteristics. I believe the human spirit and the psyche have infinite possibilities and potentialities. It is possible, albeit not typical, for a person to move from one side of the continuum to the other. Many of us are capable of overcoming our personal and relationship problems and limitations and becoming healthier people. We all experience periods in which we struggle and move a few steps backward, but we can also move forward.

EXCEPTIONS TO THE RULE

There are exceptions to the RCT hypothesis. A romantic couple who does not share a zero-sum relationship may be stable and resist breaking up because of financial dependency, medical or insurance needs, or cultural, ethnic, or religious requirements. An example of this might be an arranged marriage, which is customary in some Asian, African, and Middle Eastern cultures.

Partners in an arranged marriage may have a healthy and loving relationship resulting from their shared values, beliefs, and practices. The non-zero-balanced arranged marriage will likely persevere because of the couple's shared respect for the culturally defined institution of marriage. This couple will also maintain an enduring relationship due to strong platonic feelings for each other and shared commitment to their faith and family. However, if their RCVs are not inversely balanced, they will likely never be close, intimate lovers. Conversely, if this RCV-imbalanced couple encounters conflict or unacceptable harm that cannot be resolved satisfactorily, their culturally normative relationship configuration may become dysfunctional.

---

12 Discussed later in the book, individuals with a pathological NPD are capable of psychological growth, but the probability for such is low.

ALPHA RELATIONSHIP ORIENTATION

The RCT also accounts for a relationship pair in which two people have the same self-orientation. This commonly occurs with platonic, work, and family relationships. In this instance, the person with the higher RCV (closest to a (+5)) will be the one who exerts control in the relationship. Conversely, the person with the lower RCV (closest to a (-5)) will be more passive and relinquish control. The following case study details the Alpha Relationship Orientation with an SRO-ORO relationship.

ALPHA OTHERS-RELATIONSHIP ORIENTATION (ORO)

Judy, a passive, insecure, and apologetic (-5) RCV codependent met Alexis, (-4), at her yoga class. Alexis is outspoken and enjoys taking care of others, but worries about being taken advantage of. The two decide to go to dinner and enjoy some live music. A few days prior, Alexis emails Judy asking her to choose a restaurant since she picked the music venue. Judy says she doesn't care where they eat and asks Alexis to pick a restaurant. After a failed second attempt at getting Judy to make a choice, Alexis chooses a Mexican restaurant. The night of the dinner, after Alexis finishes her meal, she asks Judy why she barely ate. Judy responds by saying she isn't a big fan of Mexican food.

ALPHA SELF-RELATIONSHIP ORIENTATION (SRO)

Jack and Frank are brothers with a long history of going to sporting events together, especially the Chicago Cubs opening day. Jack is a textbook example of a grandiose and entitled (+5) pathological narcissist, and Frank is a self-assured, confident, charming, and sometimes dominating (+3) moderate or problematic narcissist. Although Frank loves Jack, he can only take him in small doses. The day of the game, Frank receives a text from his 17-year-old daughter, Janie, asking if he could come home early because she needs a ride to the library. When Frank suggests they leave before the game is over—it isn't even a close game—Jack looks at him incredulously and says, "No way. She should have thought of that before we left for the game." After repeatedly defending Janie and trying to get Jack to leave early, Frank sucks it up and waits until the game is over. Frank, once again, promises himself he will never go to another sporting event with his brother.

SELF-ORIENTATION CROSSOVER

Through courage, diligence, and much psychotherapy, a person who is a (-5) codependent can heal the psychological wounds responsible for the development and maintenance of their codependency. The growth of the recovering codependent's emotional, mental, and social health will almost always correspond to positive changes in their self-orientation.

Therefore, it is possible for a codependent to experiment with roles, opportunities, and relationships that are more connected to a healthy Relationship Orientation. In other words, we can transition from a caretaking personality type, career, and relationship role to one that is more focused on our own needs for love, respect, and care.

MASLOW'S HAMMER AND NAIL THEORY

As much as I attempt to define and quantify human relationship behavior using the RCT, it is neither feasible nor appropriate to rely on it alone to explain complicated human behavior patterns. There are inherent dangers in having a limited view of human psychology. According to Abraham Maslow (1996), one of the founders of humanistic psychological theory, "I suppose it is tempting, if the only tool you have is a hammer, to treat everything as if it were a nail." Let this hammer (the RCT) be one of many tools we can utilize to understand and change our dysfunctional relationships.

Maslow's quote reminds me of a myth regarding Columbus's arrival in what was thought to be the new world. The story goes that when his ships were close to land, the Native Americans couldn't see them. I don't imagine they were difficult to see, but I do believe that having never seen anything like the imposing wooden and metal ships, they were unable to make sense of them. Without a mental representation of what appeared on the horizon, they could not know how to prepare for the hostility, entitlement, and narcissistic behavior of their uninvited guests. This myth illustrates the importance of my RCT to codependency recovery. Knowing the nuts and bolts of their disorder gives codependents the necessary "vision" to resolve their lifelong problem and no longer fall prey to narcissists.

The compatible-but-opposite RO personality types are just one of many personality-type categories; other personality traits or constructs may have their own unique attraction processes. To illustrate, mentally ill, economically disadvantaged, politically disenfranchised, physically challenged, and other impaired, damaged, or oppressed groups may have their own unique relationship attraction dynamics.

Although the RCT attempts to explain and simplify complicated and multi-faceted attraction dynamics, it does not pretend to be bigger and more inclusive than it was designed to be. It measures an individual's RO, while accounting for the attraction dynamic of opposite-but-compatible personality types. The theory is not intended to be a stand-alone or comprehensive theoretical explanation. It may be useful, however, as an adjunct to other psychological theories.

I believe the RCT is both a valid and reliable psychological construct. However, as a new psychological theory, it has not yet met the rigors of scientific scrutiny. My hope is the theory, along with the other concepts discussed in this book, will add to the current understanding of human behavior, as well as stimulate further thought and discussion on the topic.

Reflections

- Where do you fall on the RCC?

- Where were you a year ago, now, and where do you want to be in a year from now?

- What will happen to your relationships should you move two RCVs toward zero?

Chapter Six

ARE WE ALL WALKING AND TALKING MAGNETS?

It has always been my ambition to explain, and even predict, the psychological and relational processes responsible for the formation of *all relationships*—not only the dysfunctional ones. The preceding opposite-attraction descriptions and theories do just that. My Human Magnet Syndrome Theory is no different, as it represents the full range of all possible chemistry-driven relationships.

The Human Magnet Syndrome's metaphorical simplicity is almost poetic. I will never forget when I first created the book's title. Despite signing a contract that took away my rights to be involved in creating its name, I would not accept a title designed more for selling books than describing its content. When my Human Magnet Syndrome "aha" moment hit me, I intuitively knew, without any doubt, that it would "kill three birds with one stone." It would please the publisher, capture the book's essence, and be catchy. I didn't need a marketing department, survey, or focus group to confirm it clearly represented the bedeviling process that pulls codependents toward hamster wheel relationships, which they believe can go somewhere good, but always disappointingly fall short.

A HUMAN MAGNET STORY

The following vignette is a mostly factual account of one of my client's experiences with the Human Magnet Syndrome. It depicts the insidious and mostly invisible magnetic power that pulls perfectly compatible dysfunctional opposites together into a dysfunctional relationship dance.

Tricia, a codependent, sought my services one year after a highly traumatic divorce with her abusive, pathologically narcissistic husband, Ken. Their marriage ended nine months after she began codependency-specific psychotherapy with me. Tricia's increased mental health put an intolerable strain on her dysfunctional marriage,[13] which motivated Ken to punish her with an aggressive and punitive divorce.

For the six-month period following her divorce, Tricia happily respected my advice to not date anyone, as she agreed it would be counterproductive to her early codependency recovery. It should be noted my Ten Stage Self-Love Recovery™ Treatment Model, which is introduced in Chapter Twelve, recommends a six- to twelve-month cessation of all romantic relationships.

Six months later, Tricia surprised me by proclaiming she was "healthy enough" to start dating. I could not convince her otherwise, despite many reminders of the pathological power of her codependency addiction, and the way it easily tricks a person into believing they can control something that is, by its very nature, uncontrollable. Despite my warnings, she signed up with an Internet dating site. A few weeks later, I received a brief email from her stating she wanted to take a six-month break from therapy.

Eight months later, I received another short email, but this time, she asked if we could resume our codependency work. In her first session back, Tricia appeared exhausted, depressed, and emotionally beaten down. Not only did she have a sad vacant look in her eyes, she looked defeated. The following is a condensed version of the story she told me, which I believe exemplifies the insidious power of the Human Magnet Syndrome. She shared the following:

> Thinking I was cured from codependency, I decided to try out my new skills
> of spotting narcissists, seeing behind their masks, and keeping very, very far
> away from them. You already know I disagreed with you about not being

---

13 This process is briefly addressed in the discussion in Chapter Five about relational disequilibrium.

ready. But I also felt a lot smarter and stronger than you gave me credit for. I had absolutely no doubt I would be able to spot and avoid narcissists. It felt like it was the perfect time to give Internet dating a try. After doing a great deal of research, I joined a dating service that seemed a lot safer than the rest. Their safety measures aligned with my needs to avoid narcissists and find healthy and compatible people to date. I can't believe I swallowed their promises that I would find the perfect soulmate.

To be completely honest, the first few days on the site gave me the same feeling in my stomach that I get when I go to Vegas . . . you know . . . that excited, "I am going to win a shitload of money, but I might lose more money than I can afford" feeling. The prospect of finally finding a good and kind man who would love me like no other had carried the day. Also, I was determined I would never let another man break my heart or mess with my head again. In fact, I was almost militant about not talking to anyone who gave me the tiniest suspicion he was narcissistic. The only men I allowed myself to talk to were those who I carefully vetted and who fit my list of "must haves," such as previously married, and of course divorced, have a child, employed, not a smoker, drinker or drug abuser, and not a gaslighting son-of-a-bitch narcissist!

I was completely shocked by how many men fit my search criteria, who seemed genuinely nice and safe. I was expecting the horror stories you always hear about. None of the five men I met floated my boat. No chemistry, zilch! It was quite disappointing. The last of the nice guys, Jonathan, was the last straw. I had grand hopes he would be the one: the guy who would set my heart aflutter, make me want to melt into him, and who would want to build a happy life with me. I thought he was a ringer for sure. He was gorgeous, employed, a great dad, clean cut, and agreed with many of my conservative values. I really wanted to feel it with him.

Unexpectedly, the blinking lights and ringing bells of chemistry didn't happen. After two hours of labored conversation, we said, almost at the same time, that it was getting late and we had to get up early the next day. Before leaving, he moved forward to give me a hug. I felt my body recoil from his advancement, simultaneously stepping backwards while stretching out my arm for a handshake instead. As much as I thought he was a nice guy, the idea of letting him in my personal space riddled me with anxiety.

Jon ignored my handshake gesture and hugged me anyway. It was a weird hug—like one you might see from two homophobic guys, barely touching each other in a guy hug. It was so uncomfortable!

On my drive home, I obsessed that I was a crazy loser. I finally met a perfect man who my heart and body didn't seem to recognize. It just didn't make sense! I felt familiar feelings of shame, despair, and pessimism. This is when the "no one will ever want me" and "I am damaged goods" tape again started to play in my head.

Once home, like a robot with no hesitation or forethought, I marched up to my bedroom and logged onto the dating site. This time, I said to myself, "fuck the filters, let's see who is really out there for me." I indulged myself, checking out a slew of gorgeous hotties that normally wouldn't show up in my searches. Despite knowing the danger of my actions, I was in an "I deserve this" mode and decided to let myself have some fun. The next thing I knew, three hours had passed, and I was happily overwhelmed with a group of potential guys. Not only were my "woe is me" thoughts gone, I was feeling quite optimistic about finding a good man.

This was when I landed on Tim Shatner's profile. The moment I saw his photo, I felt my stomach and chest tighten in the good way. My literal "gut" feeling reaction to him was a mixture of delicious excitement and a dash of danger. This is about the time my rational mind went completely offline.

Fifteen minutes after scrolling through his profile photos, all of which featured his chiselled good looks, his confident and charismatic smile, and an air of intense and slightly sad seriousness, I had feelings that are hard to put into words. He was gorgeous and seemingly perfect. The picture of him shirtless, playing Frisbee, and smiling gave me goosebumps. I was unmoved by his profile information that indicated he was "in between jobs," had no apparent professional ambitions, had never been married or had children. At this point, I went back to the photos to look for more clues. This time, I noticed that, in three of the photos, he was holding a beer and, in one photo, he had a pack of cigarettes in his shirt pocket. The warning signs were no match for my desire to meet him. As strange as this sounds, I felt an energy emanating from the computer screen that beckoned me to meet Tim—as soon as possible.

To make a long story short, I sent him an email where I probably divulged way too much personal information. Strangely enough, he responded within five minutes. It was as if he was in front of his computer, patiently waiting for me to show myself. The next thing I knew, we were sharing our life stories through email, which quickly turned into marathon phone calls, many of which were tinged with sexual innuendo, all of which were deeply personal and emotional. In one phone call, neither of us could bare saying goodbye. We agreed to just fall asleep on the phone. It was sweetly intimate.

During the call that came before our first date, I found myself sharing very private sexual information with him. Damn, I couldn't help it, as there was a boatload of chemistry going on. As strange as this sounds, I was quite sexually attracted to him. To be completely honest, I was aroused. This is when I should have run away as fast as I could, but it was too late. His energy pulled me toward him with such force I almost agreed to meet him that night. Yes, that very night. It was crazy.

We decided [she held up hand quotes] to meet for dinner at his favorite bar and grill the next evening. As soon as he suggested it, I questioned his choice. When he reacted with a rant about how warm and cozy it was and how confident he was I would love it, I just shut down—like old times. Instead of focusing on his pushiness, I found myself dreamily imagining our first meeting. It is hard to put into words how extremely excited I was. I didn't get a wink of sleep that night.

When we met, it was something right out of a storybook . . . you know, the one with fireworks and triumphal music. I was confident he was going to be everything I imagined, and more. The anticipation was so intense, I actually have no other reference point to compare it to. Pulling into the parking lot of the restaurant, my heart felt like it was going to jump out of my chest. When I caught a glimpse of him through the window, the surge of excitement made it difficult to breathe. From the parking lot, it felt like the ground tilted toward him and, if I closed my eyes, I would effortlessly slide into his arms where I would forever feel safe and happy. Sounds trippy, huh? Crazy stuff!

Once I walked in the door and ours eyes met, my stomach wrenched tight and my heart felt like it would explode. As much as I just wanted to give him a polite hug and try to slow down the revving of our engines, I literally ran into his arms and passionately kissed him like he was my husband who had just returned home from war. The intensity of the attraction was magnetic. Even if I wanted to, there is no way I could have escaped that embrace. Our bond was so complete, it would have taken a crowbar to separate us. In that moment, we were so tightly connected, so close to each other, it felt like we were just one person.

She concluded the story with the indescribable limerence experience, and the very disturbing crash of reality, when his narcissism and alcoholism moved to the forefront of their relationship. Her attraction aligns with most of the opposite attraction principles discussed thus far, especially the Human Magnet Syndrome. It was no surprise that Tricia was back in my office, deflated and depressed.

HUMAN MAGNET SYNDROME RULES

Before fully launching into the Human Magnet Syndrome Theory, I will give a very basic explanation of the natural phenomena of electromagnetism. The earth is one big gargantuan magnet and, like its smaller cousins, has two opposite poles. Each pole has opposite magnetic charges, "positive" and "negative." A metal needle in a compass is highly sensitive to the earth's magnetic field. When a compass is pointed in a specific direction, its needle's movement indicates what direction a person is facing, such as north, south, east or west (and many more combinations).

According to the Human Magnet Sydrome Theory, every human being is a metaphorical magnet, whose polarity is determined by their relationship orientation. The Others-Relationship Oriented (ORO) person carries a "negative" magnetic charge, while the Self-Relationship Oriented (SRO) person is "positive." The strength of the charge is correlated to a person's emotional and relational health. Higher, or stronger, magnetic charges (on both the negative and positive ends) indicate increased emotional and relational problems. Lower, or weaker, charges (closer to neutral) indicate the opposite—better overall emotional and relational health. When same polarities experience each other, a feeling of magnetic repulsion occurs.

RESISTIBLE VERSUS IRRESISTIBLE

The stronger the human magnet force (higher matching RCVs), the faster a new relationship comes together and the more a partner is felt to be *irresistible.* These robust human magnet pairings also result in a more intense limerence experience, which is mistaken for true, lasting, and healthy love. High RCV inverse pairings also correlate with the irresistible nature of both the new love interest and the rapidly blooming relationship.

Weaker RCV pairings account for the weakest, and *most resistible*, healthy Human Magnet Syndrome experience with a (-1) and (+1) combination. As noted previously, although both couples are brought together by the Human Magnet Syndrome, only the (-5) and (+5) couple lives, breathes, and survives by it. This dysfunctional bond is aptly explained by relationship math, which exemplifies why codependents and pathological narcissists require a relationship for feelings of self-worth, albeit distorted, and a global sense of happiness.

The dysfunctional Human Magnet Syndrome couple are consumed by the resulting shared core shame and loneliness, chemistry, limerence, and consequent addiction to each other. These two need each other to take their pain away, while promoting the false and unsubstantiated feeling of happiness. The feeling of being whole is nothing more than an illusion.

According to relationship math, the (-1) and (+1) or (-2) and (+2) matchup is healthy because the two oppositely matched lovers possess self-love, self-respect and do not need the relationship by itself to make them feel better about themselves. Despite their strong "magnetic bond," the need to preserve and protect their own emotional health has more influence and power than their Human Magnet Syndrome bond. Paradoxically, the more weakly bonded, healthy couple will likely stay connected longer as they grow and mature with age.

Although it is rare for a person's polarity to change, the intensity of its attraction and repulsion properties can. The relationships of unhealthier people ((+3), (+4), and (+5) RCVs) are directed more by the properties of the Human Magnet Syndrome. Conversely, the healthier person's weaker magnetism ((+1) and (+2) RCVs) results in a larger range of conscious influences over their relationship choices.

MAGNETIC REPULSION

Relationship logic is thrown out the window when two healthy, similar people meet. They will experience the unique combination of no magnetic attraction and mild, but imperceptible, repulsion. Despite their similarities and a mutual appreciation for their observable traits, such as physical looks and demeanor, both will experience mild discomfort and unease. The mild magnetic repulsion won't result in an alarming experience or negative judgments. Rather, while upholding their healthy emotional and physical boundaries, they won't be motivated to get to know each other better. These neutral-chemistry-connected persons will most likely adopt a "let's be friends" attitude.

The rule of thumb is the higher the matching of similar self-orientations, the stronger the *relational repulsion.* The couple's negative chemistry will likely foster harsh snap judgments, as well as discomfort, dislike, and animosity. Arguments and disagreements or mutual emotional shutdowns are the norm for this type of couple. Like its dysfunctional counterpart, the repulsion stems from an unconscious psychological process about which both are oblivious.

HUMAN MAGNETS ON THE CONTINUUM

It is no surprise the matching of a "negative" codependent's and a "positive" pathological narcissist's "magnets" follow the Relationship Compatibility Theory's principles. This can be explained with simple algebra, by the zero-sum balance: when the sum of two opposite relationally oriented individuals equals zero, they will likely be drawn together by the Human Magnet Syndrome.

The lower the matching inverse RCVs, the more freewill and conscious choices play out in relationship selections (attraction patterns). Not only does chemistry bring the healthier couple together, but limerence also impacts the early stage of the relationship. Hence, all people are unconsciously moving in the direction of their romantic partner's opposite magnetic polarity. Only healthy people are highly influenced by what they see, think, believe, and desire.

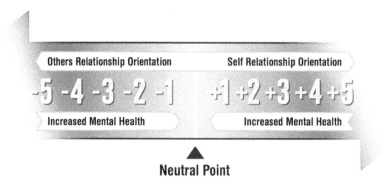

LOVE FORCE AND LOVE CHAINS

In its simplest form, the Human Magnet Syndrome is an unconscious, but formidable, magnetic-like *love force* that brings codependents and narcissists together. The *love chains* keep them bonded to each other, sometimes for a lifetime.

The force of the Human Magnet Syndrome makes the codependent-narcissist relationship virtually impossible to resist—an addiction that is one of the most difficult to treat. Without codependent-specific therapy, such a relationship is stronger than any attempt to fight it. Such treatment requires a basic understanding of brain/neurological activity, as well as theoretical and practical mastery of psychodynamic, behavioral, cognitive behavioral, addiction, and attachment and trauma theory.

YOU CAN'T FIGHT THE FEELING

The Human Magnet Syndrome makes an unhappy and disempowered codependent believe they are incapable of changing their mindset. It has the power to turn a codependent's mind against itself and convince them any attempt to escape will result in failure. The syndrome's chokehold gets tighter with each attempt to resist it. This power explains the codependent's tendency to stay in an unfulfilled dysfunctional relationship despite its repeated harm.

Promises made and life-altering consequences are no match for the Human Magnetic Syndrome. It sabotages a person's attempts to sustain their values, morals, customs, religion, and traditions. It has the capacity to turn empathic, sensitive, and nurturing adults into neglectful parents who focus on meeting the needs of their pathological narcissist partner over those of their children. The malignant force is most palpable when one does the "generational math" and calculates the exponential generational growth of codependency and pathological narcissism.

WHEN DO WE BECOME MAGNETIZED?

It is impossible to pinpoint the age at which the Human Magnet Syndrome begins to affect our intimate relationship choices. Estimations indicate it first manifests at the onset of adulthood, around age 23. Current medical research has revealed this is when the human brain's ability for insight and judgment is fully developed. Before this time, choices are mostly guided by the hard-wired influences learned in adolescence. This is a period when most people experiment personally and socially to develop *conscious preferences* about relationships. This may seem like a *contradiction* as one's *relationship template* is formed in early childhood but, in fact, normal psychosocial developmental processes are more influential.

It is not atypical for codependents to have early relationship experiments with healthier people. At the onset of adulthood, relationship preferences and choices begin to be governed by deeply seated unconscious influences. This is often the time when people make choices about long-term and potentially permanent relationships. The relationship template becomes both the relationship gatekeeper and the relationship police. Younger codependents feel a false sense of comfort and safety. This apparent contradiction doesn't emotionally register as danger, as it parallels the childhood experiences that provide the only type of "love" they have ever known.

HUMAN MAGNETISM AND THE LOVE COMPASS

Codependents and narcissists prefer old-fashioned "love compasses" over more technologically advanced GPS (satellite technology) devices. The love compass responds to the magnetic field of humans in the same manner as a real compass does to the Earth's magnetic field. In other words, love compasses are calibrated to "locate" a potential lover with an opposite "magnetic polarity."

When anyone, healthy or not, ignores or consciously chooses to *not use* their love compass, they risk getting lost and ending up in unfamiliar territory. In these situations, their relational intuition (Relationship Template) is neutralized. As a stranger in a strange land, they have little experience interacting with local inhabitants. For this "fish out of water," a new travel destination will be imminent.

RELATIONSHIP GRAVITY

Relationship Gravity is a metaphor for the psychological forces that keep our feet planted in romantic relationships. *Its vertical power weighs us down and keeps us in relationships. Synergistically connected to the Human Magnet Syndrome's horizontal influence, it irresistibly draws romantic partners together.* Both forces explain the long-term and committed nature of all relationships, from healthy to dysfunctional. Relationship Gravity is a constant force that pushes against anyone who wishes to end or leave a relationship. This *staying force* is good for healthy rela-

RELATIONSHIP GRAVITY

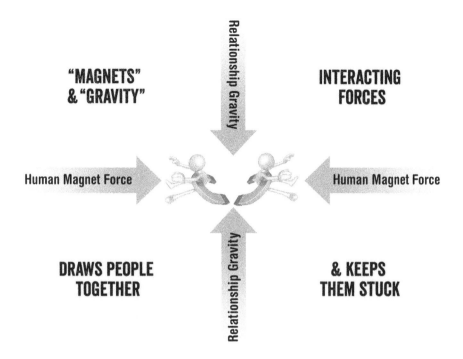

tionships, but it is bad for those inextricably connected because of their shared dysfunction, as in a well-matched codependent-narcissist relationship.

I hypothesize that Relationship Gravity, or the real psychological forces that are responsible for it, has an evolutionary purpose. It compels romantically paired individuals to remain committed to each other, while engendering feelings of comfort and connection. The magnitude of this gravitational force is influenced by one's mental health and subsequent feeling state while in a relationship. For example, this gravity is less powerful for psychologically healthy lovers who experience safety and security in their relationship. Conversely, it is more powerful, or "heavier," in one composed of unhealthy partners, such as codependents and pathological narcissists. Both experience feelings of fear, danger, and insecurity in the relationship.

A psychologically healthy couple may have problems, but neither partner is mired down in them or powerless to change them. This couple experiences Relationship Gravity as a force that helps keep them together. For the self-loving couple, the combination of Relationship Gravity and the Human Magnet Syndrome will bring everlasting happiness, meaning, and a lifetime of healthy love. Specifically, the mutual give-and-take of love, respect, and care in the relationship enhances the couple's feelings of safety. Psychologically healthy people also use their internal psychological resources to leave the relationship if they feel it is the best course of action, despite the weight of Relationship Gravity.

On the other hand, two psychologically unhealthy people will also feel the force of Relationship Gravity that keeps them together, but the force is much stronger. In the case of the codependent-narcissist couple, after the initial attraction phase, or limerence, Relationship Gravity weighs down and cements them in a dysfunctional relationship. They remain with their partners despite feeling uncomfortable, miserable, or unhappy. Without the relationship, they would float from one to another, especially when the codependent's and/or pathological narcissist's feelings of *intense attraction (limerence) subside*. This occurs at the same time their "soulmate wings" are clipped, and they fall from the euphoric sweetness of relationship heaven to the hot lava-like terrain of the newly formed dysfunctional relationship.

RELATIONSHIP GRAVITY AND THE HUMAN MAGNET SYNDROME

Relationship Gravity and the Human Magnet Syndrome, together, can be understood as compounding forces that help explain why two people remain connected in a committed relationship, independent of its health or one individual's own mental health. An example of how Relationship Gravity plays out in healthy relationships is illustrated with a healthy (-2) RCV individual who decides to break up with a (+4) RCV narcissist. Neither Relationship Gravity nor the Human Magnet Syndrome is strong enough to stop him from ending the relationship and not looking back. In other words, Relationship Gravity may put pressure on a healthy mismatched couple trying to make the relationship work, but it won't disable them from choosing to walk away if needed or necessary. The following example demonstrates how Relationship Gravity and the Human Magnet Syndrome work side-by-side in making a relationship *not* work.

UNMATCHED: DONALD AND JASON

Donald is a psychologically healthy male with a (-2) healthy ORO RCV. He started to date Jason, whose lack of emotional and relational health is demonstrated by his

(+4) SRO RCV. They had a lot in common and found each other attractive. They went on four dates, one of which was intimate. At the end of the last date, Donald decided he didn't want to date Jason anymore, as he was too self-centered and domineering. Jason had no qualms about the decision to stop dating, as he felt Donald was too opinionated and oppositional.[14] It was a clean break with little drama.

The absence of a zero-sum balance gave both the semblance of negative chemistry and the consequent Human Magnet Syndrome repulsion experience. The feelings of incompatibility and discomfort exemplify the horizontal influences of the Human Magnet Syndrome. The influence of Relationship Gravity was evident by the ease with which the new relationship ended. There was no force keeping them invested in the relationship.

The RCT also succinctly demonstrates why Relationship Gravity and the Human Magnet Syndrome work together to keep two psychologically unhealthy partners together in a relationship. To illustrate, a (-5) and (+5) RCV couple will find it virtually impossible to move beyond the confines of their seemingly permanent dysfunctional relationship. It is as if each is wearing a 75-pound backpack that renders them incapable of moving beyond the relationship, despite being unhappy or feeling unsafe. The combination of Relationship Gravity and the Human Magnet Syndrome weighing down the couple means it would take a monumental force to make any type of relational change. *Therefore, the further away from a (0) RCV (in either direction), the higher (heavier) the Relationship Gravity force. The closer to zero, the lower (lighter) the gravity force.*

For the codependent-narcissist pair, the two forces will be the cement that dries around their feet, keeping them from finding relational peace and enduring happiness. The following example illustrates exactly how these two forces work together in a relationship.

MATCHED: JOSEPH AND FRANCINE

Joseph, a (-5) ORO codependent, has been dating Francine for four months. Because Francine has NPD, she carries a (+5) pathological narcissism RCV. Not only did their relationship start off with intense chemistry, the limerence action

---

14 Typically, narcissists project their own narcissistic traits onto people who do not meet their emotional and relational needs.

was off-the-charts exciting. Within 30 days of their first date, they decided to move in together. Fifteen days later, Francine's pathological narcissistic traits began to emerge. Despite Joseph's resentment over Francine's need to always be right or have the last word on any disagreement, he couldn't bear the thought of being without her. Joseph's loyalty to Francine was equal parts distorted beliefs about the relationship, fear of being alone, and, consequently, loneliness.

In Joseph and Francine's case, the influence of the Human Magnet Syndrome worked hand-in-hand with Relationship Gravity. The dynamic of a zero-sum codependent-pathological narcissism attraction was the *horizontal* manifestation of the Human Magnet Syndrome, and Joseph and Francine's reluctance to end a dysfunctional relationship was the *vertical* force that kept them tied together.

FUSED AT THE WOUND

A memorable synchronistic "God moment" occurred in my life about 11 years ago when I first thought about writing a book. It was a time when I experienced a creative burst as a psychotherapist, especially with my codependent clientele. Clearly my psychotherapy/codependency recovery was paying off, as the personal discoveries also helped me better understand them. Because I did not want to lose any of these golden gifts, I started journaling. When I was particularly inspired, I turned those new ideas into online articles or blogs.

When my article "Codependency: Don't Dance!" received a great deal of positive feedback and attention, I began to secretly fantasize about becoming an author, telling others about my recovery journey. I didn't share my thoughts with anyone because one popular/well-liked article does not an author make. Approximately a week following my fantasy, I received a thoughtfully written letter from a man I did not know, asking if I would be interested in a complimentary copy of a book he had written 17 years earlier. In it, he explained how he had found me through an Internet search of psychotherapists who provided services to survivors of male trauma and other related disorders. His intention was to share his personal book of poems with other men he hoped could benefit from it. It was clear he was on a mission to both heal his own childhood trauma wounds and help other men try to do the same. This is no different from most psychotherapists I know, including myself.

Curious, I began my research, scouring the Internet for clues about Mr. Rick Belden, the author of the poetry. Finding almost nothing except a physical address,

I wrote him a letter introducing myself and asking a handful of searching questions like, *Who are you? Why do you want to send me a book? Of all the people online, why did you choose me?*

A few weeks later, I received a response from Rick that answered my questions as well as a copy of his book, as he had originally offered. In his poetry, he vividly shares different vantage points of a trauma survivor's journey towards hope and healing. His poetry captures the suffering and despair as much as the hope, self-acceptance, and resolution (healing). It depicts the suffering of one man, his bouts with self-destruction, and his ability to crawl out of his broken life to become a healing force in the world. His emotional vulnerability, courage, and honesty about his childhood trauma and the emotional scars it left behind makes his poetry life-changing. He is one of the few role models I have. Learning about Rick's passions opened me up to the possibility that we were brought together by divine providence.

Every so often, I get a feeling that what I am doing or have done was not by chance or luck, but instead directed by a heavenly source I believe to be my guardian angels.[16] When I decided to read Rick's book, I had one of those otherworldly feelings, as if that moment had already been scripted for me. I intuitively knew the one poem I would randomly choose would have a profound effect on my life. I just knew it. That's the moment I read the poem, "Fused at the Wound." It was an emotionally evocative rendering of magnetically connected dysfunctional lovers, whose power for emotional health was squelched by deeper, more malignant underlying forces. It was the perfect rendering of a codependent's frozen and powerless experience with his pathologically narcissistic lover.

FUSED AT THE WOUND

fused at the wound
is it love or is it addiction
    why not both
she knows tears + I know anger
together we almost made a whole person for a while
fused at the wound.

---

16 My departed mother, Mikki Rosenberg, is the one who I believe is most present in my life.

but our little house of lies isn't big enough to hold us now
she won't stand up for herself + I can't stand up
    for both of us at the same time anymore
so we ride the broken lover's seesaw of staying + leaving
    one foot in + one foot out
we dance in the kitchen like unloved children + wait
    for fulfillment of old pain's expectations.

so anxious to leave   *so anxious to be left*
so anxious to be right   *so anxious to be hurt*
so anxious to be disappointed
so anxious to be alone again.

when this whole thing started
    I wanted us to be immersed in each other
    I wanted us to fix each other
    I thought that was what people were supposed to do
I don't want that anymore
I don't need that anymore
    but I still don't know
        how to love someone I don't want to fix.

Reflections

- When did you really want to like a person, but were thwarted by the like-like "magnetism"?

- Explain your relationship gravity.

Chapter Seven

THE NEW "CODEPENDENCY"

The term "codependency" was a godsend, as it literally changed the world! Before its first incarnation, "co-alcoholism," the world saw mental health and addiction disorders one-dimensionally: provide good treatment to the alcoholic, send him home, and all will be well. Nothing could be further from the truth! The codependent and the practitioner providing treatment both know codependency, like other addictions, has a will of its own. Metaphorically speaking, it sends out "tendrils" that attach itself to, or intertwine around, other people and relationships for the specific purposes of supporting and continuing the problem.

SEEING THE FORMERLY INVISIBLE

Successful treatment outcomes require us to replace the myopic view that codependency and the treatment of it is an individual problem. Rather, it is, and always has been, a problem with the codependent, their relationships, and the interaction of the two. Family Systems Theory helps us bridge the theoretical and practical divide by explaining how such interrelated and interactive forces come to together to "create" the codependent, her codependency, and the forces that drive her toward self-destruction. A mobile demonstrates this "system" explanation and how so many aspects of the codependent's life are connected to each other.

The Family Systems Model can be illustrated as a mobile, a kinetic sculpture with a number of moving objects hanging from rods that take advantage of the principle of equilibrium. When one object in the mobile moves, it affects the other parts of the system, so they also move. This system will also pull the moving object back to the way it was before. Like family members, the objects in the mobile do not exist in isolation from one another (Shepherd and Linn, 1014, p. 67).

The following explanation of light waves and human vision will help the reader better comprehend why it has taken so long for us to recognize and understand the true nature of codependency. Light is part of the electromagnetic spectrum, which ranges from radio waves to gamma rays. We are only able to perceive the visible light spectrum. Until the theoretical and practical discoveries of electromagnetism, we mistakenly assumed what we saw represented the physical universe. With the advent of specialized telescopes like the Chandra/x ray, Spitzer/infrared, Fermi/gamma ray and Green Blank/radio wave, just to name a few, we can "see," understand and appreciate the full-magnificence of astronomical wonders.

Just as modern-day telescopes allow us to see what is out among the stars, the explanations and theories contained in this book will similarly shed new and different types of light on problems that were formerly only partially visible to us. I challenge the reader to temporarily table their current codependency-related beliefs and perceptions and step up to my "Human Magnet Syndrome telescope" where new and different "light" will illuminate your path of understanding, growth, and mastery.

THE CODEPENDENT ACTOR

Codependents are gifted actors who can slip safely into an expertly tailored, form-fitting costume. Staying in character allows them to perpetually co-star in the theatrical version of their own life. If their mask should slip, or they forget their "I'm a happy person" monologue, they risk the humiliation of being found out. They understand that, if their play should close prematurely, they would be recast in a similar role: the pathologically lonely type who floats around in a world where they are invisible and unloved. Therefore, they act their hearts out in every scene, as the end of their charade is also the end of their false feelings of safety.

Codependents go to great lengths to deny and bury their feelings of pessimism and despair. Any person or situation that makes them feel happy raises major red flags for potential danger. Experience has shown the hammer always falls. Like children who deny the existence of Santa Claus because they didn't get any Christmas gifts, they were once children who, as adults, reject the myth of happiness. Over time, they have learned not to trust their senses. What appears to be a field of emerald green grass dotted with patches of flowers is actually a war-torn field littered with landmines. The Catch-22 nature of childhood happiness requires them to guard against the experience of happiness; if they do not, they will likely experience the crushing blow of disappointment. The repudiation of vulnerability and a cautious and defensive posture is the life story of most codependents. By refusing to be vulnerable, the much-feared emotional annihilation is kept at bay . . . but at a tremendous cost.

INSANITY AND ROLLER-COASTER AMNESIA

If "insanity is doing the same thing over and over again, but expecting different results," then my former codependent self was quite "insane!" Like other codependents, I mistakenly believed I could convince, control, or influence my narcissistic loved ones to love, respect, and care for me—despite the enormous amount of evidence to the contrary. I liken this "insanity" to the love-hate relationship some people have with haunted houses and roller coasters. Let me explain.

Although they are unaware of it, haunted house and roller-coaster daredevils are addicted to the cycle of intense emotions. The sequence begins with fond recollections of the previous experience, whichever it may be. However, these memories have been sanitized and scrubbed free of any vestige of the terror or trauma involved. These memories have been compartmentalized, so only the positive elements can be recalled. The cycle continues as they anticipate and get excited about the positively remembered event. By this time, the frightening and traumatic elements of the memory have been recast as exquisitely fun, *but frightening as hell.*

The closer they get to the event, the more the positive memories are challenged by the mild-to-moderate feelings of regret and anxiety that begin to bubble up. This is when the terror of the formerly sanitized memories begins to resurface. Once the event is at hand, the *fight-or-flight response* kicks in. This is the body's response to a perceived harmful event, attack, or threat to survival. At this point, thoughts of doom and gloom take on paranoid qualities. The body and the brain simultaneously press their panic buttons and the deafening warning sirens begin to blast.

Despite experiencing acute anxiety, panic, nausea, and/or hyperventilation, the "insane" codependent person steps into the haunted house's entrance or is strapped tightly into the roller-coaster seat. As they enter the dark and claustrophobic confines of the haunted house or are pulled upward to the roller coaster's highest point, they experience a moment of "hyper-arousal": they are overwhelmed by horrifying thoughts of death and destruction. This is when the one-dimensional survival thought process takes front and center stage. For many, the norm is striking deals with God or themselves that, should they survive, they will never again repeat their mistake of poor judgment.

As the event concludes, the adrenaline junkie is eternally grateful for not sustaining a major head trauma, severed limbs, or vampire puncture wounds. This is when the "just let me survive and I will never do this again, so help me God!" promise transitions into the "holy shit, that was the most exciting moment of my life!" Now, their "dance with death" memories are conveniently reshaped into excitement and euphoria. This is what I refer to as *roller-coaster amnesia*, the number-one problem of most codependents.

Roller-coaster amnesia was responsible for my two unhappy and dysfunctional marriages to women I believe were pathological narcissists. Like a drug addict or alcoholic, I needed to hit bottom before I could fully understand the sheer pathological gravity of my codependency and how I was nearly emotionally destroyed by it. I reached my bottom when I decided to divorce my second wife. At the time, it felt like I would irreparably break if I fell in love with another narcissistic soulmate. That is when I finally decided to pull myself out of the dysfunctional muck that kept me mired in a cesspool of shame, loneliness, and self-hatred.

THE DRAMA OF THE GIFTED CHILD

Early in my codependency recovery, I could not help but notice none of the therapists I knew understood the complexities of my *roller-coaster amnesia* or predilection to *dance* with pathological narcissists. I desperately needed someone who would understand my hamster-wheel approach to unhealthy romantic love and have a prescriptive treatment plan to solve it. None of the therapists I saw had a

codependency specialty. The information they were familiar with c:
dated books on the subject and pop-psychology sources such as *Ps*

Without a psychotherapist who had the necessary background
sought any information that would shed some light on what I associated with my
codependency: stinging loneliness, unbearable shame, and a habitual attraction
to pathological narcissists. This is when a book I had read shortly after my first
divorce, *The Drama of the Gifted Child* (Miller, 1979), delivered the information
I had been seeking.

Dr. Miller hypothesizes people who identify themselves as caretaking and sacrificing adults were once gifted children. She speculates these children squelched
their need for unconditional nurturing, while learning to manipulate their reactive, temperamental, and potentially punitive narcissistic parent into taking care
of them—or at least not neglecting or abusing them. In other words, the child
who molded themselves into the "gift" that made their narcissistic parent feel
good about themselves had prevented a potentially more severe form of attachment trauma. Because the "gifted" child survived the ordeal, they were endowed
with the building blocks that would morph into an instinctively empathic adult
personality type. This person was destined to care for others who had no intention of reciprocating.

Although Dr. Miller never used the term "codependency," it was clear to me
she was describing elements of it, as well as its origins. The birth of my Human
Magnet Syndrome ideas came together after reading her book, and then merging
my codependent-narcissist dance theory with it. This holy grail connection initiated the multidimensional theoretical framework I created to explain the trans-
actional dynamics of codependency. This epiphany did not start off as an idea for
a book. Rather, I was trying to solve my own self-destructive tendencies, while
doing the same for my codependent clients. It was only after I more fully developed
my Human Magnet Syndrome ideas that I contemplated their potential to help a
much larger community of sufferers and their treatment providers.

PEOPLE ARE NOT LABELS

Many medical and mental health professionals, as well as others, have taken a
negative position against classifying people with diagnostic terms. I support their
contention that many people form inaccurate and sometimes intractable opinions

of others based solely on their diagnosis—it becomes a label. Too many practitioners focus more on getting the right diagnosis than getting to know the patient. Ultimately, it is more important, at the very least, to make sure the diagnosis explains the person's problem accurately.

To quote William Shakespeare, "What's in a name?" Well, Mr. Shakespeare, in the mental health field, *quite a bit!* Correctly diagnosing mental health disorders is crucial to both the person seeking treatment and the practitioner providing it. As previously mentioned, to treat a mental health problem effectively, it must first be understood. Only then can a valid diagnostic description and procedure be found. From there, actual results-oriented treatment techniques may be developed to resolve it.

Two examples of poorly derived diagnostic classifications are Schizophrenia and Borderline Personality Disorder (BPD). The former was created in 1910 by the Swiss psychiatrist, Dr. Paul Eugen Bleuler. It literally translates (from Greek) to a "split mind." The current understanding of BPD couldn't be any further from a split-mind explanation. The history of BPD as a diagnostic term is as follows:

> The diagnosis of Borderline Personality Disorder (BPD) has been used for over 30 years to label patients who are hopeless, those who get therapists upset, and is one of the most controversial diagnoses in *Psychology Today*. The term borderline came into existence because such patients were believed to lie on the borderline between psychosis and neurosis, with the label borderline first coined by Adolph Stern in 1938 (Al-Alem and Omar, 2008).

Too many people prefer to be spoon-fed a version of reality that fits their passive and ill-informed lifestyle. Like fake news or soundbites that are mistaken for facts, inaccurate diagnostic terms hurt countless people because of the conclusions, stereotypes, and myths often confused with the name (diagnosis) itself. Perhaps the best example is codependency. Although it wasn't a great term for the problem it represented, it was derived from actual clinical observations. Now the name itself no longer fits our clinical understanding of the problem. It promotes harmful judgments and typecasts people.

Even with the potential for misuse, such terminology is required by the researcher, educator, practitioner, and, most importantly, the patient to understand, identify, and seek help for any specific mental health-related condition. When not perceived as derogatory or belittling, the proper diagnosis can lead people to seek professional help. This has the capacity to be psychologically healing, transformational, and even lifesaving.

Like other mental health terms, codependency has been reshaped to fit its mainstream use. The original definitions are often diluted over time, especially when they pique the interest of news and media sources. Whether it is a skit on *Saturday Night Live,* a feature in *People* magazine, or a serious discussion on *60 Minutes,* the more the label is used, the more its original meaning is lost. To the general public, a codependent is a weak, needy, clingy, and even emotionally sick person who often lacks common sense, and sometimes intelligence. The idea a codependent does everything for everyone else, except themselves, eludes most people.

Codependency has taken on a life of its own. Its overuse and misuse has watered it down to the point where it is no longer accepted as a legitimate topic in most clinical discussions. Because it has evolved into a pop-psychological term, codependency no longer engenders the same amount of serious consideration as it did before 2000. In fact, many therapists, myself included, refrain from using it for fear it will be perceived as an outdated, meaningless psychological assessment.

HISTORY OF CODEPENDENCY

The origins of the term "codependency" can be traced back to the Alcoholics Anonymous (AA) movement, which was established in 1936 by Bill W. and Dr. Bob. Since physicians were the early pioneers in the treatment of alcoholism, this addiction was naturally conceptualized according to a medical model. Because of the application of such a model, treating practitioners, alcoholics, and their family and friends adopted a more realistic and sympathetic understanding of the problem.

From AA sprouted myriad other life-enhancing and life-saving 12-Step groups. Al-Anon is a recovery program for the families and significant others of the alcoholic and was founded in 1951 by Lois W. (wife of Bill W.) and Anne B. Al-Anon is a support group of peers who share their experiences by applying the Al-Anon principles to deal with the effects of having a problem drinker in their lives. It is not group therapy and is not led by a counselor or therapist; this support network complements and supports professional treatment. Al-Anon addressed the other side of the alcoholism coin—the suffering family members who, like the alcoholic, feel their lives are out of control and littered with obstacles and losses.

By the 1970s, treatment providers began to consider the one-dimensional limitations of the medical treatment model, which typically just treated the alcoholic. As treatment centers began to embrace the emerging practice of addressing alcoholism within the context of social networks and family relationships, partners of the alcoholic, or the co-alcoholic and other family members, were included in the process. This practice yielded lower incidents of relapse and longer periods of sobriety.

Beginning in the early 1980s, drug treatment programs adopted the term "chemical dependency," as it better reflected the many similarities between alcoholism and drug addiction. The term "co-alcoholic" was likewise updated to "co-chemically dependent." Being too much of a mouthful, it was shortened to "codependent." This change in terminology caused some confusion. Many incorrectly interpreted the new term as relating more to a dependent personality type who joined another dependent person in a relationship—two dependents, or codependents. In actuality, codependency denoted a person who was habitually in relationships with chemically dependent people, whom they would try to control, but were ultimately powerless over. Due to the confusion of the term itself, which continues to the present day, there have been numerous incorrect assumptions and connotations about it.

In the 1980s, codependency was used only to describe a person if they were: (1) in a love or marital relationship with an alcoholic, (2) had one or more alcoholic parents or grandparents, or (3) were raised within an emotionally repressive family (Wegscheider-Cruse, 1984). Chemical dependency facilities began to regularly provide treatment and/or support services to the addict's family members. Their primary focus was to support the codependents and/or significant others of the addict during the treatment process and teach them about their role in the problem/disease. Over time, the term codependency became increasingly accepted in the treatment and psychotherapeutic fields. It would eventually become the standard diagnostic term used for the chemically-dependent individual's partner or other individuals who enabled a chemically-dependent friend/loved one.

By the mid-1980s, thanks to many key advances within the chemical dependency and addiction treatment fields, the term codependency took on a more broadly understood meaning. It evolved to describe a person who was habitually attracted to or in a relationship with a narcissist and/or an addict. Codependents were understood to be people-pleasers who would reflexively sacrifice and care for others who would not care for them in return. They felt powerless to resist relationships with addicted, controlling, and/or narcissistic individuals. It became evident codependents came from all walks of life and were not necessarily only in relationships with addicted individuals.

Thanks to Melody Beattie, Claudia Black, John Friel, Terry Kellogg, and Pia Melody, just to name a few, the updated meaning of codependency finally saw the light of day. It came out of the closet and was no longer considered a shameful secret for which there was no help. The work of these authors helped change attitudes towards the partners of addicts or narcissists, who were no longer viewed as weak and defenseless victims powerless to leave their harmful and dysfunctional relationships.

Melody Beattie's ground-breaking book, *Codependent No More: How to Stop Controlling Others and Start Caring for Yourself* (1986), was instrumental in promoting a greater understanding of what is now seen as a universal problem. The book has sold over eight million copies worldwide. The sales figures suggest codependency is a problem that spans regional, ethnic, and cultural boundaries. Beattie and her contemporaries created a body of work that was largely influential in creating a societal consciousness of the codependency problem which, in turn, inspired the creation of programs to treat it. Beattie's endorsement of the first *Human Magnet Syndrome* was nothing short of a dream come true. I will always appreciate and cherish the advice she has so generously given me over the past few years.

By the late 1980s, codependency treatment options became more widely available. Around the same time as the publication of *Codependent No More*, Co-Dependents Anonymous (CODA) was established. CODA is a 12-Step organization that helps people deal with their codependent tendencies and develop healthy and self-empowering relationships. CODA is active in more than 40 countries, with about 1,200 functioning groups in the U.S. alone.

Because codependency shares many similarities with alcoholism, CODA effectively utilizes the AA 12 Step guidelines. Alcoholics and other addicts cannot control their addictive behavior. Their actions have negative consequences and their lives subsequently spiral out of control. Codependents are no different as they seek to control others who, by their very nature, cannot be controlled. Like the partners of alcoholics and addicts, they think they can control their narcissistic partner, who they believe has the capacity to make them happy. Codependents habitually and compulsively find themselves on a hamster wheel of relationship possibilities—but never really get anywhere.

Both chemical addictions and codependency are progressive processes characterized by loss, negative consequences, denial, and an urge to control something or someone that can never be controlled. Hence, CODA can be beneficial to codependents. Please note CODA does not replace therapy, nor does therapy replace 12 Step work.

DEFINING CODEPENDENCY

The understanding and treatment of codependency has evolved over the last 30 years and can be viewed from many perspectives. The following are a handful of definitions consistent with my own experiences with codependency.

To start, the Merriam Webster Online Dictionary defines codependency as:

> . . . a psychological condition or a relationship in which a person is controlled by another who is affected with a pathological condition (as in an addiction to alcohol or heroin); and in broader terms, it refers to dependence on the needs of or control of another.

Clark & Stoffel's (1992) research article, "Assessment of Codependency Behavior in Two Health Student Groups," describes/defines codependency as:

> A pattern of painful dependence on compulsive behaviors and others' approval in an attempt to find safety, self-worth, and identity (p. 822).
> . . . a progressive process whereby self-denial and concomitant caring for other family members is based on the assumption that doing so will foster love, closeness, acceptance, and security in the family (p. 822).
> . . . an extreme sense of responsibility to others, inability to appropriately care for the self, increased focus on others' needs, decreased focus on needs of the self, overreaction to things external to the self, under-reaction to things internal to the self, low self-esteem, low self-concept, high external locus of control, and denial (p. 822).

[A willingness] to sacrifice so much of themselves that they set aside their own physical, emotional, and psychological needs for the sake of others. They are detrimentally selfless (p. 823).

According to Beattie's (1986) book, *Codependent No More*:

A codependent person is one who has let another person's behavior affect him or her, and who is obsessed with controlling that person's behavior (p. 34).

Codependency involves a habitual system of thinking, feeling, and behaving toward ourselves and others that can cause us pain. Codependent behaviors or habits are self-destructive (p. 37).

We (codependents) frequently react to people who are destroying themselves; we react by learning to destroy ourselves. These habits can lead us into, or keep us in, destructive relationships, relationships that don't work. These behaviors can sabotage relationships that may otherwise have worked. These behaviors can prevent us from finding peace and happiness with the most important person in our lives—ourselves. These behaviors belong to the only person each of us can control—the only person we can change—ourselves (p. 37).

Codependency is many things. It is a dependency on people—on their moods, behaviors, sickness or well-being, and their love. It is a paradoxical dependency. Codependents appear to be depended upon, but they are dependent. They look strong but feel helpless. They appear controlling, but in reality, are controlled themselves, sometimes by an illness such as alcoholism (pp. 51–52).

THE NEW CODEPENDENCY DEFINITION

I place a great deal of importance on delineating the diagnostic features of codependency, while creating an expansive but precise explanation for the problem. The following is my basic definition of codependency, which applies to all personality types and possible variations of it.

Codependency is a psychological condition manifested by a compulsion to give the preponderance of love, respect, and care (LRC) in any given relationship, with the hope it will be reciprocated. Because of the Human Magnet Syndrome, codependents consistently find themselves in relationships with narcissists, who have neither the intention, motivation, nor ability to be mutually giving in most relationships. Codependents mistakenly believe the only solution to the LRC inequality problem is to try even harder to solve it, or they just give up and stop trying. The prospect of being alone—and experiencing pathological loneliness— keeps them believing that given enough time, patience, and sacrifice, their narcissist will change. If they or their partner do end the relationship, codependents perpetually find themselves on the giving end of a new relationship.

CONTROLLING THE UNCONTROLLABLE

Codependents cannot shake the unrealistic belief that happiness will only come if they are in a relationship. They look to other people to make them feel happy and fulfilled. Because of their Human-Magnet-Syndrome-driven relationship choices, their hope of a "happy ever after" disintegrates at the very moment their narcissist in hiding takes off his soulmate mask.

Since the codependent unconsciously chooses partners who are unwilling, unmotivated, or unable to meet their personal and emotional needs, they may choose the path of control to get their pathologically narcissistic partner to give them what they want and need. To some, it is counterintuitive for codependents to be controlling. There are, indeed, codependents who do give up and take a passive victim-based role in their dysfunctional relationships. However, because most codependents typically take on the lion's share of the relationship responsibilities such as child care, house cleaning, cooking, shopping, and/or financially supporting the relationship/family, they cannot afford to acquiesce and relinquish control of their family's life. Without maintaining some semblance of control, they and their family would certainly suffer. To most codependents, the idea of stopping their attempts to get their narcissistic partner to reciprocate or behave fairly and responsibly is tantamount to giving up on their relationship; something codependents are mostly reluctant or incapable of doing.

The codependent's compulsion to control someone who cannot be controlled puts them on a circular path that always brings them back to where they started: angry, frustrated, and resentful. Much like the dog chasing its tail, they run around and around, trying to get somewhere, but always ending up in the same place. Their attempts to seek the unobtainable create a series of personal and relational failures that ultimately remind them of their powerlessness over others. This pattern is self-reinforcing. The more they fail at controlling the pathological narcissist, the worse they feel. Over time, they get worn down by their failures and, consequently, give up on the hope the one-sided nature of their relationship will ever change.

CODEPENDENCY CATEGORIES

Although all codependents are habitually and instinctively attracted (and later bonded) to severely narcissistic partners, there are two categories: passive and active codependents. Both hold tight to the belief that one day their pathological partner will realize their mistakes and finally give them the LRC they so desperately want and need. It just never happens. Both try to control and manipulate their narcissistic partners, but they each go about it differently.

- **Passive Codependents** are more fearful and avoidant of conflict. For complicated reasons, mostly related to their extremely low self-esteem, fear of being alone, and tendency to be in relationships with controlling, dangerous, and/or abusive pathological narcissists, the passive codependent attempts to control or influence their partner through carefully, if not meticulously, executed strategies—most of which are intended to fall under the pathological narcissist's radar. Because of the secretive and hidden nature of their tactics, a passive codependent is perceived as more resigned, stoic, and compliant than an active codependent. The attachment trauma experience taught them that there was no benefit in fighting back, or that doing so would result in worse consequences. For this reason alone, I surmise that passive codependents suffered a higher degree of childhood trauma than active codependents and are more afraid to reach out for help.
- **Active Codependents** are overtly manipulative in their control strategies in an attempt to remedy the LRC inequity in their relationship. Not only are active codependents less insecure than their passive counterparts, but they also fall victim to what I call *the codependency delusion*. Since a delusion is a belief that is not supported by reality, an active codependent is

being delusional when they sincerely believe they can control or mitigate the harm caused by their pathologically narcissistic loved one.

Active codependents are often not intimidated or afraid of their narcissist lover. They believe their resistance and arguments will result in either modifying their partner's treatment of them, or simply teaching them a lesson. As such, they rely on an aggressive and confrontational approach to both protect themselves and get what they need. Their controlling, antagonizing, and manipulative method is rarely effective. In fact, it often results in the pathological narcissist's retaliation, which often harms the codependent even more. The defiance serves as a paper-thin attempt to feel more powerful and respected in the relationship.

PERSONALITY TYPE IS INDEPENDENT OF ONE'S RELATIONSHIP ORIENTATION

It is a common mistake to conclude active codependents are narcissists if they have negative or harmful personality traits, such as being aggressive, passive aggressive, controlling, dishonest, manipulative, unfaithful, and/or overly reactive (angry). Nothing could be further from the truth. *A person's personality type or traits, substance abuse or addiction struggles, and mental health problems are often independent of their RO.* To illustrate, it is common for both codependents and narcissists to struggle with a coexisting addiction, such as overeating, drugs or alcohol, sex, or gambling.

This "rule" applies to most mental health disorders. There are equally impaired schizophrenics who are and are not criminals. A person with Major Depression, Bipolar Disorder, or Posttraumatic Stress Disorder may or may not be an alcoholic, liar, or aggressive bully. In fact, a sweet and endearing person could very well be silently suffering from a serious mental health condition or addiction.

A CODEPENDENT CANNOT BE A NARCISSIST

Over the last ten years, I have been asked more times than I can count, primarily by codependents, "Can a codependent be a narcissist?" Since these two disorders are opposite in almost every respect, it is impossible to be both at the same time. The complex psychological dynamics at play in the codependent-narcissist relationship trigger a psychologically manipulated codependent to believe their needs, requests, and desires are either less important, or secondary, to those of their narcissistic significant other. Worse yet, they are conditioned to judge themselves as inconsiderate, needy, or selfish when asking for something the narcissist would normally deprive them of. Taking on the narcissism moniker is also explained by being a victim of the narcissist's projection. Some codependents get so worn down by the constant barrage of projections, they begin to adopt and identify with them. Hence, this is why so many obvious codependents profess to be narcissists. *Projective identification* is the term that explains this phenomenon.

Since codependents lack confidence and feelings of personal and relational efficacy, they are prone to various forms of psychological manipulation tactics, which pathological narcissists use to establish power and control. One such form of mental manipulation is gaslighting, coined from the 1944 film, *Gaslight*, which will be discussed in Chapter Eleven. Gaslighting is a form of mental abuse, like brainwashing, in which a victim is manipulated into doubting their own memory, perception, and sanity. Victims are not aware they are being covertly and methodically manipulated into believing they have a problem that renders them powerless and in need of the same person who created the problem.

Psychological gymnastics and brainwashing are behind the codependent's distorted beliefs of being a narcissist. Codependents often carry a personal narrative that condemns them for being selfish or narcissistic when wanting or seeking to meet their own needs and desires. This no-win situation, or double bind, compels them to feel selfish or narcissistic when defending themselves or when trying to take care of themselves or any person other than the narcissist. Because of the dysfunctional narrative, they submit to the belief that they are good and loving when they sacrifice and bad, selfish, or narcissistic when they seek to meet their own needs or show some modicum of self-respect and self-love. These thought distortions come from a lifelong experience of being blamed for their pathologically narcissistic loved one's narcissism.

The simplest proof I can provide to the confused codependent is most narcissists would reject the claim they are narcissistic and wouldn't invest any emotional energy feeling bad about it. Narcissists typically blame others for their problems, while experiencing little-to-no internal conflict about the harm they cause others. In contrast, codependents are quick to blame themselves for mistakes and problems, whether it was their fault or not. They are also prone to convoluted thought patterns about what they might have done wrong, what they could have done better, and how to make the people who are upset with them happy. The codependent is primed to believe any serious problem may very well be their fault. In short, a codependent will very likely believe themselves to be a narcissist; a narcissist would never consider that to be a possibility.

THE PATTERNS AND CHARACTERISTICS OF CODEPENDENTS

CODA breaks down the characteristics of codependency into five patterns: denial, low self-esteem, compliance, control, and avoidance.

Denial Patterns

 - I minimize, alter, or deny how I truly feel.
- I perceive myself as completely unselfish and dedicated to the well-being of others.

Low Self-Esteem Patterns

 - I have difficulty making decisions.
- I judge everything I think, say, or do harshly—as never good enough.
- I am embarrassed to receive recognition, praise, or gifts.
 - I do not ask others to meet my needs or desires.
- I value other's approval of my thinking, feelings, and behaviors over my own.
- I do not perceive myself as a lovable or worthwhile person.

Compliance Patterns

 - I compromise my own values and integrity to avoid rejection or anger from others.
- I am very sensitive to how others are feeling and feel the same.
- I am extremely loyal, remaining in harmful situations too long.
 - I value others' opinions and feelings more than my own and am afraid to express differing opinions and feelings of my own.
- I put aside my own interests and hobbies to do what others want.
 - I accept sex when I want love.

Control Patterns

- I believe most other people are incapable of taking care of themselves.

- I attempt to convince others of what they *should* think and how they *truly* feel.
- I become resentful when others will not let me help them.
- I freely offer others advice and directions without being asked.
- I lavish gifts and favors on those I care about.
- I use sex to gain approval and acceptance.
- I have to be *needed* to have a relationship with others.

Avoidance Patterns

- I act in ways that invite others to reject, shame, or express anger toward me.
- I judge harshly what others think, say, or do.
- I avoid emotional, physical, or sexual intimacy as a means of maintaining distance.
- I allow my addictions to people, places, and things to distract me from achieving intimacy in relationships.
- I use indirect and evasive communication to avoid conflict or confrontation.
- I diminish my capacity to have healthy relationships by declining to use all the tools of recovery.
- I suppress my feelings or needs to avoid feeling vulnerable.
- I pull people toward me but when they get close I push them away.
- I refuse to give up my self-will to avoid surrendering to a power that is greater than me.
- I believe displays of emotion are a sign of weakness.
- I withhold expressions of appreciation.

TYPICAL CODEPENDENCY TRAITS

- Low self-esteem
- Self-worth/self-esteem depends on being needed and having few needs
- Excessively complies with suggestions, requests, or inappropriate orders

- Preoccupied with the problems, struggles, and needs of others while neglecting their own
- In an attempt to be everything to everybody, loses ability to take care of their own needs
- Champions and avidly supports the needs, goals, and dreams of others while ignoring or devaluing their own
- Adept at solving the problems of others while not being able or motivated to solve their own
- Perpetually seeks to please people, always looking to help or lend a hand
- Struggles at declining a request for help—may feel guilty or needy
- Overcommits in many important relationships
- Creates excessive/impossible work and personal schedule
- Feels unable to ask for what they want or need
- Feels selfish or needy when asking for help
- Has difficulty identifying and communicating emotions
- Willingly conforms to unrealistic and unreasonable relationship expectations
- Fears and avoids disagreements and conflict
- Feels powerless to protect themselves from harm; easily manipulated and exploited by self-serving individuals
- Does not set firm boundaries (consequences) when mistreated and/or abused
- Makes attempts to control or manipulate others who typically neglect them
- In an attempt to be helpful, pushes their "help" onto others
- Confuses work and personal relationships

CODEPENDENCY ANOREXIA—STARVING ONESELF OF LOVE

Codependency anorexia occurs when a codependent surrenders to their lifelong relationship pattern with destructive pathological narcissists. The codependent often transitions to codependency anorexia when they hit bottom and can no longer bear the pain and harm meted out by their narcissist. Paradoxically, as it occurs during a moment of clarity, the codependent comes to realize they are powerless over their attraction to lovers who feel right in the beginning, but shortly thereafter hurt them. To protect themselves from the long line of soulmates who unexpectedly become cellmates, the codependent flips their vulnerability switch to off. This results in a complete shutdown of all emotional, relational, and sexual machinery.

Although their intention is to avoid getting pummeled again by the next narcissist, the codependent unknowingly insulates themselves from the very human experience of intimate romantic love. This defense mechanism serves to protect codependents from the cascade of consequences of their poor love choices. By denying their human need to connect and love passionately, in a sense they artificially neutralize the Human Magnet Syndrome. In other words, they remove themselves from any possibility of close romantic love, healthy or not.

To maintain their anorexia, codependents ultimately must divorce themselves from their emotional and sexual selves. As a result, they starve themselves from the very human need to connect romantically, intimately, and sexually. Such deprivation often leads to long-term mental and relational health problems.

In the anorexic state, codependents are hypervigilant about people or situations that could lead to a harmful and dangerous intimate relationship. In social situations, they often overcompensate to avoid showing interest in someone or accidentally reacting to someone's overtures. To that end, they avoid everyday social events so as not to accidentally bump against a vulnerable or threatening situation or person. If anything does threaten the codependents anorexic barrier, anxiety will steer them back onto their self-depriving, but safe, course.

Anorexic codependents cannot recognize their disconnection from their vulnerable relational and sexual self is harmful, if not debilitating. At the end of the day, the goal they manage to achieve is avoiding being hurt by yet another pathological narcissist. However, they also live their life in a barren desert of loneliness and fear.

The children of anorexic codependents may be inappropriately relied on to compensate for the lack of intimate adult relationships. This damaging form of parent-child enmeshment is often referred to as *emotional incest*, which is harmful to a child's psychological development.

JANICE—A CODEPENDENT ANOREXIC

Janice, a 45-year-old single mother and psychotherapist, sought my codependency treatment services due to work-related stress. Like other codependent clients, her childhood was traumatic because her father was a pathological narcissist and her mother, a codependent. All her romantic partners were pathological narcissists, always handsome, charming, confident, and bold. Despite knowing the consequences of her choices in men, she could not stop falling in love with exquisitely dangerous bad boys. In fact, her last three significant romantic relationships (two husbands and a boyfriend) were with psychologically abusive pathological narcissists.

When she became pregnant with her only child, 13 years before our therapy began, her soulmate boyfriend, Jerry, abruptly turned evil. He reacted to his impending fatherhood by breaking up with her and relapsing into alcoholism. She would later learn that, on the night he found out about their child, he went to a strip club and hired a prostitute for sex. In shock about another in a long line of relationship disappointments, she swore off men and romance. And she was serious about it. She became fiercely independent and did whatever was necessary to pursue her career as a licensed psychotherapist.

When asked about her decision to stop dating or having any form of romantic relationships, she shrugged her shoulders and said she did it to save herself from any more pain. She also unemotionally explained that what Jerry did to both her and their child was the type of trauma no person should ever have to experience twice. After being abandoned, she had nothing left to give to another man. Rather stoically, she stated, "It is better this way, as I have plenty of friends and a really good vibrator." I will never forget the vacant look on her face that accompanied this statement. When I pushed a bit harder about why she would give up the chance to experience romance, in an even more disconnected tone she insisted she didn't miss men and was grateful for the calmness and lack of drama. This is when, being the seasoned psychotherapist she was, she took charge of the conversation and changed it to something less challenging.

It took her another year of once-weekly psychotherapy sessions to reconsider her decision to starve herself of romance and intimacy. Two years later, I received a postcard announcing she had finally met the man of her dreams. For the first time, she was experiencing what had escaped her grasp throughout her life: a good man who was good to her.

CODEPENDENT MARTYR SYNDROME

Some codependents rationalize, or repackage, their codependency traits into what they believe to be positive behaviors. Their codependency becomes a badge of honor of sorts, to be worn proudly—and declared often. These individuals experience what I refer to as the codependent martyr syndrome. Codependent martyrs are intensely proud of their selfless, sacrificial, and long-suffering approach to their relationships. Their identity and self-esteem become fused with their codependency. These martyrs are proud, and even boastful, about how much they do for others, as well as how much they sacrifice in their lives. These beliefs often stem from the family values passed down from one generation to the next. This transgenerational pattern is often influenced by regional, ethnic, cultural, or religious beliefs and practices.

The martyr's self-esteem, or what I refer to as pseudo self-esteem, is built on a foundation of compliments. In other words, their codependency is reinforced by the positive attention, recognition, and even awards they receive for their selflessness; they may be referred to as a saint or "the salt of the earth." If asked why they do not ask for much, they are likely to say they really do not need much and giving to others makes them feel happy and fulfilled. Many even rationalize their selfless, giving, and generous nature as necessary for religious salvation or guarantee of an eternal afterlife. Some codependent martyrs generously and expertly guilt trip others to remind them of their sacrifice.

PSEUDO NARCISSISM (KID-IN-A-CANDY-STORE PHENOMENON)

The human spirit and psyche are malleable, and codependency recovery can literally change someone's life for the better. Therefore, it is possible to transition from a healthy ORO to a healthy SRO. On the RCC, it would look like this: The (-5) RCV codependent not only moves toward the center of the continuum, but they may also cross zero and go on to experience the world as a healthy self-oriented person.

For some, including myself, the experience is so exhilarating they may temporarily move toward a higher SRO RCV. They may experience being (and be experienced by others as) a narcissist, or what I refer to as a *codependency-recovery-induced narcissist*. A fitting analogy for this process is a kid in a candy store. The newfound experience of self-esteem, self-love, and confidence allows this person to experience a new world in which they can manifest the latent and long-buried best version of themselves. Like a teenager trying on potential identities, this overzealous person may make mistakes as the learning curve is steep. As much as they always dreamed of self-love and the absence of codependency, their overstimulation may unintentionally cause harm to others. Because they have yet to learn the skill set of modesty, they may go overboard in their expression of self-esteem and self-love. The RCV spike to a (+3) or (+4) may temporarily make the recovering codependent appear to be a narcissist, even though they really are not.

Unlike pathological narcissists, these sometimes-irritating converts are capable of self-reflection and awareness, and able to hold themselves accountable for the harm they cause. If an over-enthusiastic ORO-turned-SRO realizes they have hurt someone, they would feel bad, take responsibility for their actions, and make the appropriate amends or adjustments.

Since the goal of healthy relationships is a well-balanced distribution of LRC, it is imperative that *self-loving freshmen* get a chance to revel in their newfound mental health, while paying attention to how it may impact others. It might not be easy to dial down one's excitement about a new life without core shame, pathological loneliness, and the addictive pursuit of narcissists, but the opportunity to foster relationships with similarly self-loving people, as well as the determination to become disciplined and measured in the candy store, will be well worth the effort.

CODEPENDENT PARENTS ALSO HURT THEIR CHILDREN

Although the adult codependent parent is harmed by their narcissistic partner, their codependency should not be considered a valid excuse for not caring for and protecting their children. The unfortunate reality is when they become parents, codependents often choose to stay in the relationship with the narcissist, focusing on their needs to the exclusion of their children.

Most codependent parents do not wish any harm to befall their children. In fact, a majority will go to extraordinary measures to stop or mitigate the narcissist's harm to or abuse of the children. They are unable to stop the resulting neglect and/or abuse everyone in the family is forced to endure—except, of course, the narcissist. The codependent's inability to protect the children *co-creates* a toxic family environment in which the children are harmed, and their future psychological health is compromised.

The codependent's obsessive-compulsive desire to satisfy the narcissist's needs, while also trying to control their behavior, depletes the energy, time, focus, and emotional resources that would otherwise be given to the children. Tired and beaten down, codependents often shut down and disconnect from their responsibility to protect their children—and themselves.

Although I am suggesting codependents share responsibility for the harm of their children, caution must be taken when attributing blame. The codependent parent similarly grew up in a family where the children were held captive by the neglect and/or abuse of a codependent-pathologically narcissistic parent duo. They are clearly victims of their childhood environment as well. Without their attempts to protect their children and provide even a base amount of love and nurturing, the sum total of psychological harm to the children would be far worse compared to being solely raised by a pathological narcissist.

Many of my codependent clients have shared their anger, resentment, and even disgust about their codependent parent's unwillingness to protect them and leave their narcissistic parent. These clients have recalled numerous occasions when this parent could have protected them, but instead chose to either ignore the situation or rationalize it away. The distorted sense of loyalty to the narcissist resulted in the sacrifice of the children's psychological and relational future. Sadly, this codependent parent's selfish need for security and lifelong avoidance of loneliness (albeit sometimes unconsciously) ultimately took priority over their children.

Often, in the beginning of codependency treatment, my clients are unable to wrap their heads around the concept that their wonderfully loving and nurturing codependent parent should share any responsibility for the neglectful or abusive childhood they endured. After working hard in codependency-specific psychotherapy, there comes a time when the client is psychologically healthy enough to let go of the good-codependent-parent fantasy and realistically hold this person partially responsible for their traumatic childhood. Although this process often begins with anger and a need for accountability, it eventually transforms into a willingness to empathize with, accept, and forgive the codependent parent. In the process of being honest about who their parent really was and how much they were harmed by them, they can own their own codependency, while better understanding its current and historical impact on those who passed it down to them.

The codependent parent who disassociates from their pathological narcissist injures their children, as well as themselves. Codependency anorexia is harmful, even though it appears to protect the codependent and their children from narcissistic abuse. In reality, it ultimately deprives the children of a second parent—

another adult who loves, respects, and cares for them and is unconditionally committed to their welfare. Raising a family, while purposely avoiding a romantic or intimate partner, sends the message that such types of adult relationships may be dangerous and harmful, thus sowing the seeds for the next generation of desensitized, unemotionally attached adults.

Reflections

- Did you have a codependent parent growing up? If so, how did that impact you?

- Do you relate more to an active or passive codependent personality type? Why?

Chapter Eight

THE ORIGINS OF CODEPENDENCY

Back in the early 1980s, when I was pursuing an undergraduate degree in psychology, the nature versus nurture debate seemed to be coming to an end. Until then, the two factions were trying to convince the other that human psychology could be better explained through environmental or learning phenomenon, or by better understanding ourselves through our biological and genetic heritage.

The nature versus nurture question could never have been solved, as the answer implies an illogical and artificial developmental starting point that is mistakenly believed to be a primary process. The "give and take" relationship of biogenetics and environmental forces is what lays the psychological foundation for a developing child. Simply put, the interaction of the two impacts a child's future mental health. The synergistic relationship of nature and nurture is illustrated in the following example: Tom Nature and Jerry Nurture were very good wrestlers, but not good enough. Only after Nature and Nurture competed as a tag team did they win most of their fights and rise to the top of their league. By bringing their best into the ring and picking up the other's slack, Tom and Jerry easily defeated most of their opponents. Hence, the "what came first, the chicken or the egg" question about nature and nurture should never have been asked.

BRAIN DEVELOPMENT = PERSON DEVELOPMENT

Early neurological development and the factors that promote and inhibit it are critically important in understanding codependency. Consider that, by age 4, a child's brain will have reached 80% of its adult weight (Prabhakar, 2006). During this four-year period—a child's formative years—the most rapid physical, cognitive, and emotional growth occurs. Like sponges that do not differentiate between good and bad, children automatically soak up their environment. Anyone who has a child will attest to how quickly they absorb and learn something new. These little humans are like vacuum cleaners!

We are currently in the middle of an explosion of brain research, which has greatly enhanced our understanding of child, adolescent, and adult developmental psychology. More than ever, the puzzle pieces are coming together so we can understand the synergistic relationship among the environment, mind, and body. We now know children's physical and emotional environments, aside from their own internal feedback loop, dramatically impact the development of their nervous system. This is especially true of the brain and has profound implications for their psychological health as adults. What goes right or wrong during this delicately balanced and vulnerable stage of child development can have an everlasting impact on their life.

We have more than 200 years of examples illustrating how the environment impacts a child's physical development. Between 1780 and 1800, the height of vagrant boys in London increased by three inches in just 30 years—a growth that paralleled the improving conditions for the poor (Dougherty, 2017).

A more fundamental illustration of the interactional relationship between brain development and the environment comes from the study of human evolution. Several millions of years ago, 15 or more hominin (modern but extinct humans) species lived side-by-side. Only our species, *homo sapiens*, survived while the others perished. Paleontologists believe this occurred because of our ability to adapt to the changing conditions. The most crucial adaptation was the change in our diets—from fruits and vegetables to meat. The added protein and fat gave us more energy, which promoted the development of larger and more complex brains. Bigger and more complicated brains resulted in higher survival rates. Our larger brains gave us the ability to understand intricate planning and language and allowed us to spread new ideas from one individual to another. Planning, communication, and even trade led, among other things, to the development of better tools and weapons across the population (Mosley, 2011).

Insofar as evidence exists about how our environment enhances or quickens physical and psychological growth, there is a greater body of evidence to the contrary. This inverse phenomenon is best illustrated by Nim Tottenham (2011), who did research on deprived Romanian orphans. Tottenham found a causal connection between early childhood emotional and personal deprivation and abnormally small, structurally malformed brains. The research established little-to-no nurturing, attention, or stimulation during infancy and the toddler years prevented children's brains from developing to their fullest, genetically-determined capacity.

The orphans' brain malformations resulted in language, intellectual, and cognitive impairment. A significant number of these orphans developed Conduct and/or Antisocial Personality Disorders. This led Tottenham (2011) to conclude there is a connection between poor or absent personal and emotional nurturing (positive attachment) in childhood and irreversible mental health problems in adulthood.

Additional research (Johnson, 2012) showed the circular interaction between neurological and environmental influences and psychological functioning. This study compared a non-narcissistically reared control group with a narcissistically reared group. MRI scans revealed the latter group had less brain mass (gray matter) in the anterior insula, a subsection of the cerebral cortex, compared to the non-narcissistically reared control group. The research concluded adverse environmental factors, such as a negative attachment experience, inhibited the normal development of the brain structures responsible for compassion and empathy. Sharon L. Johnson (2012) succinctly explained the impact of environmental influences on brain development:

> Attachment, the emotional bond formed between an infant and its primary caretaker, profoundly influences both the structure and function of the developing infant's brain. Failed attachment, whether caused by abuse, neglect, or emotional unavailability on the part of the caretaker, can negatively impact brain structure and function, causing developmental or relational trauma. Early-life trauma affects future self-esteem, social awareness, ability to learn, and physical health.

VITAMIN L(OVE) DEFICIENCY

My Vitamin L(ove) Deficiency idea further illustrates the impact of that neglect and deprivation, or attachment trauma, on an adult's future mental and physical health. This awareness represents the sum of the nurturing (LRC) children receive from healthy parents during their formative years. When parents unconditionally give Vitamin L, children develop a healthy adult RO, which is indicative of adult emotional and relational health. Similar to depriving children of critically important vitamins, like C or D, Vitamin L deprivation will disrupt and harm their future development. This, in turn, will have a deleterious impact on their ability to function as adults. More specifically, it will harm a child's fragile and rapidly developing brain, which is the very foundation of their adult mental health.

Vitamin L Deficiency manifests in adulthood as either a mental health disorder or an emotional and relational deficit. In addition, it later blocks an adult's ability to metabolize or absorb vitamin L *supplements*. The adult's intention to recognize or take in another person's LRC will be thwarted by deeper psychological processes. This explains a codependent's suspicious and anxious reactions to a potential lover who is psychologically healthy (low RCVs). Not only does their system reject Vitamin L, but it also reacts to it as a toxic substance or dangerous allergen. The only viable solution is to methodically remove the trauma scar tissue that is blocking the absorption of the available Vitamin L supplements. With the scar tissue removed, a course of Vitamin L should be started, beginning at a low dose and increasing to as much as the person can tolerate. Vitamin L therapy concludes when the person can produce the vitamin themselves and no longer requires outside sources to obtain it.

ATTACHMENT THEORY

Attachment is defined as a deep and enduring emotional bond that connects one person to another across time and space (Ainsworth, 1973; Bowlby, 1969). It was created by Bowlby (1958), who demonstrated the importance of parent-child bonding. Humans require positive attachment to allow an infant's genetically programmed social, emotional, and cognitive skills to develop. The attachment process also provides the first coping system. It creates a mental representation of the caregiver that is wholly portable and can be summoned as a comforting mental presence in difficult moments. Because it allows infants to separate from their caregivers without distress and begin to explore the world around them, attachment contains within it the platform for the child to survive independently.

Bowlby (1969) hypothesized the quality of an infant's bond, or attachment, to their caregiver is correlated with, if not predictive of, adult relationship attachments. He showed how positive attachment experiences indoctrinate children with basic beliefs and thought patterns that allow them to feel valued and protected in a world that is often unpredictable, frightening, and overwhelming. Children who are well-bonded to their parents will want to explore the world, feel safe while doing it, and eventually be successful in their attempts to individuate from their parents. A positive attachment experience additionally lays the foundational building blocks for future stable and satisfying relationships. Bowlby (1969) also established that absent or negative attachment results in a child's chronic feelings of betrayal and belief they are alone and vulnerable in a world fraught with scary and dangerous obstacles. This unfortunate child will develop into an adult whose emotional insecurity and fears inhibit the growth of healthy relations.

Harlow's (1963) research on maternal separation and isolation with rhesus monkeys reinforces Bowlby's Attachment Theory. Harlow demonstrated how the monkeys mimicked and transferred their own primitive and innate child-rearing and bonding experiences to their infants. He observed the babies' need for emotional comfort was more important than anything else, including food and water. Those who were nurtured replicated that experience with their own babies. The monkeys that didn't bond with a caregiver, and were therefore deprived of nurturing, developed low levels of interest and motivation to bond with or care for their own babies. The saying "you reap what you sow" underscores Bowlby's attachment research.

Early attachment experiences stimulate growth within the brain and shape emerging neural pathways. They establish the neural pathways in the infant's brain that will sculpt what are likely to be lifelong patterns of response to many things. Neuroscientists believe attachment is such a primal need that there are networks of neurons in the brain dedicated to setting it in motion, as well as a hormone to foster the process: oxytocin (Psychologytoday.com, 2017). Researchers Hazan and Shaver (1987) expanded Bowlby's (1969) hypotheses by demonstrating an infant's attachment experience with their adult caregiver is later replicated in their adult romantic relationships. These adult relationships, like those between infant and caregiver, are deep, emotionally bonded, and indelibly connected to the early childhood attachment experience. Bowlby's attachment theory gave mental health practitioners the ability to isolate the origins of abnormal and pathological psychological behavior/disorders in order to develop viable treatment methods. The theory created a global wake-up call that firmly established the crucial importance of childhood nurturing.

ERIKSON'S DEVELOPMENTAL THEORY

Erik Erikson, a renowned developmental psychologist and personality theorist—and a personal and professional hero of mine—created an ingenious theory that rests on an eight stage model of psychosocial development. The stages, which begin at birth and end at death, include age-specific developmental challenges that, if mastered, equip a person with the experiences and abilities for potential success in the following stage. By not mastering a stage, the child remains stuck in their psychosocial development, which has a deleterious impact on their adult emotional and relational health. The name of each stage exemplifies the resulting success or failure of it. Psychosocial stunting has many faces, including codependency and pathological narcissism, as well as other pathological conditions and disorders.

ERIKSON'S EIGHT STAGES OF PSYCHOSOCIAL DEVELOPMENT

1. Trust vs. Mistrust: Birth to 12–18 months
2. Autonomy vs. Shame/Doubt: 18 months to 3 years
3. Initiative vs. Guilt: 3 to 6 years
4. Industry vs. Inferiority: 6 to 12 years
5. Identity vs. Role Confusion: 12 to 18 years
6. Intimacy vs. Isolation: 18 to 40 years
7. Generativity vs. Stagnation: 40 to 65 years
8. Ego Integrity vs. Despair: 65 to Death

Success in the first three stages requires an attachment experience imbued with unconditional LRC. Parental neglect, deprivation, abuse, and Vitamin L Deficiency result in the inability to acquire the necessary psychosocial abilities needed to move forward in Erikson's stages. A child who is unable to master one stage and move to the next will later be saddled with emotional and relational problems, such as codependency or pathological narcissism.

A child's Vitamin L Deficiency is analogous to low or absent folic acid levels during pregnancy. According to the Centers for Disease Control and Prevention (2017), women with insufficient folic acid in their diets (or supplements) risk giving birth to a child with brain and spinal defects. The following illustrates the long-term development implications of low or absent levels of folic acid.

> Neural tube defects are serious birth defects that occur along the neural tube and are a significant cause of death and lifelong disability worldwide. The two most common neural tube defects are spina bifida and anencephaly. Spina bifida happens when the backbone that protects the spinal cord does not form and close as it should. Anencephaly is a fatal birth defect that occurs when the upper part of the neural tube does not close all the way. Infants with anencephaly are often born without part of the skull and brain and die shortly after birth (Elwood, Little, and Elwood, 1992).

Other researchers confirm Erikson's developmental conclusions:

> A little like the unfolding of a rosebud, each petal opens at a certain time, in a certain order, which nature, through its genetics, has determined. If we interfere in the natural order of development by pulling a petal forward prematurely or out of order, we ruin the development of the entire flower (Boeree, 2006).
>
> Child development follows a predictable, organized course beginning with the child's mastery of physiological regulations (eating, sleeping), and continuing through the development of higher skills, such as problem-solving and peer relationships. However, under abnormal and unusual circumstances, especially abuse and neglect, predictability and organization are disrupted and thrown off course, which results in developmental failure and limited adaptation (Boeree, Marsh, and Wolfe, 2008, p. 35).

Attachment and psychosocial development theory illustrates the relationship of attachment and adult emotional and relational health. If all goes well and the child received ample Vitamin L, they will develop a psychological and neurological foundation to become a happy, healthy, and fulfilled adult, instilled with a sense of Self-Love Abundance. If the child is not so fortunate and endures deprivation, neglect, or abuse—especially during their formative years—their potential for positive psychological and relational mental health will be severely compromised, if not snuffed out. The result is the unfortunate possibility of acquiring Self-Love Deficit Disorder,™ a term synonymous with codependency.[16]

THE DRAMA OF THE GIFTED CHILD

Fifteen years ago, I was a psychologically broken man attempting to end an abusive and emotionally harrowing marriage. Determined to seek sole custody of my 3-year-old son, Benjamin, which was neither straightforward nor easy, I sought help from Jill Maling, a psychotherapist in Deerfield, Illinois. Not only did Jill help me recognize joint custody could be successful, she helped me sort through, understand, and partially recover from the trauma I had experienced. As much as I needed compassion and empathy, I required a witness of sorts to my horrific trauma stories.

Jill helped me to intellectually and emotionally connect to the deeper and more hidden nature of my post-divorce emotional pain. Rather than only focusing on what I experienced and its impact on me, she facilitated a broader awareness of how my current situation was a product of my anguished childhood. With her help, I was able to connect my adult relationships with women to my childhood and more current experiences with my parents. To drive this point home, she asked me to read Dr. Alice Miller's book, *The Drama of the Gifted Child* (1979), discussed in Chapter Seven.

Not only did Dr. Miller's astute analysis and psychological conclusions change my life, it blew my "psychological socks" off! Her book helped me understand the primary role of attachment trauma during the development of codependency. She reasoned that because pathologically narcissistic parents are incapable of unconditionally loving anyone, their children would be subjected to a traumatic attachment experience, which I refer to as attachment trauma. Dr. Miller hypothesized the child's unique coping strategies or adaptation to the attachment trauma would dramatically shape their personality development and adult relationship patterns.

16 Self-Love Abundance (SLA) and Self-Love Deficit Disorder (SLDD) are the primary concepts in my Codependency Cure™ and Self-Love Recovery™ work, on which I have accumulated a great deal of knowledge. Educational and self-help information on these concepts is available at www.SelfLoveRecovery.com

For a child to avoid severe attachment trauma, they need to be adept at a form of psychological gymnastics. This requires suppressing instinctual and reflexive emotional reactions such as frustration, anger, and disappointment, while reacting in a way that makes the parent feel good about themselves. The child who succeeds at modifying their emotional reactions to neglect, deprivation, or abuse is rewarded with the highly coveted position in the family as this parent's "favorite" child. This child becomes a long-fantasized "gift" bestowed on the parent that soothes their mostly unconscious feelings of inadequacy and core shame. The "gifted child" is rewarded by being lavished with conditional love, respect, and care, while others in the family fall prey to the narcissistic parent's damaging whims and reactions.

The narcissistic parent-gifted child relationship is psychologically and relationally inverted, as the child provides emotional comfort to the adult when it should be the other way around. Making the narcissistic parent feel good about themselves provides a treasure trove of emotional validation, praise, and attention. The child is virtually guaranteed special status in the family if they maintain the "little prince" or "princess" position. Falling from grace is not an option; the child is reminded daily that failure at their "job" will have costly and painful consequences.

A derailment or trauma to the parent-child attachment process occurs not only by what is done or not done to, or for, the child, but also through vicarious experiences—observation-based learning. Witnessing the profound abuse, neglect, and/or deprivation of people you love, like a sibling or parent, is as frightening and damaging as being the target of such harm. It is a constant reminder of the cost of slipping up in the "gifted" child role. Such survival pressure is responsible for the highly accurate, learned, emotional antennae or radar the child uses to constantly scan the physical and emotional environment for potential landmines.

The pathological narcissist's core shame and debilitating attachment trauma requires the restorative and almost medicinal value of the child's "giftedness." By siphoning feel-good "units" from the "gifted child," they can maintain a structurally weak sense of pseudo self-esteem and a veneer-thin sense of self-importance. The stakes are high for the narcissist to keep at least one "gifted" child in the family at all times. To fail will result in the conscious re-emergence of their core shame, which causes an unfathomable existential crisis.

According to my RCT, Dr. Miller's "childhood drama" is transmuted into a *relationship template*—the unconscious instruction manual for the zero-sum dysfunctional relationship. Therefore, the paradoxical sense of comfort and familiarity with narcissistic people is another explanation for the codependent-pathological narcissist relationship. To that end, Miller uses her developmental and attachment theory to clarify why "gifted" children choose adult professions that incorporate and value their built-in powers of compassion, empathy, and sacrifice.

GOOD-PARENT FANTASY AND GASLIGHTING

Critical to the child's psychological survival is the narcissist's ability to discern and adapt to a one-dimensional good-parent fantasy. They construct a fictional repackaging of their life in which their trauma and shameful memories, feelings, and thoughts are replaced with an illusion. Each good-parent narrative consists of a distorted and untrue life story that recasts the narcissist into the role of victim-turned-hero. By virtue of being a parent, the narrative allows them to experience the love, appreciation, and validation that have been absent their entire life. This narrative also gives the narcissist even more psychological distance from their malignant feelings of being fundamentally inadequate or broken.

For the good-parent fantasy to have its intended effect, the story requires the "gifted" child to abandon their actual life story for that of the narcissistic parent's. This form of psychological manipulation is considered gaslighting, and will be discussed in detail in Chapter Eleven. It occurs when the narcissistic parent forcefully places their "virtual reality goggles" onto the child, all the while coercing and manipulating them into abandoning their real/accurate perceptions and adopting the parents' skewed views. I use the following definition of gaslighting in my "Gaslighting Is Everywhere!" seminar:

> Gaslighting is a brainwashing strategy perpetrated by highly manipulative and completely or partially sociopathic narcissists who live secretly and undetected in our society. Like child molesters, gaslighters can "smell" prey, who are vulnerable to believing in their false altruism, affection, and promises of protection. Gaslighting occurs when the gaslighter systematically manipulates the environment so their victim experiences distress over an implanted dilemma that either was only mildly problematic or never even existed. The victim is rendered helpless when they are indoctrinated to believe this terrible and overwhelming problem is hopeless, and turns to the gaslighter to protect

them from it. Because the victim is coerced into believing their inculcated issue is real, they begin to demonstrate symptoms of it. The resulting power-lessness, insecurity, and paranoia creates increasing levels of helplessness and hopelessness, which serve to isolate the victim even further from anyone who could unmask their sociopathic gaslighter.

The gaslighting is complete when the child's real-life story becomes subsumed by their parent's gaslit narrative. Programming the child with the parent's own selfish narrative is not only a form of gaslighting,[17] but also another pathological brick in a wall that blocks the child from ever experiencing self-love—the anti-thesis of codependency.

GOOD-PARENT NARRATIVES

1. God . . . Giver of Life

The narcissist adopts a God-like persona, reinforced by their holier-than-thou and sanctified "creator of the child's life" storyline. Their head is in the clouds as they float in their grandiosity and entitlement about the miracle of life they produced. This reinforces their constant need for the child and others to exalt them as a God-like figure.

2. The Opposite Parent

The Opposite Parent adopts the unrealistic and illogical view that they will love, respect and care for their child in a way their parents never did. They reduce the quite complicated task of rearing a child into the simple belief that they will be a "good" parent if they raise their own children in the exact opposite way their parents raised them. In other words, by inverting their own childhood experience of abuse, neglect, and/or deprivation, the Opposite Parent believes they know exactly what a good parent should look like and how they should behave.

Hence, these narcissists unreasonably believe the inversion of their own child-hood attachment trauma will supply them with the necessary information and guidelines for healthy parenting. Predictably, the transmutation of their attachment trauma into a parenting handbook results in frustration, anger, and deeper feelings

---

17 Chapter Eleven explains gaslighting in detail.

of shame. The desire to be what their parents never were becomes an unsustainable system of theories they are unable to bring to fruition.

3. Vindication—Everyone Was Wrong About Me
This is common for adults known by most people, especially their parents and siblings, as the family's bad seed or problem child. They are thwarted by the consequences of their anger, hatred, aggression, selfishness, and impulsiveness. Although they feel justified in the harm they have caused others, they privately feel regret and shame for the loss of acceptance and relationships that followed their bad behavior.

As "good parents," they aim to prove to the people who wrote them off as bad or unlovable that they were wrong. Such narcissists mistakenly believe the narcissists to whom they are trying to make a point will experience remorse, guilt, and shame for their inaccurate harsh judgments. Their hopes that such "vindication" will reduce their pervasive toxic core shame is simply not psychologically possible. Hence, their efforts paradoxically instill deeper judgments about not being worthwhile or appreciated than before they became a parent.

4. Look at Me Now—I Was Always Good
This philosophy is adopted by narcissists who are or were shy and introverted children and adapted to their severe attachment trauma by disappearing into the background. This narrative also applies to adults who were once emotionally neglected and deprived children. Although being invisible made them feel safe, they were crushed by the fact that no one ever noticed or showed appreciation for how good or talented they really were. This good-parent version allows them to finally put themselves front and center in the lives of the people whose attention, appreciation, and love they always wanted, but never received. Putting the spotlight on themselves, they can showcase their "good parenting" abilities and finally get the accolades and acknowledgements they always deserved.

5. This Will Heal My Trauma
By being what they believe is a "perfect parent" who raises a "perfect child," the attachment trauma they are aware of will miraculously be healed.[18] Not only is this

---

18 This is an exception, as many pathological narcissists do not remember or want to remember their attachment trauma.

expectation unrealistic and nearly impossible, but the child ends up being resented or held responsible when it, predictably, doesn't happen. Once the child temporarily relieves their parent's core shame and deep longing for recognition and affirmation, they are placed on the highest of pedestals as the miracle child. Because shiny trophies eventually tarnish, the child's healing properties will ultimately diminish over time.

6. Let Me Show You My Perfection

This parent's narcissism is so severe they aren't conscious of their core shame. Like most people with NPD, they keep the focus on themselves, while downplaying the contributions of others. This situation is used by the "professional parent," who does almost everything while making sure everyone knows it. They are a natural at marketing and publicizing their perfect parenting. The child is the lead actor in their meticulously written, feel-good script. The lonely and neglected child behind the scenes is never seen.

7. Someone Finally Needs Me!

Pathological narcissists who are conscious of their very low self-esteem and loneliness daydream about the happiness a child will bring them. Unconsciously, they become reliant on the child's dependency on them. Every sacrifice or good deed reminds them of their self-worth. Like drug addicts, they crave the opportunity to coddle and care for the child as it fills them with feelings of existential worth, hope, and contentment. Being recognized as the perfect parent is the primary motivation for their kindness, affection, and nurturing. When the child attempts to individuate from the parent, the house of cards comes tumbling down—that is when the narcissists' core shame re-emerges. This is also the type of narrative that is responsible for the extremely toxic nature of an overly enmeshed parent-child relationship.

8. My Child Will Make Me Immortal!

The severely narcissistic and potentially sociopathic parent is more emotionally invested in their bloodline and the child's role in carrying it forward than in the child themselves. The child is the golden ticket who will legitimize their life, assuring them of their imagined legacy. The fact the child will outlive them provides hope that the world will never forget them and their fictional contributions.

THE PLEASING TROPHY CHILD

To be a narcissist's treasured trophy, the gifted child must maintain their valuable and coveted object status; on command, they can generate "oohs" and "ahs" for their compliment-starved parent. They are happiest when boasting about any of their child's accomplishments or outstanding traits. Only a trained eye can see the child has no intrinsic value to the parent. Rather, the parent's off-the-charts pride for the child is nothing more than a ruse that generates a steady stream of self-esteem boosters. Sadly, there is no level of perfection that will make this child loved any more than a shiny trophy.

Aside from maintaining their first-place position in any real or imagined competitions, this child must mold and sometimes contort themselves into a person who is instinctively pleasing. Quick on their feet and psychologically agile, they have the never-ending responsibility to make their parent happy. To accomplish this feat, the child must discern the dos and don'ts for the purpose of maintaining their "good-parent fantasy" status. They must keep a vigilant eye out for any potential accidental injury to their parent's fragile ego. Like a dog who instinctively displays puppy-dog eyes, this child learns tricks and strategies to be likable and adorable on cue.

The trophy child must be careful not to overdo their boastful or showy behaviors. Should they inadvertently take the spotlight away from their parent, they may unintentionally spark feelings of resentment, embarrassment, or shame, all of which are punishable by crushing narcissistic rage. Their value would plummet and then they would have to work their way back into the parent's display case. As this child ages, their good-child nature builds an identity and an unstable form of pseudo self-esteem that requires them to stay in their pleasing role in all future relationships.

THE CHILD'S SURVIVAL ROLES

It is no easy task to manage, control, and be responsible for a narcissistic parent's emotional fluctuations. Hence, a "gifted" child goes to great lengths to be perfectly accommodating with a caretaking persona. They become a superb actor in their narcissistic parent's "stage adaptation" of their life. By repackaging their feelings and their expression of themselves into twisted but acceptable versions, they are spared the worse fate of later becoming a pathological narcissist.

The following pleasing child roles illustrate the necessary façade-like personalities and masks gifted children must adopt to find a sustainable purpose and role in their narcissistic parent's shame-ridden and lonely world.

PLEASING CHILD ROLES

1. The Great Pretender

Maintaining the identity of the fantasy child requires the child to suppress their natural desire for unconditional love. Smiling when they want to cry, acting calm when frightened, complying rather than rebelling, and behaving affectionately when angry and resentful are all common feelings. By controlling both their inner emotional involvement and the physical manifestations of it, they are able to avoid being a target of abuse or lessening its impact on them. Like professional actors, they fake a happy, understanding, and empathic face. This tells the narcissist this little person not only knows them inside and out, but also loves them completely and unconditionally, unlike others who trigger their narcissistic rage.

Mastery over their facial expressions is a protective technique used by adult codependents. Unbeknownst to them, it is often an obvious clue they suffer from codependency. It is quite common for codependents to smile or laugh when anxious, sad, and even angry. For example, many of my clients recount their childhood abuse or neglect with a smile and a smattering of laughter. If they are confronted with the incongruence of their facial expressions and the descriptive content, they often are not aware of it and are unable to stop. I can recall at least two examples of clients contorting their faces into a smile while sobbing or crying. In both cases, when I observed the incongruent happy face, I was able to connect it to a deeper and often unconscious experience of childhood attachment trauma.

2. Calmness Under Fire—The Hostage Negotiator

This face is that of an unshakably tranquil and emotionally-disassociated child who can calm and de-escalate a potentially dangerous person to ensure no one gets hurt. Like an actual hostage negotiator, this is a child who is unnaturally talented at the following skills:

- **Empathy:** conveys understanding, compassion, and a realistic understanding of another person's emotional state, especially when it is negative.

- **Active Listening:** allows the other person to talk, making them believe they are completely understood and appreciated.
- **Use of Time:** slows things down instead of pushing for a quick resolution, which produces a soothing and calming effect.
- **De-escalation Techniques:** calms down agitated and angry people by making them feel understood, less angry, protected, and hopeful.
- **Rapport Building:** conveys knowing the person inside and out and can calm them down, while instilling a feeling of confidence and trust.
- **Facilitating Self-Control:** makes the person in crisis, who has lost self-control, feel less emotionally fragmented, while helping them think through their plans to hurt others. By including the person in the process, instead of making demands or arguing with them, the narcissist becomes more open to accepting feedback or suggestions.

3. Feeling Illiterate

Most codependents struggle with understanding the language of feelings. Not only do they not know how to identify their feelings at any given moment, but they are also not well-versed in the differences between one feeling and another. A joke I tell my seminar audiences best sums up this pleasing child face:

> Two codependents have sex. In the afterglow, one says to the other, "Well, I know it was good for you, how was it for me?" (Source unknown)

It is common for codependents to have never learned feeling words or felt safe expressing them. These adults were once children whose fear of their narcissistic parent's rage taught them from a young age to either be careful and judicious in expressing their feelings or to suppress them completely. As a result, they became adults who describe their feelings with overly-simplistic and poorly-descriptive words such as good, bad, or so-so. In addition, they often mistake thoughts, behaviors, or conditions for feelings. The obviously angry codependent will respond to "How are you feeling?" with "Busy and harassed." When pushed to be more descriptive, they become either defensive or resistant and might even emotionally shut down. Codependents with a deficiency of "feeling words" fall into two primary groups: those who are irrationally anxious and afraid of expression and those who have no idea how they really feel.

4. The Quicker Picker Upper™

The child who is an emotional sponge communicates a sympathetic willingness to sacrifice their own psychological health in order to clean up their parent's frequent emotional spills. Paradoxically, they are valued for their unnaturally tough and resilient nature, while being appreciated and needed because of their soft and sensitive side. They can absorb their parent's problems, while not emotionally falling apart, assuring them of the favorite-child status. Proctor & Gamble's advertising slogan for Bounty paper towels sums up the cleanup utility of this child. The slogan is, "And with Bounty by your side, even the biggest messes are no big deal. Because Bounty is the Quicker Picker Upper."

This super-absorbent, but resilient, child will likely develop into an adult whose boundless capacity for empathy and sensitivity makes them the go-to person when someone is upset and in need of advice or support. Such adults choose the term "empath" to describe their acute sensitivity to the emotional energy of others. Empaths feel, experience, and reportedly absorb the physical, mental, and emotional pain of others. Many of these adults will not identify with being codependent, but will adopt the softer, more benevolent, less-stigmatizing "empathy" moniker. It should be noted, while codependents are almost always empaths, empaths are not necessarily codependents.

5. Old Soul

The Old Soul children are wise, tolerant, and patient beyond their years. These worldly-seeming children possess adult-like interests, preoccupations, and even worries. They have an uncommon ability for boundless empathy and compassion, while having an advanced understanding of complex social, psychological, and even spiritual concepts. They also are able to understand and give advice about grief, sadness, and heartbreak. These children know exactly what they want to be as an adult and plan for it. Sometimes, but not always, they are social misfits, whose adult-like persona alienates them from peers in their age group. When given a choice of hanging out with a roomful of kids or adults, the adults almost always get the nod.

Pathologically narcissistic parents proudly showcase these mini-adults, whose maturity, calmness, and reflective personality brings them feelings of pride and accomplishment. The child's old soul is caused by the emotionally incestuous and inverted parent-child relationship in which the parent needs the child as much as the child needs to be needed by the parent.

Not until my son told me one of our relatives referred to him as an "old soul" did I connect it to his attachment trauma. During my first year as a full-time parent after my divorce, I noticed how even-tempered, calm, and reasonable Ben was. He responded well to explanations and seemed to have an uncanny knack for understanding adult relationship matters. Not only did he prefer the company of adults over children, he didn't seem motivated to make new friends. Ben's premature maturity was driven by a deeply enmeshed mother-child relationship that rewarded his ability to be an adult-like companion to her. Because of his patience, sympathy, and consideration, he was rewarded with his mother's positive attention. However, he was burdened by not having the freedom to be a normal, healthy, irrational, immature, and self-centered child. After living with me for a year, Ben was able to embrace his childhood, which made being a dad so much fun! His normal immaturity gave me the opportunity to mirror my own back at him!

6. "Sorry" Child

Children destined to be codependents learned early in life the value of being reflexively remorseful and apologetic. Not only does their "sorry" reflex help them avoid being the target of their narcissistic parent's rage and retaliation, it helps them defuse or de-escalate it. The "sorry" reflex triggers their narcissistic parent's conditional tolerance and forgiveness. In turn, they are made to feel like a benevolent and forgiving parent. This reflex is a dead giveaway of a codependent. Not only do they have no control over it, they are prone to apologizing when they did nothing wrong. Worse yet, they even apologize for other people's mistakes.

7. Radar Operator

To avoid triggering a narcissistic injury and the consequential narcissistic rage, the pleasing/gifted child develops radar that quickly and accurately picks up on potentially dangerous emotional situations. This is no ordinary tracking system, as it is so finely tuned it detects the subtlest shift in a pathological narcissist's emotions or mood—from the barely detectable or disguised to outwardly debilitating anger. Predicting their parent's moods, identifying their triggers, and flying "under the radar" staves off humiliation, deprivation, and potential harm. They learn their needs will never be as important as those of their pathologically narcissistic parent and other narcissists in their life.

To manage the "emotional radar system" and survive their narcissistic parent, the child must learn to split off from their feelings. Without this split, they would realize they are not worthy of unconditional love and are inherently lacking in importance and value. Experiencing the full breadth of their feelings would be too big of a blow to their young and fragile mind. Therefore, by pushing these feelings, thoughts, and memories into the unconscious mind or repressing emotionally evocative events, their mind can defend itself from what it can't manage and process. Repression is an unconscious protective strategy, or defense mechanism, that protects the human brain from the destructive effects of trauma.

Out of a need for survival, the "gifted" child develops acute hypersensitivity to any minute or subtle shift in their narcissistic parent's mood. In addition, they can accurately predict an oncoming emotional meltdown and/or episode of narcissistic rage. In terms of a metaphor, the child's highly accurate emotional radar system and their ability to identify the family's weather patterns serves as an early warning system that informs them and others to board up the windows to prepare for the big storm. These hyper-vigilant children have a distinctly serious and anxious look about them, as missing obvious clues could have disastrous consequences.

8. Poker Face

This is the face of disassociated codependents who learned early in life the danger of expressing or daring to feel their negative affective (feeling) states. This lack of expression is common for "gifted" children of a parent with Borderline Personality Disorder. With a hypersensitive and emotionally dysregulated parent, the smallest emotional misstep can unleash a damaging barrage of punitive narcissistic rage. By developing a poker face, the children learn to avoid being the accidental target of their parent's unpredictable and lightning-quick emotional meltdown.

TURNING LEMONS INTO LEMONADE

Like taking a lemon and making lemonade, a future codependent takes a selfish, self-obsessed, critical, and abusive parent—a pathological narcissist—and convinces themselves they are loving. This resourceful survival strategy assures a level of protection that is greater than that of other people. A "gifted" child is no different than one raised by healthy parents, as all children want to feel good about themselves. The child takes great pride in their selfless, sacrificial, and unassuming personality.

The positive attention, praise, and compliments they receive create pseudo self-esteem and a distorted sense of self-confidence. These children are subtly coerced into believing their sacrifices are noble and for the greater good. To guarantee the narcissistic parent's favor and avoid their rejection or wrath, they learn to excel at their adult-like responsibilities.

By becoming a sibling's caretaker, the family's cook or house cleaner, or maintaining a part-time job to help pay the bills, this pleasing child twists their sacrifices into something to be proud of. This pseudo self-esteem allows them to feel good about a life that is, and always will be, in the shadow of a narcissist. These gifted and pleasing children may never know what they lost as they sacrificed their childhood to make their pathologically narcissistic parent happy.

IDENTITY FUSION

In order to continue to be the fortunate recipient of their parent's attention and kindness, the "gifted" child must acclimate to the narcissist's mercurial selfish and self-centered temperament, while allowing their identity to be incorporated into that of their parent's. This child's individuality is absorbed into the pathological narcissist's insatiable need to bring attention back to themselves. Ultimately, this child is subsumed into their parent's ego, as everything they do reflects on the parent. Instead of being the child who is wonderful and lovable just because they are who they are, they become a valued acquisition.

The codependent child becomes their narcissistic parent's "feel-good appendage." Consequently, for the narcissist, compliments about the child are no different than receiving a direct compliment. Even worse, the child's "appendage" identity reduces them to a possession or prized object, like a piece of jewelry or a new car.

EMOTIONAL AND SEXUAL INCEST?

With several of the good parenting narratives, the child is required to give up normal healthy boundaries to compensate for their parent's emptiness and neediness. Such a child is burdened with the highly unrealistic expectation of being that parent's only source of happiness and hope. As their parent's emotional caretaker, their psychological health is commandeered and driven into the ground. This type of traumatizing and developmentally harmful relationship is often referred to as emotional incest.

Emotional incest occurs when a parent sabotages a child's intellectual or emotional development by demanding they partake in deeply personal, intimate, and private interactions that are typically reserved for a spouse or adult partner. Confiding in children about personal, occupational, financial, or sexual problems puts a damaging burden on the child who is not emotionally equipped to handle them (Kelley and Kelley, 2006). For fear of retaliation or unfavorable consequences, the emotional incest victim resigns themselves to their forced role as their parent's best-friend, confidant, and counselor. They end up giving the type of emotional comfort to their parents that the adult parent should be giving to them.

To better understand the long-term implications of emotional incest and highlight its extremely traumatizing nature, learning basic information about sexual incest is necessary. Naturally, a "gifted" child is chosen as the stand-in for the adult who would normally fulfill the narcissist's sexual desires/needs. This "special" child is a preferred target; their belief systems are already geared towards sacrifice and selflessness. Despite a grooming process that prepares them to not resist the upcoming sexual advances, the child is systematically manipulated to believe they are a normal expression of parent-child love. The child's innate psychological and physical boundary systems are broken down by being manipulated into believing good girls and boys want to make their parents happy and such happiness requires the fulfillment of their sexual needs.

Typically, the psychological or physical trauma (pain and suffering) are consciously and unconsciously compartmentalized and often not remembered, so it doesn't sabotage their survival-induced desire to maintain the favorite child role. Such mental gymnastics also enables the victim-child to appreciate, enjoy, and even desire the incest. Despite the sex being physically and psychologically traumatic, the child adapts to it, as it has been fused with feelings of importance, love, and care. The early sexualization of the "gifted" child will have profoundly devastating psychological implications that follow them into adulthood. Intimate relationships will be confusing, awkward, frightening, and, consequently, avoided. There are several other possible negative implications. The most common is the child becoming prematurely sexual with other children. Another is becoming an adult with out-of-control sexual compulsions satiated by narcissistic adults—unconscious representations of their abusing parent.

Apart from the physically/sexually traumatic violations, emotional incest mirrors sexual incest identically. The implications are almost as severe, but worse, in some ways. The emotional incest victim is likely to continue the toxic and dysfunctional relationship, sometimes well into adulthood.

THE RELATIONSHIP TEMPLATE AGAIN

Over time, the coping strategies that help these future codependents emotionally survive will crystalize into a relationship template. Forged out of the early attachment trauma experiences of being invisible and low-maintenance children, they learned how to survive on minute morsels of LRC. Although a codependent's relationship template might seem irreparably broken, the human spirit has remarkable transformative potential, much like muscle memory. We do not have to be the torchbearers of our parents' life sentence. We all have the capability to grow and learn from our mistakes. Many of us—armed with knowledge, dedication, and the appropriate professional services—have a fighting chance to overturn what once seemed like a never-ending road of dysfunctional relationships. That's the beauty of being a codependent, as hope does exist. It is just very difficult to achieve.

GENERATIONS OF ATTACHMENT TRAUMA

Dysfunctional family patterns are passed down from one generation to the next. This transgenerational movement is not news to most people. Common sense dictates our adult mental health is often only as good as the environment in which we were raised and that of our parents. Despite the wealth of exceptions, most of us can accurately attribute some of our best and worst traits to something our parents did or didn't do for us when we were young and impressionable. Although I am not advocating that you blame your parents for your codependency (or narcissism), it is critically important to understand the transgenerational nature of the problem.

The cause of codependency and its resistance to change can be explained by Family System Theory. This model is based on the idea that all families, especially dysfunctional ones, resist change, as it is quite uncomfortable, if not extremely painful. Both healthy and dysfunctional families experience discomfort when the openly or implicitly agreed-upon rules or roles are challenged or broken down. In a healthy family, one member who is unable to fulfill their role or responsibilities will cause the other members to feel threatened, afraid, and uncomfortable. This family will do anything they can to remedy the problem, including nurturing the person back to health while being compassionate, empathic, and supportive. The family will breathe a sigh of relief once the person heals and can return to their "normal" and "healthy" role in the family.

DYSFUNCTIONAL FAMILIES DON'T LIKE GETTING BETTER

The dysfunctional family that breeds codependency and pathological narcissism is not terribly different from the healthy family. With a major role disruption, they will fight to re-establish the lost equilibrium. The following story illustrates why dysfunctional families resist change, including change they thought they always wanted.

John, husband of Mary and father of Sam, successfully completed a 90-day, inpatient alcohol treatment program, but without any family participation. Mary could not take time off work to attend the couple's workshops and sessions; she is the family's primary breadwinner and they are in severe debt. Sam, a resentful and entitled 16-year-old, openly refused to attend the family sessions. He was not willing to break the promise he had made to himself to never again speak to his father after he broke his mother's arm during the last drunken rampage. Sam demanded proof of his dad's changes before he would consider trusting him again.

Upon his return home, John walked into a home that was imbued with tension and anxiety. Instead of being greeted with appreciation and hope, he felt like he was walking on eggshells. Both Mary and Sam were suspicious of his ability to remain sober and feared being hurt again. Neither were interested in hearing about his life-changing experiences in rehab. The tense, angry, and distrustful family environment quickly whittled away John's new-found self-esteem and optimism.

By the third day back home, hopelessness, insecurity, and negative thoughts started to creep back into John's mind. Trying to practice what he learned in rehab, he decided to go to an Alcoholics Anonymous meeting. A suspended license for a prior DUI forced him to rely on Mary or Sam to drive him to the meeting. Mary couldn't because of her work schedule. Sam, having no intention of helping his father, let his dad's calls repeatedly go to voicemail. Alone and in despair, John stormed out of the house and walked to the nearest bar, his former hangout, where he knew he was appreciated. Later that night, he returned home inebriated.

Dysfunctional families, like healthy ones, actively defend against and proactively disable anyone's attempts to label them as bad, harmful, or dysfunctional. They will go to extreme lengths to defend their collective "good family" narrative. Someone who attempts to question the legitimacy of that moniker will be recast as enemy number one and ultimately the recipient of the family's wrath. These dysfunctional families, like healthy ones, have a seemingly permanent connection to the generation that preceded them and the ones that will follow.

Like a virulent codependency virus, both an individual's dysfunction and the family's overall dysfunction spreads from one host to another. To stop the spread of this sickness or stop handing off the codependency baton from one generation to another, each person must courageously fight their inner demons, while developing strength and increased capacity to neutralize the dysfunctional power of the outer ones. Be forewarned: it may seem impossible to prevent this runaway train from reaching its next-generational stop, but it will always be possible to disembark if you put in the work. Remember that.

Reflections

- If one of your parents was a pathological narcissist, which good-parent narrative was used?

- As a child, did you adopt any of the pleasing child roles? If so, which one and why?

Chapter Nine

THE ORIGINS OF PATHOLOGICAL NARCISSISM

The saying, "The apple doesn't fall far from the tree," illustrates both the transgenerational nature and developmental implications of a child born to a pathologically narcissistic parent. Perhaps a better question would be, "On what side did that apple fall?" Both the question and its answer account for the divergent paths to which attachment-traumatized children are assigned. Gifted children are given travel papers that send them to codependent adulthood. The destination of the "disappointing" child is more bleak and disturbing, as his child-victim self will be given an adult-narcissistic *identity*. Sadly, the developmental path of the future pathologically narcissistic adult is more traumatic and psychologically damaging than its gifted counterpart.

"THE CHILD IS BAD, NOT ME" NARRATIVE

Children's temperaments are highly influenced by uncontrollable environmental factors, as well as genetic makeup. Therefore, a parent can never know how a child's personality or temperament will unfold. For the pathologically narcissistic parent, their good-parent narrative is a risky proposition. A betting man might place the odds at 3 to 1 that any given child would match up with their parent's unreasonable expectations. Since the chances of winning a hand of blackjack are much higher than having a child who conforms to the narrowly defined parenting fantasy, most end up being consigned to the alternative "the child is bad, not me" narrative.

Unfortunately, normal healthy children with challenging personality types activate their narcissistic parent with a narcissistic injury, which induces anger and resentment against the child. Possible disappointing scenarios include: "She doesn't coo and smile like the babies in the commercials do." "He looks exactly like his asshole father and nothing like me." "She is so needy, I can't leave the room without her crying or begging me to hold her." The narcissistic parent-child fantasy could have been blown simply because the child was the wrong gender, had the wrong shade or color of skin, or forced the parent to put an end to their college/career ambitions.

As previously explained, the pathological narcissist unconsciously believes their children are an extension of themselves.

> In a sense, the narcissist views others and the world around him as an extension of himself, perhaps as you might view your arm or leg. He unconsciously expects you to conform to his will, just as his own arm or leg would do. When your behavior deviates from his expectations, he often becomes as upset with you as he would be if his arm or leg were no longer under his control (Payson, 2002, p. 22).

The pathologically narcissistic parent reacts to their "bad" child as if a horrible trick was played on them, a bait and switch of sorts. Instead of giving birth to the baby of their dreams, whom they were so sure they would create, they gave birth to a seemingly damaged, ungrateful, difficult, and willful one who appears hell-bent on preventing them from actualizing their long-held fantasies of parenthood. Their hope that a beautiful bundle of joy would deliver them from their own personal misery and traumatic past would most certainly be derailed. The failure of the child to provide their parent with the necessary good-parent narrative becomes the kiss of emotional death: they are imprisoned in the attachment trauma dungeon, with no hope of parole.

A "BAD" CHILD FOREVER

A grudge will be held by the pathologically narcissistic parent against their broken and imperfect child, by whom they will forever feel embarrassed and disappointed. Because of this child's perceived imperfections, the narcissistic parent's self-serving needs for affirmation, recognition, and praise will not be realized.

Unable to live up to parental fantasies, these children will be unfairly labeled as disappointing and difficult. This egregiously damaging verdict will eventually become the basis for their self-contempt and deeply damaged self-esteem. Over time, they will internalize their parent's mistreatment and begin to agree with the pathologically narcissistic parent that they are, indeed, inadequate. This label will likely stick for a lifetime.

The pathologically narcissistic parent is harshly judgmental and reactive to what they perceive as their child's negative traits and deficiencies. It is not that they hate this child; it is more that the child's inadequacies painfully remind them of what is wrong with themselves. These parents unknowingly project their own personal shame and disappointment onto their child. As psychologically impaired and unconsciously shame-based individuals, they find it easier to recognize these traits in others, especially their disappointing child, than to see it in themselves.

These disappointing children are placed in a harmful double bind by the expectation that they not be upset by the maltreatment they experience. The narcissistic parent will never take responsibility for the harm caused, as to do so would ignite the powder keg of repressed and deeply buried rage and self-hate for being parented in the very same manner. Therefore, externalizing and blaming away their child's apparent "badness" serves to protect them from realizing their own worst nightmare—they have become the next generation of abusive or neglectful parents who have created their own traumatized and damaged children.

When a pathological narcissist is unable to tolerate their child's acting-out, they may resort to punishing or abusing the child. Since this parent takes the negative behavior personally and, consequently, experiences a narcissistic injury, they feel justified in their retaliation. Worse than neglect or deprivation, the narcissistic parent may verbally, emotionally, or physically harm this child.

The reality for these children is they are being punished for behaving as any child would if brought up by a similarly hostile, unsafe, and unloving parent. Instead of being a natural recipient of unconditional love and kindness, they will be a moving target for unmitigated abuse and neglect and become the narcissistic parent's and other siblings' "punching bag."

Not only is this "displeasing" child unable to fulfill their parent's fantasies, their own accumulated bitterness manifests into increasingly angry and hostile behaviors. Prolonged abuse or neglect encourages this child's negative behaviors to likely escalate in frequency and severity. This cycle of acting out and punishment results in a perpetual Catch-22 where the actions will justify the parent's continued deprivation, neglect, and abuse, which reinforces their distorted view of the child. This child is not fighting back per se, but trying to survive a confusing world of mixed messages, broken promises, and disappointment. Over time, they internalize and identify with the label. Eventually, they give up and submit to the inevitable: never being able to transform their parent's anger, disappointment, and resentment into some form of appreciation, affirmation, and, most importantly, love.

Even if the child could surprise their narcissistic parent and begin behaving as a fantasy child (the pleasing child) should, it would never be enough to change their parent's predetermined opinions of them. Paradoxically, they would be unintentionally challenging their parent's justifications and excuses for their punishing treatment. If the pathologically narcissistic parent's deprivation, neglect, and/or abuse were confronted, a defensive and vindictive response would result. The parent would angrily rationalize their actions, blame others for the child's problems (including the child), and punish the child even more.

Drew Keys, author of *Narcissists Exposed* (2012), writes about the displeasing and disappointing child who identifies with his mistreatment. Keys refers to this child as a "scapegoat."

> Because narcissistic parents cannot accept personal faults, they spend their days trying to convince themselves that everything they do is perfect. When their personality causes distress within their family, and their children's issues begin to reflect this, these parents are forced to make a choice. They must either acknowledge that they are making mistakes that are affecting their children negatively, or they must try to convince themselves and others that the problems are coming not from themselves, but another source . . . In their minds, by blaming another, they absolve themselves of any wrong-doing, and they can continue to believe—and strive to convince

others—that they are in fact, perfect. But they must first have someone to blame . . .

. . . For defenseless children made to play scapegoat, the burdens of being labeled "bad" no matter what they do are heavy. The scapegoat soon learns he or she cannot win; there is no sense struggling to improve the family's opinion of them, because that simply cannot be allowed to occur . . . In a desperate attempt to reduce their parents' active oppression and derision, the scapegoat succumbs to the roles of underachiever, troubled one, loser, black sheep, or troublemaker. This presents the parents with exactly what their mental disorder is making them feel they must have—an external object upon which to place blame—so that they can continue the reassuring fantasy that there is nothing wrong with themselves or their family on t he whole.

In an effort to alleviate to some degree the distress of her narcissistic mother's wrath, the scapegoat eventually gives in and agrees with the family's assessment of her as inferior and worthy of blame. She internalizes the belief that she is inherently bad, worthless, and defective, and believes that everyone she contacts can clearly see this and will reject her as completely her family does (Keys, 2012).

Without unconditional love, this child eventually learns they are essentially unlovable and unworthy, and the world is an unsafe place. Humiliation, shame, and anger accumulate as they realize the abuse and neglect may never stop and they will never be loved unconditionally. To temper the loss of hope and despair, and to survive their living nightmare, they will need a psychological strategy to protect themselves from the stark realities of life. They can attain this protection by using an array of defense mechanisms. Someone who was violently traumatized by rape or war trauma would use the same type of defense mechanisms.

REPRESSION AND DISASSOCIATION: THE BRAIN'S CIRCUIT BREAKER

The human mind has distinct limits of how much trauma it can manage. Comparable to a circuit breaker, the mind has properties that protect it from experiences that are too painful and threatening to handle. Its virtual on and off switch protects a person from what they are unable to process and store in their short-term memory. Repression and disassociation are the primary defense mechanisms that help a person cope with unbearable trauma. Repression is defined as the unconscious exclusion of painful impulses, desires, or fears from the conscious mind. When a traumatic episode is repressed, that person simply forgets it ever happened. Disassociation is defined as the psychological experience in which someone feels disconnected from their sensory experience, sense of self, or personal history. One of several forms of disassociation is to feel detached from a situation, as if you were merely watching yourself while the abuse is happening.

Repression and disassociation are essential to the psychological survival of most trauma victims, especially the neglected and abused child of a pathologically narcissistic parent. Without these defenses, the child, and the adult they will become, will not only remember the trauma, but will also emotionally re-experience the shame, anger, loss of hope, and desperation they experienced during the abuse. The resulting self-hatred, neediness, and expansive reservoirs of wrath are too unbearable to accept. Instead, we relegate them to the dark expanses of our unconscious mind, locked behind concrete walls of denial, resisting any attempts at expression or recovery. These repressed feelings and memories will only see the light of day through bouts of depression, narcissistic rage, or incorporating the skills of an experienced psychotherapist.

Because of their traumatic history and the resulting psychological damage, these children will grow up to become adults who are unable to create or sustain healthy romantic relationships. More specifically, their abusive and neglectful childhoods will manifest into a mental health disorder, notably one of the three NPDs. As a pathological narcissist, they will naturally be hyper-focused on getting their needs met first or being adept at getting others to meet their needs without feeling compelled to reciprocate. As narcissists, they will be oblivious to any harm they cause other people.

The childhoods of these pathological narcissists taught them that only through a selfish and egotistical approach to others (relationships) could they feel good about themselves. The ability to manipulate or exploit others, combined with an exaggerated sense of their own importance, helped them survive their own traumatic childhood. Forming healthy, reciprocal attachments is not likely to occur, as these future pathological narcissists will unknowingly follow the dysfunctional path of those who created them.

THE SUBJECTIVE NATURE OF TRAUMA

To explain why some people with NPD came from families who did not treat them harshly or abusively, it is necessary to clarify the subjective nature of trauma. I have often explained to my clients, and those who I have clinically supervised, that trauma is not defined by what happens to a person, but rather by their personal experience of it. For example, if a child was lost in the mix of a pathologically narcissistic parent's personal or psychological absence, they would more than likely suffer the fate of the abused child. These deprived or neglected children similarly experience an unloving and emotionally barren childhood in which they internalize feelings and beliefs of inadequacy, unimportance, and unworthiness.

Both NPD and codependency can be caused by a sterile, neglectful, or unsafe childhood environment. This can result from absent parents, a debilitating medical or mental illness, poverty, or living in a crime-infested community. Living in an orphanage, foster home, military school, boarding school, or other similar emotionally-scarring environment may also result in the development of Narcissistic Personality Disorder.

Although I have presented viable explanations for the origins of codependency and pathological narcissism, it is not possible to account for every condition or factor that causes these disorders. Moreover, it is not written in stone that pathological narcissists always create mentally unhealthy children. There may be mitigating circumstances that offset the child's early traumatic experiences. For example, if the pathological narcissist parent relied on childcare from a consistently loving and nurturing adult caregiver, then the child's early-life experiences may have been sufficiently equalized. Such a substitute parent could include a close relative, a nanny, or a long-term babysitter. Even an involved and caring coach or teacher could sufficiently buffer the damage caused by a pathologically narcissistic parent. An older sibling who took on the role of a protective, encouraging, and affirming parental surrogate may have similarly counterbalanced the possibility of codependency or an NPD.

Reflections

- If you have a sibling who is a pathological narcissist, how does this chapter explain their personality development?

- Does the information in this chapter make you feel more empathy for any specific pathological narcissist? Explain your answer.

Chapter Ten

PATHOLOGICAL NARCISSISM: NPD, BPD, AND ASPD

The purpose of this chapter, and for that matter the book, is not to denigrate or demonize narcissists while upholding the codependents as the innocent victims of their harm. The premise is, and has always been, that it takes two to tango. Both codependents and narcissists have equal stakes in the relationship, as they need each other to feel whole or complete.

IS NARCISSISM ON THE RISE?

I am frequently asked if pathological narcissism is on the rise. My simple answer is no, it is not. It is an illusion caused by major changes in Western society, culture, and politics that, in combination, have made it easier for pathological narcissists to rise to positions of influence and power. The media's coverage on the topic puts the terms and problems of "narcissism" and "narcissists" in the forefront of our daily life.

After decades of the clashing and pulling apart of society, the ground on which everyone stood finally fractured and, in some cases, disintegrated. The resulting landscape shifts and changes caused cracks and chasms. These, in turn, resulted in a further separation between the haves and have-nots, which unleashed a series of aftershocks responsible for what I call the "Decade of Pathological Narcissism." This period began in 2007 and continues.

The metaphorical great earthquake that kicked off this decade of pathological narcissism was the 2007 financial meltdown, which for the U.S. was the worst since the Great Depression. Due to the rampant irresponsibility, laziness, and corruption of the government, its regulatory arm, and the banking industry, the world's financial infrastructure collapsed. The resulting shock waves were felt all around the globe. It was within this sociopolitical time of upheaval that pathological narcissists seized opportunities that, before these disasters, were less readily available. Their ascent to positions of influence and, in some cases, moral authority can be directly attributed to a series of small, but catastrophic, societal earthquakes.

ORWELLIAN DOUBLESPEAK

The manipulative choreography of a society's belief system, emotions, and political candidates is scored based on the treatment of language. An example of this can be found in George Orwell's futuristic dystopian novel, *1984*. The protagonist, Winston Smith, works at the "Ministry of Truth," the state-run propaganda department where inconvenient news is discarded and substituted with state-accepted propaganda. The government's official doublespeak language deliberately obscures, disguises, distorts, or reverses the meaning of words with the intent to deceive or confuse.

The Orwellian society also has a "Ministry of Peace," whose sole purpose is to create war, and a "Ministry of Love" that dispenses torture. This arrangement is intended to ensure the state's propaganda-infused explanations of public and military policy, or even its own history, are not challenged or called into question. A prime example of doublespeak in the political forum is Ronald Reagan's reference to a massive land-based missile as "the Peacekeeper." Another example is a 1997 bipartisan deal that Bill Clinton, Trent Lott, and Newt Gingrich promoted to balance the government's budget that, in reality, raised spending and cut taxes.

HAIL TO THE NARCISSISTIC CHIEF—THE TOP 10 LIST

An Emory University study, "The Double-Edged Sword of Grandiose Narcissism: Implications for Successful and Unsuccessful Leadership Among U.S. Presidents" (Watts, 2013), revealed that, typically, U.S. Presidents are more narcissistic than the average American. The research ranked all the U.S. Presidents according to their levels of grandiose narcissism, a subcategory of NPD. The grandiose narcissist is flamboyant, assertive, and interpersonally dominant; has an inflated sense of self; overconfident in making decisions; and has a seeming inability to learn from their mistakes (Riggio, 2015). To understand this narcissism subcategory, the definition of "grandiosity" should be understood.

Ronningham (2005) describes grandiosity as "an unrealistic sense of superiority —a sustained view of oneself as better than others that causes the narcissist to view others with disdain or as inferior—as well as a sense of uniqueness—the belief that few others have anything in common with oneself and one can only be understood by a few or very special people."

The study revealed grandiose narcissism in U.S. Presidents has increased in recent decades. This subcategory of NPD correlates with a president's success, or lack of it, especially in the ethical domain; hence, the double-edged sword. The contradiction was most notable when considering these presidents were associated with "superior overall greatness." This was measured by historians' rankings of presidential stature and was "positively associated with public persuasiveness, crisis management, agenda setting, and allied behaviors" (Ronningham, 2005). In addition, they won a larger share of votes and initiated more legislation than less narcissistic presidents. On the other hand, these same men were more likely to be the targets of impeachment resolutions and to engage in unethical behavior.

The research suggested the election of narcissistic presidents is related to the heightened demands on political figures to be publicly charismatic, as media coverage has become more intense. Additionally, the study suggested the noticeable increase in presidential narcissism could be tied to greater numbers of narcissists in the general U.S. population. Due to the year the research began, neither Barack Obama nor Donald Trump were included in the results. In order from most to least grandiosely narcissistic, Lyndon Johnson topped out at number one. Following him were: Theodore Roosevelt, Andrew Jackson, Franklin Delano Roosevelt, John F. Kennedy, Richard Nixon, Bill Clinton, Chester Arthur, Andrew Johnson, and Woodrow Wilson, which illustrates neither the Democratic nor Republican Party has cornered the market on grandiose narcissism.

Wolven's (2015) research sheds additional light on "grandiose narcissism" and its implication for U.S. politics:

When grandiose narcissists experience or perceive potential threats to their achievements, they are likely to use explicit externalizing behaviors to react, such as the derogation or devaluation of others and/or physical aggression towards others. By demanding recognition of their entitlement and use of externalizing behaviors like aggressive tactics, individuals high in grandiose narcissism are able to dispute any perceived weaknesses or invalidations of their inflated self-views. Furthermore, these individuals may also implement internalizing behaviors in order to gain the recognition they "deserve."

Grandiose narcissists may act empathetic and supportive of others, but will simultaneously harbor disgust and contempt for the vulnerable person. By providing the instrumental support, the grandiose narcissistic individual is using the situation to reinforce his or her self-view of specialness . . . Additionally, when grandiose narcissists do not succeed, they react confrontationally and use externalizing behavior to blame others for their shortcomings to displace their failures (pp. 21–22).

THE "GIFT" OF A PERSONALITY DISORDER

Not only do I support research findings regarding presidential grandiose narcissism, but I also believe some politicians who have an NPD enjoy a distinct advantage over their non-NPD opponents/adversaries. In a twisted sense of fate, the dysfunctional forces responsible for their NPD also formed personality traits that enable them to succeed in the cut-throat and exclusive world of politics. In other words, by surviving severe childhood attachment trauma, they developed specific characteristics and "abilities" that were instrumental in their future political success.

By adopting a mask-like personality type that matches the needs of others, they are able to wrangle from their competitors what they never had, but believed was always their birthright. Their pathological narcissism was converted to a paradoxical "gift" that would manipulate the masses into mistaking their charm, boldness, and leadership appeal for the real thing. The ability to hide their true malevolent and self-serving agenda, while believably promoting their people's representative persona, is the "best" of the pathologically narcissistic politician's "worst" traits.

In addition to having a variety of masks to choose from, their lack of empathy and absence of guilt are handy resources that keep them from getting sidetracked as they rise to the higher echelons of their profession on the backs of others. Still, competing narcissistic agendas continue to crash into each other, creating the same logjam they promised to change. This is no different than any other group of massively opinionated narcissists who are compelled to work together in the same office; very little tends to get accomplished. Because compromise and deal making make the political wheels go 'round, their promises to fulfill the people's mandate is no match for the clashing of self-interest and competing aspirations.

REDEFINING NARCISSISM

The darker, or psychopathological, side of narcissism is, of course, pathological narcissism. My favorite concise definition of narcissism is provided by the international expert and author of my favorite book on the subject. Eleanor Payson, author of *The Wizard of Oz and Other Narcissists* (2002), explains that in its most fundamental sense, narcissism means a tendency to self-worship.

Narcissism is one of those ubiquitous pop-psychological terms, like codependency used to be. It simply means too many things to too many people. Because of this, among other reasons, I created the Relationship Compatibility Theory (RCT) and the Relationship Compatibility Continuum (RCC). These provide a concrete definition for the person with an SRO that is considered "narcissistic," that is, in the (+3) to (+5) RCV range. For the sake of simplicity, the paragraph below defines narcissism, while tying it to my (RCT) explanation.

The term "narcissism" should only be used to describe a person who, because of their narcissistic personality traits, causes another person some form of harm. Such harm ranges in severity, beginning with selfishness or self-preoccupation, escalating in severity to the condition I refer to as *pathological* narcissism.

NARCISSISM AND THE RELATIONSHIP COMPATIBILITY CONTINUUM (RCC)

The person with an SRO is not automatically considered a narcissist, nor are they considered harmful or psychopathological. SROs with a (+1) or (+2) RCV are not narcissistic, as the term itself implies. However, those with a (+3), (+4), or (+5) RCV absolutely are narcissistic. The (+3) RCVs are considered moderate narcissists, while the (+4) and (+5) are considered dysfunctional. For a person to be considered a pathological narcissist, they must have a (+5) RCV and fit the diagnostic criterion for Narcissistic, Borderline, and Antisocial Personality Disorders and/or be a selfish and harmful addict.

We all know someone, whether a friend, sibling, coworker, or acquaintance, who is the life of the party, a know-it-all, a comedian, or an on-the-spot performer. Such individual values and seeks recognition, praise, and affirmation, while exuding confidence and a healthy drive for success and appreciation. This person might be your favorite athlete, musician, or even author, who passionately pursues fame and notoriety, reveling in the moments of being on stage or the center of attention. This person may be exceptionally motivated to pursue lofty personal and professional goals that energize their focus and determination, and they may spend a significant amount of time in achieving them.

In relationships, the focus for a healthy SRO leans more towards the acquisition of LRC from others than on giving the same amount back. However, because of their (+1) or (+2) RCV and closer proximity to the (0) RCV, they may be very capable and motivated to give adequate and, at times, generous amounts of LRC to others, despite it not always being equal to the amount their partner (or others) gives. An SRO in this range is not only empathic, but also capable of receiving constructive feedback about the LRC inequality and will happily make the appropriate adjustments. This is not a narcissist, but a healthy and well-adjusted individual.

DOES HEALTHY NARCISSISM EXIST?

Healthy narcissism doesn't exist, as narcissism, according to my definition, is always mildly to severely harmful to others. There is, however, healthy self-love, which in no way is indicative of any form of dysfunction or psychopathology. Consider the goal of my codependency treatment, which I refer to as the Codependency Cure™ and Self-Love Recovery™ (SLR).[19] The goal is to solve the reason for one's Self-Love Deficit Disorder™ (SLDD) and to achieve Self-Love Abundance. Therefore, the ability to love oneself is absolutely a positive trait and should never be pathologized. Narcissism should not be confused with self-love. With that said, a person who is infatuated with themselves loses track of the importance of other people's needs for attention and affirmation. This person does not have a self-love problem, but instead

---

19 Information and educational resources on Self-Love Abundance (SLA) and Self-Love Recovery (SLR) are available at www.SelfLoveRecovery.com.

is a narcissist. I reject any definition of narcissism that uses the term or explanation of excessive self-love.

MODERATE NARCISSISM OR JUST "NARCISSISTS"?

Moderate narcissists, who are defined by the Relationship Compatibility Theory as having a RCV of (+3), are a group of people who I consider non-pathologically narcissistic. Such narcissists are tilted toward the self-centered and self-obsessed side of the continuum, and they may be mildly to moderately irritating to others. Their need for praise, affirmation, and recognition often becomes the central point of their relationships. This results in others feeling neglected or not as important. Although these narcissists are self-consumed, over-the-top confident, and mildly entitled, they are still able to turn the attention around to others when needed.

Self-awareness for moderate narcissists is possible, and they can be successful at controlling or moderating their self-indulgences. At the point their narcissism has upset or offended someone, or if they are criticized for it, they experience a combination of shame and empathy, which together motivates them to make amends and curtail their hurtful behavior. Despite the moderate narcissist's periodic self-centeredness, selfish quirks, and personality traits, they can be cognizant of them and have moderate success in modulating them. These narcissists are typically neither malicious nor intentionally harmful in their pursuit of acknowledgment and admiration. Unlike the more severe group of narcissists, they are able to respond positively to constructive criticism without reflexively striking back with a narcissistic injury or hurting the person giving it to them.

Moderate narcissism could be a product of immaturity, as it is a normal personality type of young adults. Still learning about social norms and age-appropriate behavior, they simply do not yet have the life experiences to understand the negative aspects or consequences of their narcissistic tendencies.

Many of us know and even love these narcissists; they are our friends or loved ones who consistently expend a great deal of energy making sure we know their value, importance, and uniqueness. Thriving on any positive attention and recognition, they excessively value and are consequently overly motivated to seek admiration, status, understanding, and support. They are often cherished for their affable, charming, humorous, and confident natures. Their mildly off-putting desires, combined with a tendency to seek the spotlight, is likely to make them endearing. After all, in our culture, confidence and self-assuredness are respected personality traits.

The value of sharing and giving is not lost on them. Even though they struggle with regulating their narcissistic traits, they can be loyal friends—just ones who are more oriented toward the *mes* in any given conversation than the *yous*. In a relationship, these narcissists may be exhausting, as they require frequent affirmation and validation. However, unlike those with a diagnosable narcissistic personality disorder, they have insight into and control over their narcissistic traits.

Unlike dysfunctional/pathological narcissists, these people have limited empathy to offer others but can still have moments of being unconditionally giving. They are also capable of participating in and sustaining lower-level reciprocal and mutual relationships. Moderate narcissists are able to meet some, but not all, of their loved ones' emotional and personal needs. When necessary or demanded, they will suspend their self-centered, self-obsessed, and selfish ways. They can benefit from therapy, as they are able to take limited responsibility for their behaviors and the treatment of their partner.

These narcissists thrive in careers where they can be the center of attention, perform, and openly showcase their talents and successes. Their professional achievements can, in fact, be enhanced by their tendency to seek success, while making sure everyone is aware of it. Professions that require public demonstrations of their abilities such as music, acting, academia, business management, and politics are not only appealing to them, but naturally fit their personality. Nonetheless, moderate narcissists walk a fine line between robust self-confidence, arrogance, entitlement, and egotism and a more pathological and harmful form of narcissism—NPD.

DYSFUNCTIONAL/PATHOLOGICAL NARCISSISM

Dysfunctional or pathological narcissists, who are defined by the Relationship Compatibility Theory as having a RCV or either (+4) or (+5), hurt others and are unable, unmotivated, or simply refuse to stop. Such narcissists are typically unaware of how their narcissism and selfishness hurts those they claim to love. Consumed with their own need for LRC, they tend to completely ignore the same needs in others. In their relationships, reciprocity and mutuality are nonexistent. The only exception to this rule is when there is a personal, relational, or tactical advantage of temporarily meeting the needs of others.

PERSONALITY DISORDERS

Personality disorders are a class of pathological personality types, categorized as mental health disorders in the DSM-5 (2013). Inherent in all personality disorders are deeply ingrained maladaptive patterns of behavior, emotions, and thinking, which may be identified as early as adolescence and often persist for a lifetime. A personality disorder can be diagnosed if there are significant impairments in self and interpersonal functioning together with one or more pathological personality traits. In addition, these features must be:

1. relatively stable across time and consistent across situations,
2. not better understood as normative for the individual's developmental stage or sociocultural environment, and
3. not solely due to the direct effects of substance abuse or a general medical condition (DSM-5, 2013).

Pathological narcissists often do not realize or admit to having the disorder. If they do admit to a problem or a problematic element of their personality, it is usually because they were caught red-handed in a lie or were trying to manipulate their way out of being held accountable for a hurtful act.

PATHOLOGICAL NARCISSISM DISORDERS

Four personality disorders—Narcissistic, Borderline, Antisocial, and Addiction—are grouped in my diagnostic category of pathological narcissism. Despite these being demonstrably different than each other, they all share core pathologically narcissistic personality traits. This does not imply other psychological disorders or issues do not have pathologically narcissistic traits. Pathological narcissism disorders cannot be understood without seeing how they manifest within a relationship. Think about this: if you were going to attempt to understand the problems of alcoholism, you would have to look at the alcoholic's relationship with their partner—the co-alcoholic, or codependent. The relationship portion of the equation is crucial when dealing with addiction. The same holds true with pathological narcissists and their codependent partners. As described in the "Codependency: Don't Dance!" essay on page 38, both sides of the dysfunctional coin need each other to enact their dysfunctional Relationship Orientation. The following categories of narcissism will provide a better understanding of the nuances I use to define narcissism and what traits constitute someone I would consider harmful.

NARCISSISTIC PERSONALITY DISORDER (NPD)

According to a 2008 national epidemiologic study in the *Journal of Clinical Psychiatry*, slightly more than 6% of the total population qualifies for an NPD diagnosis. This includes 7.7% of men and 4.8% of women. As with other personality disorders, those with NPD are generally unaware of and oblivious to their psychological condition. These people are considered pathologically selfish, self-absorbed, grandiose, and egotistical. Motivated by a long-standing and insatiable desire for admiration, praise, and validation, their relationship partner is often worn down as there can never be enough compliments and affirmation to satisfy them.

A PATTERN OF GRANDIOSITY

NPDs honestly believe, and hold others accountable to, an exaggerated belief of their own importance, which is typically not based on reality or facts. They expect others to share their inflated and unrealistic appreciation of themselves. The narcissist's grandiosity often results in viewing others as unequal competitors who are naturally inferior. They are consumed with their special, unique, and gifted status, which they consider imbalanced in the world in which they live. Due to their inflated sense of self-importance, they are prone to exaggerating their achievements and talents. They expect to be recognized as superior or exceptional, despite not having the requisite experience or contributions. Preoccupied with fantasies of unlimited success, power, brilliance, beauty, or ideal love, they believe they can only be understood by, or should associate with, other exceptional people or institutions.

ENTITLEMENT

Another primary attribute of an NPD is their sense of entitlement, which is defined as a personality trait driven by exaggerated feelings of superiority. Entitled narcissists believe they deserve special treatment and unearned privileges. They are often perceived as having a "chip on their shoulder" and, as such, believe they are owed a measure of success like other successful people, even though they lack the same background and accomplishments.

A DEEP WELL OF SHAME

People with NPD carry a heavy unconscious burden of shame and deep feelings of inadequacy. Compensating through an obsession with power and status, they are excessively proud of and fixated on their own achievements and appearance. Their vanity, whether it be with their physical or personality attributes, often rises to a level of obsession. Because of their inflated self-appraisal and consequent need to show others their positive qualities and contributions, they are typically viewed as arrogant and conceited.

These narcissists are incapable of sustaining mutual and reciprocal relationships. They have a limited capacity for empathy and sensitivity to others, especially when they feel threatened. Additionally, NPDs are generous to others only when personal gain is imminent. Their strings-attached approach to relationships exemplifies their self-serving nature. These one-sided relationships are aggravating and offensive to anyone except a severe codependent.

As a direct result of their unstable personality and very low self-esteem, people with NPD often overreact to their mistakes or perceived flaws. They are acutely sensitive about making errors or the possibility they may be criticized or judged. They internalize the constructive criticism as if the critic is purposefully and maliciously trying to embarrass them; their fragile self-esteem simply cannot handle the humiliation. They instantly feel anger and contempt for the judgmental person. Instead of processing the value of the critical feedback, they react smugly and angrily—sometimes even aggressively. Alternatively, they may shut down emotionally, sulk, or become passive-aggressive.

The pathological narcissist's aggressive reaction to the narcissistic injury is called "narcissistic rage." Once enraged, they are typically unable to stop or control their destructive behavior. Because they are unaware of, and can't take responsibility for, their harmful reactions, they are quick to blame others. These individuals rarely apologize for their wrongdoings and do so only when cornered or when a positive result may occur from an act of contrition.

Because of their unreasonable expectations and over-inflated egos, NPDs believe they should automatically receive preferential treatment and routine compliance with any request or desire. From the NPD's point of view, they naturally should always come first. The entitled NPDs are the ones who cut in a long line or insist they get a table at a restaurant immediately, despite the others waiting in line. One person with NPD took his disabled parent's handicapped parking permit and shamelessly used it for himself, to obtain preferential parking.

NPD SUBTYPES

NPD can be further categorized into four subtypes: covert narcissism, productive narcissism, malignant narcissism, and addiction-induced narcissism.

NPD SUBTYPE: COVERT NARCISSISM

Covert narcissists are masters of disguise—successful actors, humanitarians, politicians, clergy members, and even psychotherapists—who are beloved and appreciated, but are secretly selfish, calculating, controlling, angry, and vindictive. They create an illusion of selflessness while benefitting from their elevated status. Although they share basic traits with the overt narcissist—the need for attention, affirmation, approval, and recognition—they are stealthier about hiding their egocentric motives. Unlike the overt narcissist who parades their narcissism for all to see, the covert narcissist furtively hides their real intentions and identity. These narcissists are able to trick others into believing they are honest, altruistic, and empathic. They are successful at pretending to be a more likable version of themselves, knowing if their true characters were uncovered, they could not maintain the respect, status, and prestige they so desperately desire.

A common variation of the covert narcissist is the parent who expends an inordinate amount of time and energy taking care of all aspects of their children's lives. These individuals are admired and held in high regard for what appears to be their tireless and dedicated efforts to be the best possible parent. Their frequent complaints about the personal and emotional costs of their sacrifices are manipulative ploys orchestrated for attention and praise. To the outside world, they seem like an unconditionally giving and generous parent when, in reality, all their moves are carefully calculated by an insatiable need for recognition and respect. The child's emotional needs are ultimately secondary to their own narcissistic requirement for validation, affirmation, and attention. Unfortunately, the only person who has a bird's-eye view of this covert narcissist's real intentions is their child. As is the case with all covert narcissists, only close friends and family members are privy to their shameful and hidden agenda.

Compared to overt narcissists, they are more reserved and composed. By not advertising their deeper narcissistic values and motives, they achieve their goals while protecting their innermost insecurities. Unlike overt narcissists, they expend an excessive amount of psychological energy hiding their callous and manipulative inner selves. Covert narcissists repress the magnitude of their personality disorder because, on a semi-conscious level, they are aware their fantasies are embarrassing and unacceptable.

Because covert narcissists create and maintain a façade of altruism and unconditional positive regard, they can function in positions traditionally unattractive to narcissists. Even though they are able to replicate the known qualities of these positions, they are often deeply insecure and secretive about their lack of knowledge or inability to perform the most essential tasks.

For example, a covert narcissist who is a psychotherapist will have mastered the stereotypical career-specific, idiosyncratic behavior patterns such as reflective listening, supporting, accepting feedback, and making gestures that mimic unconditional acceptance. Although they will attempt to demonstrate honesty, sympathy, and empathy with their clients, they will ultimately fall short. They will be deficient in the most critical area of their job as they simply are unable to master the key elements of the position. Often, when they are challenged or questioned, they become agitated with their clients.

NPD SUBTYPE: PRODUCTIVE NARCISSISM

Michael Maccoby (2004), a noted anthropologist and psychoanalyst, coined the term "productive narcissist." According to Maccoby, productive narcissists are extraordinarily useful and even a necessary manifestation of NPD. Although similar to overt narcissists, productive narcissists are responsible for society's greatest achievements. Because of their fervent desire to make the world a better place, they task themselves with the responsibility of coming up with important inventions, achievements, and contributions to humanity. They are supremely gifted and creative intellectuals, inventors, business leaders, and politicians who find great meaning in improving the world and leaving behind a profound legacy. Andrew Carnegie, John

D. Rockefeller, Thomas Edison, and Henry Ford are examples of this subcategory of narcissism. Productive narcissists are driven by an unwavering passion to achieve and build great things, not for themselves, but for the betterment of mankind.

Like overt and covert narcissists, productive narcissists are hypersensitive to criticism, exhibiting overcompetitive, grandiose, and pompous tendencies. As a direct result of being recognized and praised for their profound intellectual and creative accomplishments, they come close to fulfilling their elaborate ideals and fantasies. Their successes give them the opportunity to bypass the limitations that entangle many narcissists. They are completely consumed by their quest to make a difference. Their obsession to contribute is still a narcissistic process, as it is ultimately motivated by their tireless pursuit to convince themselves of their greatness.

Even with all their abilities, productive narcissists are prone to self-destruction. As a result of their successes, they start to believe in their complex fantasies and feelings of invulnerability. Consumed by their achievements and beliefs that they are invincible, they take less advice. Over time, increasing levels of motivation lead them to take unnecessary risks and become increasingly careless. As they lose perspective on their human limitations and start to identify with their elaborate ambitions, they begin to behave as if they are beyond reproach and unaccountable for their mistakes. Their entitlement and flagrant disregard for rules and laws eventually lead them to catastrophe. Fallen productive narcissists are often successful at redemption, since the very same gifts that brought them to their creative and productive apex can be utilized to get them back on track with their imagined greatness.

NPD SUBTYPE: MALIGNANT NARCISSISM

In 1984, Dr. Otto Kernberg, a Cornell University psychoanalyst, created the diagnostic term "malignant narcissism." Kernberg believed there is a narcissism scale, with NPD at the low end and malignant narcissism with psychopathic features at the high end. Malignant narcissism appears to be a hybrid of NPD, as it is a combination of four pathological extremes: narcissism, psychopathy, sadism, and paranoia. Even with the other forms of psychopathology, they are still distinctly narcissistic as they demonstrate most narcissistic traits/symptoms. The difference is malignant narcissists force their elaborate fantasies onto others.

While malignant narcissists are entitled and grandiose, they take it to a more extreme level because they believe they have a special destiny in life. This reinforces their dangerous sense of dominance and impenetrability in their relationships. They are outwardly selfish and unapologetic, while also feeling compelled to direct the lives around them. They are often suspicious of others, especially those who could remove them from their position of power. They are belligerent and scheming, while manipulatively casting themselves as the injured party. They often rise to influence by claiming they are victims of oppression. As a direct result of their charm, popularity, and calculating nature, they can sympathetically rally support for their cause. With legions of dedicated followers, they lead and inspire rebellions that, in turn, secure their leadership and authority structure.

Because malignant narcissists are fundamentally insecure and paranoid in their relationships, they counter by maintaining total control over others. Once they have achieved control, they will do almost anything to maintain it, including rape, murder, and even genocide. As a direct result of their paranoid and psychopathic tendencies, they challenge, defy, and demean anyone who is either an authority figure or has the power to hurt them. Examples of malignant narcissists include Adolph Hitler, Joseph Stalin, Muammar Gaddafi, and Saddam Hussein. Their cruel and harmful treatment of others is reinforced by their need to maintain power, domination, and a sense of superiority. Although they seem similar to psychopaths, they are different in that they can internalize right and wrong, form meaningful personal and social relationships, and rationalize their actions as a desire to advance society. They may be loyal in relationships, but because of their paranoia, may hurt or harm those who pledge loyalty to them.

NPD SUBTYPE: ADDICTION-INDUCED NARCISSISM

People who are addicted to a drug or behavior often act in narcissistic and self-serving ways, just like someone with NPD. The difference between an addiction and NPD becomes apparent once the person has been detoxed and has had a few months of sobriety. This is when the addict's RCV corresponds to their RO, and not their addiction. A person diagnosed with NPD and a harmful and aggressive addict have similar narcissistic tendencies. While the pathological narcissist's narcissism reflects their underlying personality, the addict's narcissism reflects their selfish desire to seek their drug of choice despite its potential damage to anyone else. If the recovering or sober addict maintains their narcissistic symptomatology, they likely have a co-occurring narcissistic personality disorder—having both NPD and an addiction.

BORDERLINE PERSONALITY DISORDER (BPD)

It is estimated 1.6% of the U.S. adult population has Borderline Personality Disorder (BPD) (Lenzenweger et al., 2007). According to the National Alliance on Mental Illness, the figure may be as high as 5.9% (2017, NAMI.org). BPD is more common than many other recognized mental illnesses, such as Schizophrenia and Bipolar Disorder (Nordqvist, 2012). It is common among adolescents and young adults, with the highest rates occurring between the ages of 18 and 35 (Oliver, 2012). It was once believed to be more prevalent in females. However, recent research by the National Institute of Mental Health indicates BPD is equally distributed between the sexes (Grant et al., 2008).

According to a compilation of BPD-related statistics, it is the only personality disorder to have suicidal or self-injuring behavior among its diagnostic criteria. The self-injuring behaviors symptomatic of this disorder can emerge in a child as young as 10 to 12 (SAMHSA, 2011). A prospective study showed a 3.8% completed suicide rate—a dramatic reduction from earlier reported rates of 8 to 10%. Still, this is approximately 50 times greater than that of the general population. The work of Grosjean and Warnick (2009) dispelled the notion that a person with BPD attempts suicide just for attention and not to end their life. They reported no demonstrable differences in the degree of lethality and intent to die when comparing the suicide attempts of BPD and non-BPD individuals. They also dispelled the myth that a person with Major Depression is more motivated to die than a suicidal BPD individual.

According to Insel's (2010) report, 85% of BPD sufferers have concurrent mental health disorders, such as:

- 61%: At least one anxiety disorder, most commonly a specific phobia or social phobia
- 49%: Impulse-control disorder, most commonly intermittent explosive disorder[20]
- 38%: Substance abuse or dependence disorder, most commonly alcohol abuse or drug dependence
- 34%: Mood disorder, most commonly dysthymia (mild, chronic depression) or Major Depression

---

20 A behavioral disorder characterized by explosive outbursts of anger and violence, often to the point of rage, that are disproportionate to the situation at hand.

BPD may be among the most stigmatized of mental disorders. Currently, there are rumblings in the mental health field about the negative implications of the term itself, as many consider it misleading and fraught with negative associations. It is often undiagnosed, misdiagnosed, or treated inappropriately (Porr, 2001). Clinicians may limit the number of BPD patients in their practice or drop them altogether because of their resistance to treatment. If the person with the condition repeats self-harming behavior, frustration among family, friends, and health professionals increases and may lead to decreased care (Kulkarni, 2015).

BPD is characterized by volatile moods, self-image, thought processes, and personal relationships. When unable to regulate their emotions, borderlines tend to engage in wild, reckless, and out-of-control behaviors such as dangerous sexual liaisons, drug abuse, gambling, spending sprees, or eating binges. A prominent feature of BPD is the inability to regulate mood, which is often referred to as mood dysregulation. Symptoms include rapidly fluctuating mood swings with periods of intense despair and irritability and/or apprehension, which can last a few hours to a few days. Borderlines become overwhelmed and incapacitated by the intensity of their emotions, whether it is joy and elation or depression, anxiety, or rage. They are unable to manage these intense emotions. When upset, they experience a flurry of emotions, distorted and dangerous thought processes, and destructive mood swings that threaten the safety of others, as well as themselves.

Their love/hate approach to relationships is entirely a narcissistic process, as the direction of the relationship is always determined by the BPD's feelings at any given moment. Unlike someone with an NPD, a BPD has a limited capacity and willingness to be genuinely empathetic, sensitive, generous, and sacrificial. However, those positive attributes are not without the proverbial strings attached; when the BPD explodes with vindictive rage, all they said or gave to their loved one may be taken away in one fell swoop of aggression.

LIFE IN EXTREMES: LOVE/HATE

BPDs experience the world in extremes: black-and-white or all-or-nothing. When they are happy, the world is a beautiful and perfect place. The joy they experience is as perfect as any person's joy could be. On the other hand, they reflexively experience reckless rage, paranoia, and feelings of hopelessness when they perceive they are being rejected or abandoned. Their swing into red-hot, out-of-control fury brings them to the brink of harming themselves or others. In extreme circumstances of depression, agitation, or rage, the person with BPD may spontaneously behave violently and lethally—towards themselves and/or others.

BPDs typically don't intend to cause harm to anyone, including themselves, but their reflexive emotional rampages create a form of temporary insanity. During moments of a complete emotional meltdown, their thought processes, insight into their emotional state, and ability to make sound and rational decisions become severely impaired. They will put themselves and loved ones in harm's way because of an irrational and uncontrollable wave of hatred, rage, or paranoia. This is not due to a lack of love, but because, in that moment, they have been triggered to experience the wrath and anger connected to repressed memories of their abusive, neglectful, and traumatic childhood.

BPDs are rarely capable of sustaining stable long-term relationships. Their romantic relationships begin quickly, intensely, and with a great deal of excitement, euphoria, and sexual chemistry. Their volatile emotions move in one of two directions: love and adoration or hate and destruction. Because this person has had little-to-no experience with healthy relationships, the euphoric "perfect love" feelings that occur in the beginning of the relationship are neither realistic nor lasting. The early euphoric love experience is transient as their psychological fragility leads them to an eventual emotional crash and burn. This black-and-white approach to their romances creates a teeter-totter effect of extreme behavior; they either shower their partner with love and kindness, or rage at them with disgust and violence. Their love/hate processing of relationships places an impossible burden on the partner.

ABANDONMENT: THE CORE ISSUE

Often individuals diagnosed with BPD are preoccupied with real or imagined abandonment, which they frantically try to avoid. The perception of impending separation or rejection can lead to profound changes in the way they think about themselves and others, as well as in their emotional stability and behavior. Whether real or imagined, any reminder causes them to strike back at their romantic partner with rage and aggressive hostility. A mistaken comment, a benign disagreement, or an expression perceived as disappointing can quickly transform their loving feelings toward their "soulmate" into a raging retribution against an enemy. People with

BPD are chronically unsure about their lives, whether it is with their family, personal relationships, work, or future aspirations. They also experience persistent uncertain and insecure thoughts and feelings about their self-image, long-term goals, friendships, and values. They often suffer from chronic boredom or feelings of emptiness.

According to Marsha Linehan (1993), one of the world's leading experts on BPD, ". . . borderline individuals are the psychological equivalent of third-degree burn patients. They simply have, so to speak, no emotional skin. Even the slightest touch or movement can create immense suffering." According to Kreisman and Straus (2010), the authors of *I Hate You, Don't Leave Me: Understanding the Borderline Personality*, "A borderline suffers from a kind of 'emotional hemophilia'; she lacks the clotting mechanism needed to moderate her spurts of feeling. Prick the delicate 'skin' of a borderline, and she will emotionally bleed to death" (p. 12).

The BPD's fear of abandonment or rejection creates a self-fulfilling prophecy. This is defined as "any positive or negative expectation about circumstances, events, or people that may affect a person's behavior toward them in a manner that causes those expectations to be fulfilled." To feel safe and secure, they form romantic relationships quickly and intensely. A quickly formed emotional and sexual union temporarily shields them from terrifying feelings of loneliness and worthlessness. These attachments can only temporarily relieve or decrease their anxiety and fears of abandonment, as the person with BPD is profoundly psychologically impaired.

In relationships, BPDs are often clingy, insecure, and needy as they seek frequent reassurances of their value and worthiness. When they react with harmful and damaging retribution, typically if their partner is not codependent, they will have caused the relationship to fail, creating the very situation they fear most: abandonment. If the partner happens to be codependent, a cycle of love, destruction, and reconciliation will be repeated.

ANTISOCIAL PERSONALITY DISORDER (ASPD)

According to the DSM-5 (2013), people with Antisocial Personality Disorder (ASPD) habitually and pervasively disregard or violate the rights and considerations of others without remorse. ASPDs may be habitual criminals, engage in behavior that is or is close to grounds for arrest and prosecution, and manipulate and hurt others in non-criminal ways regarded as unethical, immoral, irresponsible, or abusive of social norms and expectations.

This disorder is characterized by a pervasive pattern of disregard for and violation of the rights of others that begins in childhood or early adolescence and continues into adulthood (DSM-5, 2013). ASPDs possess distorted and destructive patterns of thinking, perceiving, and relating to others. They often have an impaired moral compass and make decisions driven purely by their own desires, without considering the needs or negative effects of their actions on others. They lack empathy, demonstrate little guilt or remorse, and will unscrupulously do whatever is necessary to meet their self-serving desires. They are typically dishonest, calculating, and selfish. Impulsivity and unpredictability are very common.

The DSM-5 (2013) approximates the prevalence of ASPD is 3.3%. The lifetime prevalence in two North American studies was 4.5% among men and 0.8% among women (Robins et al., 1991). Not surprisingly, ASPD is common in prison settings: 47% of men and 21% of women (Fazel and Danesh, 2002). The U.K. ASPD prisoner population accounts for 63% of male remand prisoners, 49% of male sentenced prisoners, and 31% of female prisoners (Singleton, Meltzer, and Gatward, 1998). It is estimated 50 to 75% of the prison population in the U.S. meets the criteria for ASPD, but only 15 to 25% exceed the cut-off point for psychopathy (Hare, 2008).

Of all the pathological narcissists, ASPDs are by far the most insidious, manipulative, and harmful. For that matter, they are the most narcissistic of the pathologically narcissistic disorders. Note: even though all ASPDs are narcissistic, not all NPDs are antisocial.

ASPDs are indifferent to the needs of whomever they are in a relationship with. As pathological liars and cunning manipulators, they are typically unfaithful and exploitative. They lack consideration for others and are irresponsible in most of their relationships, including chronic employment problems, as they are either fired, quit, or simply walk off their jobs when bored or annoyed. ASPDs often have a history of legal problems and have a capacity for belligerence, aggression, and violence.

Other diagnostic terms associated with ASPD include "sociopathy" (sociopaths) or "psychopathy" (psychopaths). The DSM-5 (1994) replaced the diagnoses of "sociopathy" and "psychopathy" with "Antisocial Personality Disorder (ASPD)." The psychological and psychiatric communities deemed the change necessary because the primary diagnostic trait/symptom for sociopathy was a "violation of social norms," which was considered subjective and ever-changing. The updated ASPD diagnosis required more behavior-specific and concrete diagnostic criteria.

PSYCHOPATHS VERSUS ASPDS

Before 1980, the terms psychopathy and sociopathy were used interchangeably. Although they share behavioral similarities, such as being dishonest and manipulative and lacking empathy and remorse, they are considered different diagnoses. While most psychopaths meet the criteria for ASPD, not all ASPDs are psychopaths. Psychopaths are generally understood to be dangerous, violent, and controlling. They rely on violence and intimidation to dominate others and satisfy their selfish needs. They are unable to feel/experience guilt, remorse, or anxiety about any of their actions. Moreover, ASPDs and psychopaths internalize and externalize their pathological behavior differently. For example, "[ASPDs] are seen as disorganized and rash, making extreme responses to normal situations. They lack impulse control. Psychopaths, by contrast, are highly organized, often secretly planning out and fantasizing about their acts in great detail before actually committing them, and sometimes manipulating people around them" (wiki.answers.com).

In an article on Chris Weller's website, MedicalDaily.com (2014), he differentiates between these two variants of ASPD:

> Psychopaths are dangerous. They're violent and cruel, and oftentimes downright sinister. They show no remorse for their actions, usually because of a lesion on a part of their brain responsible for fear and judgement, known as the amygdala. Psychopaths commit crimes in cold blood. They crave control and impulsivity, possess a predatory instinct, and attack proactively rather than as a reaction to confrontation. A 2002 study found 93.3% of the psychopathic homicides were instrumental in nature (meaning they were planned), compared with 48.4% of the homicides by people who weren't psychopaths.
>
> Sociopaths are a different breed. They, too, may suffer from their mental illness because of lesioned brain regions. Upbringing may also play a larger role in a child becoming a sociopath versus those who are diagnosed as psychopaths, or they slide into dementia on the other end of the spectrum. Sociopathic behavior is manifested as conniving and deceitful, despite an outward appearance of trustworthiness or sincerity. Sociopaths are often pathological liars. They are manipulative and lack the ability to judge the morality of a situation, but not because they lack a moral compass; rather, their existing moral compass is greatly (yet not always dangerously) skewed.

Although psychopathy is associated with conduct problems, criminality, and violence, many psychopaths are not violent. Despite having "psycho" being a root word of the diagnosis, psychopaths are rarely psychotic. For the purposes of this book, psychopathy, sociopathy, and ASPD diagnoses will be treated as one disorder—Antisocial Personality Disorder.

LIVING BY THE PLEASURE PRINCIPLE

ASPDs live their life by the pleasure principle. If it feels good and they can avoid consequences, they will do it. They live their life in the fast lane, to the extreme, seeking stimulation and excitement wherever they can get it. Every day brings new opportunities to feel good. Whether it is sex, drugs, alcohol, or spending, they live like there is no tomorrow. Their never-ending search for gratification may evolve into an addiction, which often exponentially increases the levels of chaos and dysfunction in their relationships. Adding an addiction disorder to ASPD is like throwing gasoline onto a fire. Therefore, it should be no surprise that ASPD is more common with alcohol and drug abusers (Lewis, Cloninger, and Pace, 1983). Approximately 15 to 20% of male alcoholics and 10% of female alcoholics would qualify for an ASPD diagnosis, compared with 4% of men and approximately 8% of women in the general U.S. population (Cadoret, Troughton, and Widmer, 1984; Anthenelli et al., 1994).

More than the other pathologically narcissistic disorders, those with ASPD are unwilling or unable to participate mutually and reciprocally in any relationship. As pathological/compulsive liars and con artists, they are easily able to conceal the truth from others. Relying on deception and fraudulence to maintain their façade of likability, they disarm others. For some ASPDs, conning others is a sport. Not only do they gain from their exploits, but they also experience the pleasure of the hunt, often utilizing aliases to cover up their secrets, including multiple identities and secret lives.

Some ASPDs have honed their superficial wit and charm into a precise skill set that, when used well, will fool almost anyone, including those who have known them their entire life. Their victims, or those who have confused their likable charm with who they really are, are often oblivious to their enigmatic agendas. These master choreographers, or actors, are so believable, they could earn an Oscar. Charm is the metaphorical mask that enables ASPDs to blend in with society and achieve their dishonest and sociopathic goals. When their secret plans are uncovered, often through an accident or mistake, their victims are mortified and shocked at their gullibility.

Ted Bundy (a psychopathic serial killer) was described as handsome, charismatic, articulate, and very likable. He exploited his victims by saying exactly what they wanted to hear. Charm got him close to the people he would eventually brutally murder. He was convicted of 30 homicides in seven states; the true total remains unknown.

Bernie Madoff is another example of a charming, clever, and highly exploitive ASPD. A white-collar businessman, he stole $50 billion from unsuspecting investors, including friends, family, charities, senior citizens, and others. Many of his victims lost all their personal reserves and some their entire retirement nest eggs. Friends and family were shocked when they learned of Madoff's crimes. It was reported virtually no one suspected he was capable of such grievous wrongdoing, as he was well-known for being kind, sensitive, generous, and trustworthy.

ASPDs are capable of using a person as a cover, or camouflage of sorts. Through a fake "normal" relationship, they give themselves legitimacy—a perfect alibi for their clandestine side. They act the part of a loving and caring person, especially when it helps them obtain what they value most: sex, financial security, someone to care for them—or just the status of being in a relationship. The dual lives enable them to freely engage in furtive and despicable activities without detection. This is why so many people are shocked when they hear about the sociopath next door.

MASTER MANIPULATORS

ASPDs easily, and without guilt or shame, exploit their partners for financial and/or personal gain. They often justify their dishonest, manipulative, and harmful actions through a distorted and bizarre set of beliefs, such as "take what you want, or someone will beat you to it," "it's a dog-eat-dog world . . . get what you can when you can," or "sometimes you're the bug and sometimes you're the windshield."

When confronted by their victims or even by the law, typically they vehemently and believably deny any wrongdoing. ASPDs get the spotlight off themselves and generally blame the victim for their antisocial behavior because of their ignorance or gullibility. ASPDs are intolerant of anyone who tries to prevent them from getting what they want or believe they need. They can be dangerously threatening, aggressive, and abusive to anyone who attempts to get in their way. When confronted or provoked, they are easily enraged to the point of violence. They behave physically, verbally, psychologically, or sexually abusive in this manner because they feel entitled to do so and are unable to regulate their aggressive or violent impulses. Naturally, codependents are susceptible to the ASPD's beguiling and manipulative charms. By nature of their others-oriented psychopathology, codependents are susceptible to a domestically violent ASPD's strategy to systematically weaken, deflate, and, consequently, strip them of real and perceived feelings of personal efficacy and power.

ADDICTION DISORDERS

Addiction Disorder is a catch-all phrase for the persistent and compulsive dependence on a habit-forming substance or behavior. People who are addicted to a drug or behavior, such as sex or gambling, qualify for the pathologically narcissistic diagnosis only if they tandemly demonstrate significant pathological traits of any of the three pathological NPDs. If they don't have any other diagnosis, the addiction, rather than an underlying psychological disturbance, is responsible for their psychopathological or dysfunctional behavior. Despite negative consequences, people with Addiction Disorder are compelled to continue the use of a specific mood-altering substance or destructive and repetitive behavioral patterns. This is a progressive disorder that has its origins in the brain.

Reflections

- Do you know someone who is a covert narcissist? What would they do if their mask was taken off?

- Have you ever personally encountered anyone with ASPD? If so, how did you know?

- For you, what would be some of the most difficult aspects of being with someone with BPD?

Chapter Eleven

GASLIGHTING AND NARCISSISTIC ABUSE SYNDROME

NARCISSISTIC ABUSE SYNDROME (NAS)

Lately, an increasing number of books, articles, blogs, YouTube videos, and social networking sites are focusing on Narcissistic Abuse Syndrome (NAS), also known as *Narcissistic Victim Syndrome*. Like most newly recognized and understood psychological or relational phenomena, descriptive and diagnostic data must be developed so it can be accepted in broader clinical/mental health circles. The more that is researched and written about it, the higher the probability that effective treatment and support services will be developed. Although it occupies just a few paragraphs in this manuscript, its importance and relevance to the Human Magnet Syndrome material is significant.

Narcissistic Abuse Syndrome and the Human Magnet Syndrome are unrelated, and bear little resemblance to each other. NAS focuses on a pattern of abuse perpetrated by a narcissist onto a codependent victim. HMS, in its simplest form, explains why opposite personalities are attracted to each other, and why relationships persevere despite one or both people being unhappy. Regardless of differences, I estimate that at least 75% of codependents experience some form of NAS in relationships.

NAS is a chronic pattern of physical, emotional, and/or sexual abuse perpetrated by a pathological narcissist against weak and more vulnerable individuals. Because NAS victims typically lack confidence, self-esteem, and social supports, they are prone to feeling trapped by the perpetrator. The experience of being trapped may be an accurate assessment or a result of carefully implanted "trapped narratives," otherwise known as gaslighting. NAS victims come from all walks of life. However, the ones who either feel trapped, believe they can control or mitigate the abuse, or actually believe they deserve it are codependent or have a Self-Love Deficit Disorder.™

NAS is a chronic condition because of the Human Magnet Syndrome. HMS's complicated psychological and relational dynamics are responsible for the formation and maintenance of the perpetrator/victim relationship, and the inability to terminate it. The NAS victims, the codependents, are either unable to or *believe* they are unable to end the abuse and/or the relationship because of the following:

1. Uncertainty about the true dangerous nature of the abuser
2. Fear of actual consequences
3. Fear of threatened consequences/retaliation
4. Fear of social and familial rejection and isolation (siding with the abuser)
5. Physical entrapment
6. Financial entrapment
7. Various forms of active, passive, and covert coercion and manipulation
8. A successful gaslighting campaign
9. Codependency addiction withdrawals, especially pathological loneliness

As pathological narcissists, perpetrators of NAS have either a Narcissistic, Borderline, or Antisocial Personality Disorder, and/or Addiction Disorder. The less empathy an NAS perpetrator has, the more effective they are in controlling and dominating their codependent prey. They maintain power and control over their victims by beating or wearing down their resolve to defend themselves or to reach out for protection or help. The various forms of direct, passive, and covert manipulation and aggression ensures the victim stays in the relationship, while the codependent neither fights back nor exposes them.

The most potent form of NAS entrapment comes from a sustained brainwashing and/or gaslighting campaign perpetrated by a pathological narcissist who is either a sociopath (Antisocial Personality Disorder) or one with sociopathic traits. Because a categorical explanation of NAS is beyond the scope of this book, I recommend viewing my full-length seminar videos on the subject.[21]

LIKE PEDOPHILES…

Like pedophiles (who sexually abuse children), NAS perpetrators have a "nose" for codependent victims who are naturally unable to recognize their scheming and highly manipulative ways. As with a pedophile at a playground, their laser-guided vision identifies and locks onto people who are the most oblivious to their nefarious intentions and most incapable of defending themselves. NAS offenders also possess an uncanny ability to discern whether potential victims are pathologically lonely or encumbered by core, real, or perceived beliefs of powerlessness and weakness. They seize upon anyone in a given crowd who appears isolated from others or whose loved ones, despite their protective and loving pronouncements, are uninterested in them and/or absent. The perfect NAS victim has been taught the futility of fighting back, as doing so often makes matters worse.

These cunning perpetrators, who often are sociopathic, purposely choreograph their victim's Human Magnet Syndrome experience, so the victim falls helplessly head over heels in love with them. Once in the "soulmate fog," the codependents invite the malicious individuals into their vulnerable areas—both physically and emotionally—where the scheming pathological narcissists take up permanent residence.

BRAINWASHING

Brainwashing and gaslighting are just a few of the many mind-control tactics used in NAS. The primary difference between the two is brainwashing relies on forceful and obvious mind-control strategies, while gaslighting is carefully cloaked in secrecy. A combined Cambridge, Oxford, and Merriam Webster gaslighting definition is as follows:

---

21 "Pathological Narcissists: Who They Are & What to Do About Them—The Observe, Don't Absorb Technique" (six hours) and "Gaslighting Is Everywhere! How and Why Pathological Narcissists Brainwash Others" (four hours) are both available at www.SelfLoveRecovery.com

1. Making people believe only what you want them to believe by continually telling them it is true and preventing any other information from reaching them.
2. Pressuring someone into adopting radically different beliefs by using systematic and often forcible means.
3. Persuading by means of propaganda or salesmanship.

BRAINWASHING IS MIND CONTROL

Brainwashing employs secret, but covertly forceful, psychological strategies with the purpose of changing a person's belief system, perceptions, attitudes, and analytical abilities. Through repetition and purposeful confusion, intimidation, and a regimented campaign of propaganda, victims unconsciously relinquish their version (perceptions and analysis) of reality and accept the forced version.

It is a methodical and controlled system of indoctrinating a specific set of beliefs that, before the brainwashing, was not held by the victim. Brainwashing relies on the systematic application of isolation, verbal and physical abuse, and mind-clouding techniques like sleep deprivation and malnutrition to reduce comfort levels and feelings of hope. Shifting from cruelty to seemingly altruistic concern creates psychological instability and increased levels of uncertainty, despair, and hopelessness. These culminate in the adoption of the forced set of ideas, views, and beliefs. Brainwashing often takes place in an environment of isolation, meaning all "normal" social reference points are unavailable. There is often the presence or constant threat of physical harm, which adds to the victim's difficulty in thinking critically and independently (Leighton, 2017).

GASLIGHTING EXPLANATION

Gaslighting is an insidious mind-control method sociopathic pathological narcissists covertly use on their vulnerable codependent prey. They target individuals who believe their false altruism, affection, and promises of protection. Gaslighters are most successful when casting themselves as loyal, dutiful, and unconditionally invested in defending and caring for their victims.

Gaslighters systematically manipulate a codependent's environment so they are powerless to fight back, isolated from anyone who could help them, and convinced their gaslit impairment makes them inadequate and unlovable outside their carefully choreographed false, but realistic, relationship with their captor.

They implant narratives, or revised and distorted versions of reality, to weaken their victim, neutralize their defenses, and turn their own mind against them. The scheming gaslighter chooses a problem that either did not previously exist, or was only a mild or moderately bothersome problem about which the victim was already aware. The gaslighter carefully and methodically choreographs the victim's environment, so they repeatedly experience the staged problem.

Whether "new" or pre-existing, the gaslighter seizes on these staged moments by implanting a narrative to make the victim feel guilt for what they did, shame for who they've become, and a belief they are unable to control the "problem" on their own. Over time, this scenario further inculcates them with insecurities and paranoia.

The methodical barrage of false narratives about the problem, their inability to control or stop it, and the impact it is having on others purposely manifests as thoughts and feelings of hopelessness, powerlessness, and a deepening of the pre-existing core shame. This cements their desire to isolate into the safe world inhabited only by them and their captor.

Not only does the gaslighter make the codependent victim inaccessible to anyone who could protect or rescue them, they convince them these people don't care, love, or want to be with them. Moreover, they are effectively persuaded that, if they should visit their friends and loved ones, more harm than good would come of it. In severe cases of gaslighting, the victim will defend the gaslighter, as well as sound an alarm if someone should try to intervene in their relationship. Not only does the gaslit person defend these new self-narratives, but loyalty to the "loving" and "protective" gaslighter is paramount. These misperceptions, together with a sense of allegiance and appreciation, would prevent the victim from accepting help. All the while, the gaslighter is feeding their victim's loved ones false information for the sole purpose of further alienating or severing the relationships.

As previously discussed, codependents are primed for gaslighting by virtue of their childhood attachment trauma, the consequent relationship template, and their life-long mental health and self-love deficit problems. Sadly, their childhood "gift" or "trophy" experiences set the stage for them to fall victim to and identify with implanted stories about who they are, how they feel, what they think, how valued and loved they are by others, and how little power they have at putting an end to their own problems.

INCULCATION AND NARRATIVES

Inculcation: a more descriptive word for "implant." It is the perfect gaslighting word because it specifically describes its primary manipulation process. Dictionary.com (2017) defines it as "to implant by repeated statement or admonition; teach persistently and earnestly. To cause or influence someone to accept an idea or feeling." The Cambridge online dictionary defines it as "to cause someone to have particular beliefs or values by repeating them frequently." I define gaslighting as "to implant false and/or distorted narratives that are specially designed or formulated to manipulate a person into a destructive web of deception, loss of control, and the surrender of personal freedom and beliefs of self-worth, self-esteem, and productivity."

Self-Narrative: a person's "self-story" that is believed as fact and which is communicated to others. Self-narratives are comprised of autobiographical information that is factual and anchored in accurate memories. It is formed by the organic interaction of the person with the people and events in their lives. The self-story is formed by the competing forces of experience and memory, which by their very nature are in a constant state of evolution.

Self-narratives are the subjectively understood and communicated stories that account for a person's assessment of their total self—strengths, limitations, and everything in between. This narrative is a metaphorical mirror that, in real-time, accurately reflects a person's self-reality. When communicated, it relays a person's internal belief structure, thoughts, perceptions, and feelings. While precisely accounting for a person's past and present, it also predicts the future. They reflect a person's subjective evaluation of their self-worth and significance to others. Self-narratives have the capacity to confirm and strengthen one's self-appreciation/self-love as much as they can weaken or challenge it. They are, therefore, predictive of emotional/mental and relational health.

Self-narratives are analogous to a person's "life painting," which they must look at to understand and explain who they are. Lastly, they create the foundation upon which the relational-narrative rests.

Relational-Narrative: the story a person tells themselves that paints a picture of their worth and value to others in general or to specific people. The positive or healthy relational-narrative is comprised of beliefs, thoughts, and feelings that make a person feel worthy of love, respect, and care. It often takes the shape of a projection of self-worth onto others. To illustrate, if a person has good self-esteem and believes they are likable and lovable, then they project that story to a person or people who they believe like and love them. Naturally, the relational-narrative is highly impacted by a person's self-narrative. Both are similarly anchored in accurate autobiographical information—recollections constantly reinforced by experiences and memories.

Gaslit **Self-Narrative:** stories that are manufactured and systematically implanted, covertly and malevolently re-packaged into gaslit narratives, to replace, challenge, or degrade a person's natural beliefs and sell as truth to the gaslit victim. These inculcated stories reinforce a person's feelings and opinions about being defective, incompetent, and/or unlovable. They are implanted in a cunning and methodical manner so the victim doubts, forgets, and casts aside healthier and more self-promoting narratives. This covert form of mind-control and personal and relational manipulation is motivated by an over-arching plan of isolation, control, and domination.

Gaslit **Relational-Narrative:** a story that is anchored in and intertwined with the carefully engineered and choreographed gaslit self-narrative. Using a modern term, it is the inculcated "fake news" relationship story that gaslighting victims are convinced is the truth. Like the gaslit self-narrative, it is a methodically implanted suggestion that convinces a person they are unlovable, disliked, or that creates stress and discomfort in the lives of their friends and loved ones. The gaslighter also disseminates distorted, incomplete, and untrue negative information about the gaslit victim's friends and loved ones. This is specifically designed to drive a wedge between the person and the outside world. Without an outsider to pull the mask off the gaslighter and reveal their true identity to the victim, the gaslighters end-game of complete isolation and psychological control can come to fruition.

Gaslit self- and relational-narratives reinforce one another. The person who falls prey to their inculcated mental health problem(s) is more likely to believe the fabricated relational-narrative. Hence, the shattered self-narrative makes the indoctrinated relational-narrative fit, like a hand in a glove. Similarly, the deeper the fictional relational-narrative is imbedded in a person's psyche, the more it proves the implanted self-relationship narrative.

The following two vignettes illustrate how individuals with mild-to-moderate problems can be gaslit into believing they are much worse than they really are, and how they are systematically led to trust people who cause them harm in the first place.

GASLIGHTING JACK

Jack is a successful, 35-year-old wedding photographer, who is in a committed long-term relationship with Robert, a 46-year-old entrepreneur and CEO of an accounting firm. Since the age of 8, Jack has struggled with a slight-to-average case of social anxiety. His narcissistic father didn't "believe in" any form of anxiety treatment. He thought it could be controlled with a little effort and didn't allow Jack to get help. Once in college, he started to take medicine and periodically sought the help of a counselor. Despite his roller-coaster relationships with jealous and controlling men, he did well in college and all his subsequent jobs. After being replaced with another man by his last boyfriend, Jack's anxiety issues began to spike. These included intermittent minor panic attacks, which did not necessitate outside intervention.

When Jack met Robert, the "I can't feel my feet . . . I am floating on air" sensation of their new love was overwhelming. Not only was Robert highly intelligent, charming, and handsome, he seemed to have a knack for coming up with simple solutions to complicated problems. His "can do" and "take charge" qualities were most endearing to Jack. Like many new lovers, Jack quit talking to his friends and family members; all he wanted to do was be with Robert.

Jack was completely taken off guard by Robert's complete lack of judgment and unconditional acceptance of his anxiety. In fact, early in the relationship, Robert often told him he was cute and lovable when anxious. Having never experienced this level of patience, tolerance, and emotional freedom, this led Jack to feel more comfortable when being his normal anxious self. What was most appealing was Robert's willingness to coach him in overcoming his lifelong anxiety.

In the first few months of the relationship, Jack experienced intermittent anxiety spikes and a few mild panic attacks, for which he sought help from a psychotherapist and psychiatrist, just like he did before meeting Robert. Unbeknownst to Jack, Robert was a sociopathic gaslighter, convincingly casting himself as an understanding and sympathetic confidant invested in helping Jack deal with his anxiety.

Jack's anxiety didn't subside. In fact, the frequent discussion about it, combined with Robert's suggestion to keep an active log of any occurrences, made him even more nervous. During one late-night heart-to-heart discussion, Jack told Robert about his preoccupation and fear that his therapy and medicine were no longer working. Robert pointed out they not only seemed to have become ineffective but were also possibly making matters worse.

Because of Robert's insistence that psychotherapy and medicine didn't work—they were "the lazy man's solution"—Jack decided to stop seeing his therapist and psychiatrist and discontinue his medicine. It was an easy decision to make after listening to Robert's advice that "because a person's problems begin and end in their mind, the only solution is mind-control." Jack was optimistic about Robert's promise to teach him mind-control techniques.

Although Jack wanted to have one more session with his psychotherapist and psychiatrist, to say thank you and goodbye, he heeded Robert's warning that such a discussion would only anger and insult them. This would then provoke both of them to conspire together to keep him in treatment. Jack also believed Robert's prediction that the sessions by themselves would provoke a major panic attack. Protecting himself from the therapist and psychiatrist's intentions to rope him back into treatment, Jack ignored their phone calls and emails.

Jack felt affirmed and protected by Robert's purported understanding of anxiety and the loving care he gave him. He seemed to be truly dedicated to helping Jack remove all his triggers, which included most of his close friends and family. Even though his social network slowly shrank, Jack felt more understood and cared for than ever before.

The only other questionable area in Jack's life was his job. According to Robert, wedding photography was a naturally anxiety-provoking field and none of his advice or coaching would be able to address it. He suggested Jack quit, take a break from work, and try to find his "calm emotional center." The decision was an easy one, as Robert offered him a sizable loan that would cover his living expenses. The cherry on top was Robert's apparent selfless and generous insistence that Jack move in with him. Robert told him to stop throwing away money on his "rat-trap" one-bedroom apartment, of which Jack was quite fond.

Three months after moving in with Robert, Jack became increasingly worried about his escalating anxiety, about which Robert was constantly reminding him. Robert convinced Jack that he wasn't giving the mind-control plan enough effort and accused him of unintentionally sabotaging it. This was when Robert began to deride and blame Jack for his impatience and pessimism. Despite not agreeing with Robert, Jack would never challenge the person who had made so many sacrifices for him.

Jack received several emails from his mother and sister, begging him to leave Robert's home. They were afraid he was being brainwashed. Jack sought Robert's comfort and support. Robert helped him understand they didn't know him anymore and were more concerned about their own selfish interests than what was best for him. Once again, Robert's wisdom made logical sense, and Jack doubled down on his efforts to avoid his family. A month later, on separate occasions, Jack's best friend and his mother spoke to Robert on the phone and asked him to relay messages of love and concern. Robert explained Jack was "fine . . . and very happy," but needed some more time to gather his thoughts before contacting them. Robert promised to encourage Jack to contact them.

Three weeks later, following his family's failed intervention to rescue Jack from Robert's home, Robert finally convinced Jack about the duplicitous and selfish nature of his family. They both agreed to keep these "invading" people a safe distance away from their "happy family."

After months of further psychological programming, Jack began to wonder if the safe bubble he lived in was now making him feel worse. He begged Robert for permission to go back to his therapist or start taking medicine again. Robert was profoundly disappointed and resentful that Jack would give up on their plan. He also threw down a reminder that he had invested over $100,000 of his own money to help Jack with his anxiety problems. Jack started to cry and begged Robert's forgiveness, while promising to never ask about psychotherapy or medicine again. Jack's belief that his anxiety caused everyone to not like him and made him a bad person was now set in stone.

A year into the relationship, Jack became increasingly paranoid about his anxiety and the possibility Robert might put him out on the street. Any form of intimacy between them stopped, and Robert became overtly disinterested and annoyed with Jack. With his anxiety at its highest, he became severely depressed and secretly wished he were dead.

Jack soon discovered Robert was having an affair. Robert instantly denied Jack's accusation and, in a fit of rage, pushed Jack into the kitchen wall and almost broke his shoulder (and the wall). Robert's threat to leave Jack should he not get a better handle on his anxiety and paranoia, was enough to ensure Jack would never again make a similar accusation.

Three months later, Jack called 911 after trying to kill himself by swallowing a bottle of pain pills. Despite his protests, he was transferred to a psychiatric hospital for intensive treatment. Thanks to a persistent psychotherapist and the outpouring of love and support from his friends and family, Jack finally awoke to the two years of his gaslighting prison. He never saw Robert again. Two years later, after a great deal of psychotherapy, Jack is psychologically healthy and in a safe and loving relationship with another healthy person.

GASLIGHTING KENDRA

Kendra and Frank have been married 15 years. Like most relationships, it started off with plenty of excitement, fun, and sex. In the beginning, Frank constantly praised Kendra for her athletic, size-zero physique. However, in the first trimester of their first pregnancy, Frank began to make comments about her weight gain. At first, they were subtle observation-like remarks, but as the pregnancy progressed, he became increasingly judgmental of her extra weight. Three months after delivering the baby, Frank's criticisms became mean-spirited and mocking. He went so far as to call her fat, chubby, and a tub of lard. At this juncture in their marriage, Frank lost all interest in sex.

Kendra was unable to lose the extra 15 post-baby pounds and Frank's insults became more frequent and intense. He even asked her who she thought would want to have sex with a "repulsive whale." He often told her she was lucky to be married to him, especially after she had pulled a "bait-and-switch" on him, and most men would leave their wife for that alone.

The verbal and emotional abuse and feelings of powerlessness to lose the baby fat resulted in bouts of depression and anxiety, which Kendra self-medicated with her favorite drug of choice—food. Predictably, Kendra became heavier. The larger she became, the worse Frank's verbal abuse became and the more he justified his lack of interest in having sex with her. By the time their child turned 2, Kendra had gained another five pounds. She no longer thought of herself as a beautiful woman with a weight problem, but a "morbidly obese pig."

Around this time, Kendra began noticing Frank's pattern of late nights at the office and recurrent "guys only" trips with his friends. As much as Kendra was afraid of confronting Frank about her suspicions of his infidelity, she was also afraid it was all in her mind and she was over-reacting. Self-blame and criticism seemed natural to her, as she grew up with highly judgmental and critical parents who also gave her a hard time about her weight.

One night after a few glasses of wine, Kendra briefly bolted from her prison of self-doubt and confronted Frank about her suspicions of him having an affair.

Outraged at the suggestion, Frank screamed at her, calling her paranoid and inse-cure. When Kendra produced proof of the affair, he instantly calmed down and showed no signs of anger. He broke down in tears and said he never would have cheated on her if she hadn't let herself go. It was her fault she was not exciting to him anymore. He apologized profusely, said he was ashamed of himself, and begged for another chance. He then explained how "he was only a man" and had to take care of his sexual needs.

As a consequence of being blamed for the affair, Kendra's depression and anxiety kicked into high gear, landing her in bed frequently or drowning her humiliation with food. Thoughts of Frank with another woman, coupled with her embarrass-ment of being fat, triggered her Catch-22 lifelong feelings of shame and preoc-cupation with being abandoned. This further escalated her emotional eating. For Kendra, there was no escaping the "fact" that she was a disgusting pig who deserved to have a cheating husband.

ADDITIONAL GASLIGHTING TERMS

Circular Gaslighting: when the gaslighter uses the implanted problem, which has escalated to pathological proportions, to justify harmful actions to the victim. They feel both bad and fortunate the gaslighter hasn't abandoned them, as their friends and loved ones (supposedly) did. This is when the nuts and bolts of the gaslighting process have been tightened to the point where they have no chance of escaping—that is, if they ever would want to. Both previous vignettes demonstrate the double-bind control maneuver.

Gaslighting Logic: the distorted and flawed reasoning ability of a gaslighting victim. A sustained campaign of inculcated false narratives results in the scrambling of the gaslit prey's thoughts, emotions, and intellectual capacities to the point of becoming impaired. This results in *brainwashing out* the victim's logical thoughts and reasoning skills, replacing them with the carefully and systematically engineered false versions. Gaslighting logic renders the victim unable to recall their former critically thinking self, believing subconsciously the instilled principles, reasoning, and rational think-ing are their own. This implanted system of reasoning is resistant to another person's attempts to break it down or dispute it. The following represents the semi-linear nature of gaslighting logic:

- My beloved wouldn't hurt me because he always shows me how much I matter to him.
- I completely believe he has my back and will protect me.
- He proved to me he understands my low self-esteem and insecurity problems.
- I believe him when he says he wants to help me with my self-esteem and insecurities.
- If he says something is true, then it must be. He would never lie to me.
- When he says there is something wrong with me, I believe it.
- He protects me by calmly letting me know when my anxiety affects our life.
- He tells me he unconditionally loves me despite my bad and sometimes annoying habits.
- He protects and defends me from all the people he says don't like me.
- He keeps me focused by reminding me I am getting worse, while saying I should not lose hope.
- He promises to never leave me, despite my debilitating psychological problems.
- He tells me my friends and boss confided in him about being annoyed by my insecurities.
- With his encouragement and promise of financial support, I quit my job.
- He took me to a counselor who agrees I am getting worse.
- I stopped seeing the counselor because I heard him complaining about our bills.
- I stopped taking my antidepressant medication, as it is expensive and was clearly not helping me.
- Everyone except my beloved has abandoned me because of my paralyzing insecurities.
- My beloved is right; I am so lucky to have him, as no one else could deal with my craziness.
- I agree with him about not seeing my backstabbing sister, who has been begging to talk to me.
- I am grateful for his support, especially since we now don't have much money.
- After I confronted him about my suspicions of his infidelity, he took me to the emergency room to get help for my out-of-control paranoia.

- I was diagnosed with depression-induced paranoia and was prescribed anti-psychotic medication.
- The doctor agreed with my husband about my need to be more trusting of him.
- I am so fortunate to have the unconditional love and protection of my beloved.

As gaslighting is a broad and diverse subject, only a few approaches will be presented here. The reader may benefit from my four-hour seminar, "Gaslighting Is Everywhere! How and Why Pathological Narcissists Brainwash Others," which is available at www.SelfLoveRecovery.com. [22]

GASLIGHTING MANEUVERS

The Gaslighting Catch-22: any attempt to disprove the plot or uncover the gaslighter's duplicity proves the narrative. When Jack shared his worries with Robert about his continued anxiety, despite stopping the "counterproductive" medication, psychotherapeutic, and psychiatric services, Robert convinced him he was at fault for not doing enough to prevent it from happening.

Gaslighting Secrecy: when the victim is convinced the outside world and formerly trusted people have a vested interest in hurting them. Gaslighting can only work if the victim is manipulated into a covenant of secrecy. Robert was able to convince Jack his family did not have his best interests at heart. Because of this, Jack had little problem cutting them out of his life.

Bridge Bombing: when a gaslighter convinces their victim that others don't like, love, or care about them and have plans to hurt them. They coax the victim to confront these offending individuals, which creates the intended severing of those relationships. An example is a gaslighter who convinces his girlfriend to confront her boss, who has written her up because she has been late three times during the last two weeks. She is encouraged to stand her ground and not let the "bully" push her around. When she repeats what she was coached to say, she is fired. Now that she is unemployed, she will need to move in with her gaslighting boyfriend because she cannot afford to pay bills.

Exponentiating the Narrative: the crack cocaine of gaslighting techniques. It is the most powerful, effective, and harmful. It occurs when the implanted narrative is aggravated through a carefully planned campaign of triggering and activating events. The gaslighter methodically instigates these events to make the victim accept the implanted problem, becoming powerless and in need of the gaslighter's "protection" and "care." This gaslighting strategy crushes the resolve of the victim to protect themselves, while galvanizing a belief of powerlessness. It moves the victim into a state of desperation and hopelessness. At this point, they not only give up on their reality, but seek further comfort and protection from the person who is hurting them the most.

FIVE TYPES OF GASLIGHTERS

Although the following five types of gaslighters appear to be demonstrably different, they all utilize similar mind and behavior-control strategies. The gaslighter type does not determine the degree of harm perpetrated on an unsuspecting victim. Rather, it is determined by the level of depravity and sociopathy of the perpetrators and the degree of susceptibility, weakness, and psychological impairment of their victims.

Sociopathic/ASPD: the most criminal of the five types. They are naturals at gaslighting because of their diminished capacity for empathy, remorse, or regard for another person's welfare. The combination of their cunning con man abilities and complete absence of compassion makes them perfectly suited to choreograph every aspect of their meticulously manufactured selves/lives. Their gaslighting "dungeon" is nearly impossible to escape. True to their ASPD form, they can destroy a person's life inside and out, without guilt, and only stop if they are caught. Not hamstrung by culpability or cognitive dissonance (stress about bad deeds), they are unimpeded in the pursuit of dominance and control. As such, they prey on susceptible individuals who believe in their false altruism, affection, and promises of protection.

Bully Malignant Narcissist: an aggressive, menacing, and punitive persona. These gaslighters exploit their real story of being abused, maligned, and/or forgotten, and recast themselves as saviors or martyrs with heroic moments where they defeat their "enemies." More angry and outspoken than others, they flaunt their "stick it to the man" mentality, while reframing their campaign of harm and terror as necessary actions of a loyal and protecting person.

They play to codependents who are trapped by another narcissist's or group of narcissists' webs of coercion and deceit. Wearing this mask, they pose as the strong and aggressive protectorate who will rescue their codependent prey. Through their apparent idealism, strength, and professed courage, they befriend their victims. Their sociopathic abilities to do almost anything to attract victims and keep them ensnared may result in great harm to others.

This type of gaslighter prefers the shock-and-awe approach to mind control. They are unabashedly negative, critical, contemptuous, and controlling. The reality-bending and patient, manipulative exercises of the covert gaslighter wear down or compel their victim to comply. In contrast, the bully malignant narcissistic gaslighter forcibly shoves their victim into a mold, where they must find a way to fit.

Slippery Covert Narcissist: charismatic, charming, and considered quite likable. They are typically employed in positions where they flaunt their fabricated altruism, patience, and kindness, which earns them status, attention, and praise. Their best disguise is their professional role. They use subtle and undetectable forms of mind control, while maintaining complicated systems of deniability over their sociopathic-like manipulation of others. In their personal relationships, they are perceived as over-the-top concerned and doting caretakers. They perfectly play their savior role, engendering sympathy or respect from the unsuspecting people who have been fed their contrived narrative. If someone should attempt to take their mask off or reveal their true motives, there will be hell to pay! Gaslighters will do anything and everything to undermine or cast doubt on the person who attempts to reveal their true identity, reestablishing their altruistic reputation (re-gluing the mask to their face).[23]

"Wallpaper" Gaslighters: master manipulators who are painfully shy and expend a great deal of energy to avoid attention. They often have jobs that keep them out of the public eye and maintain a reclusive lifestyle. Described as the quiet, nice, and seemingly harmless neighbor who minded their own business and kept to themselves, unlike other pathological narcissists, they neither like nor want attention.

---

23 I wrote an article and produced a video on this topic. The article, "Unmasking Your Counterfeit Friend, The Covert Narcissist," is published on Huffington Post. The YouTube video is "When You Unmask a Covert Narcissist, RUN, But Quietly!"

In fact, they crave just the opposite. They go to great lengths to create and uphold their subterranean worlds. Like the ASPD and covert narcissist gaslighters, they are masters of invisibility. As "wallpaper" gaslighters, they are adept at blending into the background, while not making much of an impression on those they meet. However, behind the scenes, they are anything but meek and harmless. Like other gaslighters, they systematically manipulate their victims and the environment, so they gain complete control. The primary difference between this mask and the others is, when it is inadvertently removed, most people are in utter disbelief.

Reflections

- Have you ever been gaslit? When and how did you escape it?

- Do you know anyone who has been gaslit? If so, explain.

- Which of the personalities best fit a gaslighter you know?

Chapter Twelve

INTRODUCING THE CODEPENDENCY CURE™ AND SELF-LOVE RECOVERY™

THE JOURNEY IS JUST AS IMPORTANT AS THE DESTINATION

In writing the Human Magnet Syndrome books, my overriding goal was to provide explanatory and theoretical information about codependency, pathological narcissism, and their dysfunctional relationship "dance." I have stayed true to this goal, despite the multitude of desperate pleas from others to write about the solution or treatment of it.

Despite the obvious need for such information, especially since I have most of it developed already, I remained resolute in my mission to answer the critically important "what is this?" and "why me?" questions before addressing the "what do I do?" inquiries. As a reminder from an earlier chapter: codependents, and the mental health practitioners treating them, cannot overcome codependency *if they don't know what it is*. Moreover, if it's misunderstood, mislabeled, or confused with another problem, issue, and/or disorder, its treatment will surely have limited results or will fail altogether.

Now that this book is completed and the "whats" and "whys" have been answered, it is time to deliver on a promise I have made repeatedly since the 2013 publication of the first Human Magnet Syndrome book and my first seminar on the topic. In approximately six months from now (early summer 2018), I plan to begin writing my third book—the book that finally answers the ultimate question: *What do I do?* But first, I will take a much-needed break. This is necessary, not just for my own mental health, but also to organize the vast library of information I have gathered regarding my methods of treating codependency. I estimate my next book, which will most likely carry the title, *The Codependency Cure: Recovering from Self-Love Deficit Disorder,* will be published in the summer of 2019.

COMING SOON!

Please understand that the delay in publishing my next book does not mean I have not been working tirelessly on the material; nothing could be further from the truth. I have been developing, writing, and perfecting it for many years. Consider that I first provided psychotherapy services to a codependency client in 1988. Twenty-six years later, in 2014, I came full circle and provided educational seminars on codependency treatment as it relates to my Human Magnet Syndrome work. In addition, I have compiled 12 seminar videos (ranging from two to six hours each) focusing on various Codependency Cure related topics. These are available on my Self-Love Recovery Institute website.[24]

The Codependency Cure content, like my previous work, was fashioned from my own codependency recovery/psychotherapy blood, sweat, and tears; the vast contributions of the psychological and medical sciences; the generous support of coworkers, colleagues, and mentors; as well as the synergy of everything combined. My work is rooted in the medical and psychological disciplines, the bulk of which were inspired by many psychological theories. Although the collection of theories and techniques may seem divergent and contradictory, they are not. I have brought them together into a comprehensive psychotherapy/treatment theory that has enabled me to create a unified codependency treatment protocol. *The Codependency Cure*'s homegrown theories, explanations, and new definitions, as well as its treatment paradigm, are things of which I am quite proud.

MY WORK IS NOT ORIGINAL

I am not embarrassed to say the majority of what I write about is not original. Everything can be traced back to the brilliant contributions of great authors, theoreticians, researchers, and practitioners, all of whom have greatly influenced my own theoretical and practical work. If I am going to take credit, it would be for how I repackaged seemingly contradictory psychological and neurobiological theories into a simpler and more user-friendly codependency model. This model has provided relief to many people. I feel blessed and incredibly fortunate that the sum total of my life—"the good, the bad, and the ugly"—has merged into the creation of the Human Magnet Syndrome and Codependency Cure information. It seems like yesterday I was a dreamy idealistic 22-year-old psychology major at Towson State University, hell-bent on changing the world for the better. I couldn't be happier that I have made some headway toward this ambition.

THE CODEPENDENCY CURE AND SELF-LOVE RECOVERY

The mental health and addiction treatment communities have never completely agreed on the exact nature of codependency and how to effectively treat it. The mental health and addiction treatment communities have never completely agreed on the exact nature of codependency and how to effectively treat it. For this reason, and more, the mental health condition known as "codependency" has not been recognized in either the DSM-5 or ICD-10, the two most highly-regarded mental health diagnostic manuals.

Thirty-five years after the term "codependency" was first used in the mental health and addiction fields, it is even more ambiguous than when it was originally introduced. It is now a caricature of itself, barely recognizable from its alcohol abuse treatment origins. Despite the gallant efforts of many a learned and scholarly author, researcher, and educator, there is still no accepted and concretely defined codependency definition. It was my intention to create such a definition in my 2013 *The Human Magnet Syndrome*. Below is the simplest and clearest version of my HMS codependency definition:

> A problematic mental health and relationship condition that manifests in the chronic disparity of the distribution of love, respect, and care (LRC) in most emotionally and sexually intimate relationships. Despite the codepen-

dent chronic pattern of giving most, if not all, the LRC to the narcissistic takers, struggling emotionally with it, trying unsuccessfully to change it, and self-promises to end the relationship, they choose to continue the pattern. The absence of LRC equality is forever sacrificed so chronic core shame and pathological loneliness is kept a bay.

GOODBYE "CODEPENDENCY!" HELLO "SELF-LOVE!"

According to many of my clients, the word "codependency" is shame-inducing. With my recent Codependency Cure work, I have given this word a well-deserved "retirement." Although "codependency," or as some call it, "codependence," is the best word we had at that time, it has still (unintentionally) shamed and stigmatized three generations of sufferers. My new, updated terminology for this age-old problem and the development of techniques to treat it has modernized the mental health and substance abuse/addictions treatment fields, while giving hope to a new generation of chronically suffering "codependents."

DISCOVERING SELF-LOVE

Little did I know my quest to rename "codependency" would take me to New York City where, on June 2, 2015, I participated in a panel discussion with several well-respected members of the mental health community. Harville Hendrix, an international relationship and psychotherapy expert (and endorser of my English language books) is a personal hero of mine and I genuinely am thankful for the opportunity to learn from him during that event. Of the six panel members, I formed an immediate connection with Tracy B. Richards, a Canadian psychotherapist, artist, and wedding officiant. While my portion of the discussion consisted of the codependency, narcissism, and Human Magnet Syndrome concepts, Tracy's focused on the healing power of self-care, self-acceptance, and, most importantly, self-love. We instantly bonded while sharing a warm, synchronistic feeling of comfort and familiarity. It also seemed apparent our "children"—my Human Magnet Syndrome and her "Self-Love is the Answer"—fell in love at first sight.

Once back at work, I couldn't stop thinking about and referring to Tracy's thoughts on self-love. Over time, her simple, but elegant, ideas took up more and more real estate in my head. It was no surprise when her concepts began to crop up in both my personal efforts regarding my family-of-origin challenges and my codependency psychotherapy/treatment work. In no time, her theories found their way into my instructional articles and videos, as well as several of my seminars. The importance of Tracy's self-love concept to my already-formed theoretical and practical work on codependency treatment/recovery cannot be overstated. In fact, it would be the primary catalyst for my Codependency Cure and Self-Love Recovery material. The following statements illustrate the logic of my new self-love discoveries:

1. Codependency is impossible with Self-Love Abundance (SLA).
2. Codependents have significant deficits in self-love.
3. Childhood attachment trauma is the root cause for Self-Love Deficiency (SLD).
4. Self-Love Deficiencies are rooted in chronic loneliness, shame, and unresolved childhood trauma.
5. The fear of experiencing suppressed or repressed core shame and pathological loneliness convinces the codependent to stay in harmful relationships.
6. The elimination of Self-Love Deficit and the development of Self-Love Abundance are the primary goals of codependency treatment.

"CODEPENDENCY" NO MORE

Remaining true to my conviction to retire "codependency," I first needed to come up with a suitable replacement. I would not stop my search until I discovered a term that would describe the actual condition/experience, while not triggering a person to feel worse about themselves. My luck changed in the middle of August 2015, while writing an article on codependency. In it, I penned the phrase, "Self-Love is the Antidote to Codependency." Recognizing its simplicity and power, I created a meme, which I then posted on several social networking sites.

I could not have predicted the overwhelmingly positive reaction to my meme and its meaning, as it provoked deep and reflective discussions about how and why the lack of self-love was intrinsically connected to codependency. This was when I knew I was on to something big! Like other codependency-related discoveries, it would marinate in my mind before delivering its most important lesson—the follow-up epiphany.

My *eureka* self-love moment came to me almost two months later. While developing material for my new Codependency Cure seminar, I created a slide entitled "Self-Love Deficit is Codependency!" Once it was in print, I was carried away by a flood of exhilaration and anticipation. This is when I heard myself say, *Self-Love Deficit Disorder is Codependency!* I am not exaggerating when I say I almost fell out of my chair with excitement.

Instantly realizing the importance of this simple phrase, I immediately started including it in articles, blogs, YouTube videos, trainings, and with my psychotherapy clients. I was absolutely amazed at how many codependents, recovering or not, comfortably identified with it. I was consistently told how it helped people better understand their problem, without making them feel defective or "bad." About that time, I made a conscious decision to replace "codependency" with Self-Love Deficit Disorder. Despite it having many more syllables and making me tongue-tied numerous times, I was intent on carrying out my "codependency" retirement plans. Fast forward to one year later: tens of thousands of people, if not more, have embraced Self-Love Deficit Disorder as the new name for their condition. The consensus has been that Self-Love Deficit Disorder is not only an appropriate name for the condition, but it has also motivated people to want to solve it.

SLDD THE PROBLEM/SLD THE PERSON

In a matter of weeks, I decided to embark on a worldwide campaign to retire "codependency," while simultaneously building a broader awareness and acceptance for its replacement. I executed my plan through YouTube videos, articles, blogs, radio and TV interviews, professional trainings, and educational seminars. If there was an official codependency association, I would have besieged them with requests to allow me to replace it with the more appropriate term, Self-Love Deficit Disorder (SLDD), with the person being Self-Love Deficient (SLD). I am proud to say SLDD and SLD slowly seem to be catching on.

THE CODEPENDENCY CURE *IS SELF-LOVE ABUNDANCE*

As much as I do not approve of the use of negative words typically found in mental health diagnoses, I firmly believe "Deficit" in Self-Love Deficit Disorder is essential, as it specifies the problem for which treatment is needed. Unlike other disorders that require daily medication, once SLDD is successfully treated, *it's cured*—requiring neither subsequent treatment nor any worry about recurrence or relapse.

With the resolution of any disorder, I believe the diagnosis assigned to a person should be revoked, or replaced with another that indicates positive or improved mental health. This thought was inspired by my work with the Major Depression diagnosis, which shows no signs or symptoms once properly medicated. The same idea applies to SLDD: why hold onto that diagnosis? This line of thought inspired me to create a term representing the permanent resolution of SLDD—the Codependency Cure.

The next step was to create a name for SLDD treatment. In February 2017, I began to refer to such treatment as Self-Love Recovery (SLR), as it was a natural extension of my new self-love terminology. With the updated diagnostic terms for "codependency" in place, I began to revise my treatment-oriented material to accommodate them.

My renaming efforts spurred a wave of additional theoretical and treatment discoveries. In an effort to better explain my emerging theoretical and practical material of SLDD and SLR, I developed The Self-Love Deficit Disorder (SLDD) Pyramid. This pyramid clearly illustrates that codependency is not the primary problem requiring treatment. Rather, codependency is, and always has been, only a symptom of foundational pathological forces responsible for it. In this vein, the pyramid linearly and hierarchically represents the progression of the problem. Beginning with attachment trauma and continuing with core shame, pathological loneliness, codependency addiction, and finally, the symptom known as codependency, the SLDD

The Pyramids of Despair and Hope

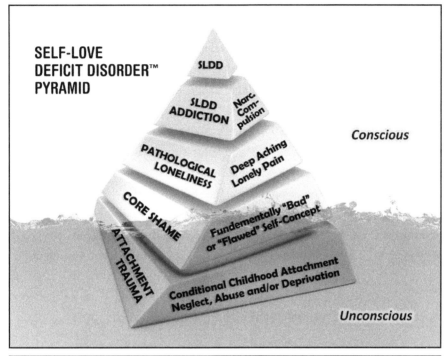

SELF-LOVE DEFICIT DISORDER™ PYRAMID

SLDD

SLDD ADDICTION

Narc-Com-pulsion

Conscious

PATHOLOGICAL LONELINESS

Deep Aching Lonely Pain

CORE SHAME

Fundamentally "Bad" or "Flawed" Self-Concept

ATTACHMENT TRAUMA

Conditional Childhood Attachment Neglect, Abuse and/or Deprivation

Unconscious

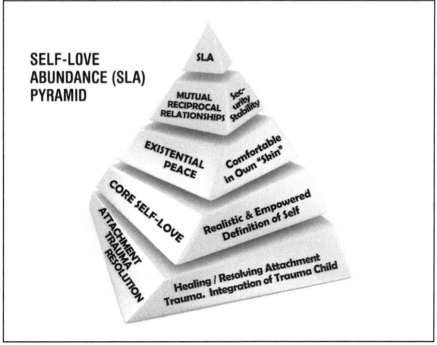

SELF-LOVE ABUNDANCE (SLA) PYRAMID

SLA

MUTUAL RECIPROCAL RELATIONSHIPS

Security Stability

EXISTENTIAL PEACE

Comfortable in Own "Skin"

CORE SELF-LOVE

Realistic & Empowered Definition of Self

ATTACHMENT TRAUMA RESOLUTION

Healing / Resolving Attachment Trauma, Integration of Trauma Child pyramid gives a 3D illustration of codependency, that is both clinically correct and intuitively accessible.

As much as the Pyramid demonstrates the levels of the hierarchical nature of SLDD, it also illustrates the path of its development. The lowest tier is Attachment Trauma, the root issue, which is responsible for causing core shame. This, in turn, creates pathological loneliness, which fuels the addictive need for a narcissist (SLDD Addiction), represented at the top of the Pyramid as a set of symptoms known as Self-Love Deficit Disorder (SLDD). The Pyramid represents that most SLDD treatment is focused *only* on the symptoms and not the underlying causes, some of which are unconscious/unknown to the client seeking help.

No doubt my yin-yang theoretical leanings influenced the creation of the subsequent Self-Love Abundance Pyramid. It communicates the Self-Love Recovery possibilities on which a suffering codependent could base their future goals. The power of this graphic was exponentiated when accompanied by my two favorite quotes:

"And the day came when the risk to remain tight in a bud
was more painful than the risk it took to blossom."—Anaïs Nin

"It is never too late to be what you might have been."—George Eliot

The two pyramids served to contrast the problem and its solution. Not only did the SLDD Pyramid explain the multidimensional nature of the problem, it did it in a way that struck an emotional chord. The Pyramid drives home the point that SLDD is an invisible and treatment-resistant addiction, a symptom of deeper, more foundational attachment trauma, which manifests the additional symptoms of core shame and pathological loneliness. These Pyramids serve to demarcate *a starting and finishing point* of the Self-Love Recovery/Codependency Cure treatment experience. It has been amazing and rewarding to observe how just two graphics can change a person's life.

ORGANIZING "THE CURE"

One of my more daunting challenges in developing the Cure was the organization of a wide array of divergent and eclectic explanations, theories, and treatment techniques into a coherent, logical, and intuitive treatment model. For the treatment to work and later be replicated, I needed the power of the SLDD and SLA Pyramids, coupled with an overarching scaffolding of sorts onto which I could sequentially organize my toolbox of Self-Love Recovery treatment techniques. This organizational structure would need to be dialectical in nature, as it would require the integration of seemingly dissimilar and contradictory psychological theories and practices, into a compelling, unified, linear, stage-based explanation of, and blueprint for, Self-Love Recovery. Most importantly, it would need to appeal and make sense to both a prospective client and the treating professional.

Like my other homegrown theoretical and real-world successes, it reflected how I made sense of the inner and outer workings of codependency. It would, therefore, also need to embrace the seemingly paradoxical nature of my SLDD/codependency treatment worldview: specific, measurable, behavioral, and direct, while retaining its free-flowing, analytical, and flexible characteristics. The first Three Stage Model was created shortly after the 2013 publication of my first book. One stage at a time, the treatment model advanced—keeping pace with my growing understanding of Self-Love Recovery. The following graphic depicts the Ten Stage Self-Love Recovery Model and represents the Codependency Cure's resolution of SLDD.

A LINEAR AND PROGRESSIVE PARADIGM

Like the Erikson Eight Stage Psychosocial Model described earlier in this book, my Ten Stage Model contains sequential beginning and ending points. Linear and progressive, they both require specific conditions and challenges be met and overcome before moving up. Completing each stage provides a person with the needed information and experience to be successful with the next stage's challenges. If a stage is not sufficiently mastered or is skipped, the person's mental and relational health will be compromised and attempts to succeed in the next stage will likely be unsuccessful. Achieving SLA requires each of the nine stages (SLA is Stage 10) to be successfully worked through, absorbed, and completed. Unfortunately, there are no shortcuts.

THE TEN STAGE MODEL OF SELF-LOVE RECOVERY TREATMENT

The following is a condensed introduction of each of the ten stages in my Self-Love Recovery Model. The length of time to complete the Ten Stage Self-Love Recovery Treatment process is between one and two years, depending on many variables.

10	Achieving Self-Love Abundance or Self-Love Recovery
9	Practicing & Enjoying Self-Love-Driven Relationships
8	Transitioning from SLDD to SLA— Self-Love Abundance
7	Resolving/Integrating Unconscious Trauma *Healing Attachment Trauma*
6	Maintaining Safe & Secure Boundaries
5	Setting Boundaries in a Hostile Environment
4	Preparing for the Narcissistic Storm *Mastering Power & Control Dynamics*
3	Understanding SLDD Addiction & Pathological Illness
2	Understanding the Human Magnet Syndrome—Relational Chemistry
1	Hitting Bottom: Introducing Hope

STAGE 1: HITTING BOTTOM

Introducing Hope

This is the moment in time when the cumulative damage of the Self-Love Deficient's painful and dysfunctional Human Magnet Syndrome fueled relationships with pathological narcissists becomes overwhelmingly evident. A lifetime of accumulated defeats has worn the SLD down and pushed them to the bottom of the sinkhole that has become their life. This is the "bottom," when the SLD realizes they can no longer stand up, much less live under the painful burden of their SLDD. Hitting the lowest point compels them to do something bold, uncomfortable, and hopeful: seek help to end their lifelong indentured servitude to the pathological narcissists in their life. This is when the SLD starts talking to trusted friends and/or a psychotherapist about their secret shame, loneliness, and pain. They come to understand the paradoxical nature of hitting bottom: the life-saving breaking point.

STAGE 2: HUMAN MAGNET SYNDROME EDUCATION
Breaking Free from the "Dance"

A massive amount of educational recovery material is introduced, most of which is included in this book. This is when people learn about the complicated forces that shaped their SLDD and those that maintain it. Stage 2 requires a "schooling" on pathological narcissism and narcissistic abuse, including gaslighting, and the other overt and covert manipulative strategies their pathological narcissists employ to keep them powerless to leave the damaging relationships. The education begins with both Pyramids and then the Ten Stage Self-Love Recovery Treatment process is presented. Crucial discussions occur regarding the "birth" of their SLDD and how and why attachment trauma, core shame, and pathological loneliness are its core elements. Addressing and breaking down denial systems are critical to this stage. The diverse topics relating to the Human Magnet Syndrome are discussed, processed, and discussed again. Lastly, the transgenerational nature of the Human Magnet Syndrome is explored, and discoveries are made about their family tree and its long history of "infection" with codependency and narcissism.

STAGE 3: WITHDRAWING FROM SLDD ADDICTION
Battling Pathological Loneliness

In this stage, the SLDD Addiction concept is discussed, processed, and mastered. Only with a complete understanding of the addiction, its origins, its withdrawal symptoms, and the impossible-seeming odds of overcoming it can a person be prepared to begin the process. The concepts of pathological loneliness and core shame are important discussion points, as both are primary conditions to the secondary addiction. The concept of pathological loneliness—SLDD Addiction's most potent and treatment-resistant withdrawal symptom—is studied, broken down, and eventually understood. The simultaneous use of a 12 Step Program is suggested, while its structure, tenets, and philosophy are discussed.

During this time, intimate relationships, including casual sex, are prohibited. Making progress in fighting the SLDD Addiction is impossible if the SLD believes they are healthy enough to spot narcissists and take periodic tastes of their addictive drug. It should be noted that "selling" this rule is quite challenging for even the best psychotherapist, which is why having an addiction or substance abuse background is advantageous.

STAGE 4: PREPARING FOR THE NARCISSISTIC STORM

This stage was conceived in reaction to the dangerous and difficult nature of Stage 5. Like Stage 2, this is an educational phase when the SLD delves deeply into their pathological narcissist's strategies. Here, concepts like gaslighting; triangulation; parental alienation; and power, control, and domination strategies are deconstructed. "Predictive awareness" is this stage's most important concept. It is defined as the ability to accurately predict how the pathological narcissist will react when boundaries are put into place. Such a skill set requires the recovering SLD to learn a great deal of information about their SLDD, their partner's narcissism, and how the two have always interacted.

For the sake of safety and the long-term viability of SLDD recovery, SLDs are taught the interactional mechanics and consequences of placing boundaries on narcissists. The Observe, Don't Absorb (ODA) Technique enables SLDs to safely disconnect from and set boundaries with their pathological narcissists. ODA is a set of defensive tools and strategies that is effective in neutralizing the pathological narcissist's tactics, while not engaging them in any form of a fight. ODA is proven to work, as I developed it to overcome the harm of pathological narcissists in my personal life. My clients tell me of its positive impact on their recovery, and my YouTube ODA videos have been viewed over 600,000 times.

STAGE 5: SETTING BOUNDARIES IN A HOSTILE ENVIRONMENT
Courage and Commitment

This is the stage in which the SLD implements well-planned boundaries that are intended to ensure their safety and/or to break free from their narcissistic partner's control and domination of their life. As a direct result of the lessons learned in the previous stage, they are well prepared for the potentially harmful and dangerous reactions of the angered and, more than likely, agitated narcissist.

Since being "forewarned is forearmed," this stage includes my "Surgeon General's Warning," which prepares SLDs for the pathological narcissist's angry and retaliatory reactions to their newfound boundary-setting abilities. The primary focus of this stage is to safely and strategically set and maintain boundaries with the pathological narcissist. During this "earthquake" stage, the SLD's behavioral changes cause seismic shifts in their relationship with the pathological narcissist. With the help of a qualified, trained, and experienced psychotherapist, the SLD metaphorically peels the pathological narcissist's fingers away from their throat. One boundary at a time, the SLD begins to insulate and protect themselves. This is when the SLD experiences, some for the first time, the taste of self-respect and hope.

This tumultuous stage feels particularly unsafe due to the predictable withdrawal symptom of pathological loneliness. The aching and persistent loneliness is the bane of every SLD and will seem like an impossible habit to break. Involvement in a 12 Step program is especially important at this time.

During Stage 5's upheaval, the SLD either terminates their relationship with the pathological narcissist or the narcissist abandons ship. In either case, Stage 5 leaves few-to-no pathological narcissists "standing," except those to whom the SLD has little choice but to remain connected, such as an elderly parent or a husband who controls the finances. To all who survive the SLD's process and remain in the SLD's inner circle, their message is clearly delivered: "There's a new sheriff in town, one who is going to get rid of all pathological narcissist outlaws."

STAGE 6: MAINTAINING SAFE AND SECURE BOUNDARIES
Protection, Security, and Self-Care

Stage 6 begins in the rubble of the earthquake-affected vicinity, where SLDs decide the fate of the remaining buildings: demolish them or ensure they are brought up to code. In less metaphorical terms, the more empowered and confident SLDs choose to either terminate the relationship with the lingering narcissist or require them to follow the new boundaries and rules. In the case of loved ones with whom terminating the harmful situations/relationships is not an option, the usefulness of ODA is reinforced. They learn how to manage boundary intrusions or breaches, as some pathological narcissists do not give up easily. To maintain the boundaries, recovering SLDs may need to establish a no-pathological-narcissist-contact rule.

STAGE 7: RESOLVING/INTEGRATING UNCONSCIOUS TRAUMA
Healing Attachment Trauma

Resolving the unconscious attachment trauma requires the SLD to dredge up long-forgotten suppressed and repressed memories and core shame. Attachment trauma is the foundational cause of SLDD, and its resolution the basis of SLA. This knowledge is important to all the work in the preceding stages. The challenge of the resolution, however, is it should only be facilitated by an appropriately qualified, trained, and experienced trauma psychotherapist. I highly recommend my Healing the Inner Trauma Child psychotherapy method, which I present and explain in a four-hour training video.[25]

Through the trauma-based psychotherapy work, the SLD's unconscious/forgotten attachment trauma and core shame is first safely exhumed. These are transformed into memories that are acceptable and conscious, but painful and sad. The goal is to acknowledge, share, process, and integrate these memories and feelings into the SLD's conscious self. The aim is also to integrate the unconscious forgotten attachment trauma and core shame, which is the invisible glue that has kept the SLD perpetually attached to a familiar, albeit dysfunctional, self-image. This is a seemingly miraculous stage: when it is accomplished, the burden of the repressed attachment trauma is lifted, allowing the client to see the SLA light at the end of the tunnel.

STAGE 8: DISCOVERING SELF-LOVE

Building an Internal Self-Love Foundation

If SLA is a house where the SLD plans to enjoy the rest of their life, its groundwork must be sturdy and resilient. This is when they create and fortify the foundation. The "seeds" planted in the previous stages begin to bear fruit in Stage 8. This stage is my personal favorite because the radiant side of SLA begins to poke through the formerly dark and opaque SLDD clouds.

Now that boundaries are intractably set and the SLD is experiencing greater levels of safety, glimmers of self-love begin to appear. They finally begin to "fall in love" with themselves. They are no longer held captive by their former distorted thought patterns. They have learned to understand self-love is not only far from selfish, but is also the best gift they could ever give themselves. By this time, pathological loneliness and SLDD Addiction have been permanently eradicated. The smiling, self-loving person is a far cry from the lonely, shame-based, and broken person of the past. Often, these clients experience what I call "the infectious nature of self-love." Because it feels so good, it spreads quickly and completely to other areas of their life.

---

25 Available at www.SelfLoveRecovery.com, Self-Love Recovery Institute's online store.

STAGE 9: BUILDING AN EXTERNAL FOUNDATION OF SELF-LOVE
Achieving Self-Love Driven Relationships.

Stage 9 is the experimentation stage where the intimate relationship and sex prohibition is finally lifted. Believe it or not, by this stage, the craving of intimacy for the purpose of taking pain away has disappeared. The reverse is actually the case: a feeling of nervous energy is experienced about bringing someone new into their highly-guarded romantic circle. Like learning to ride a bicycle, the excitement of being independent and mobile is often tempered by occasional falls and skinned knees.

Armed with a rock-solid foundation of self-love, this person is encouraged to invite visitors into their newly-constructed home and test their new set of emotional and relational skills and abilities. Mistakes are inevitable in this stage, as most emerging SLAs have little-to-no previous frame of reference with a self-love-driven relationship. Learning, mastering, and practicing healthy emotional and physical intimacy is both extraordinarily frightening and exciting. This is when they realize sex is an act of unconditional love, respect, and intimate caring that has the capacity to synergistically bond two self-loving partners in a long-term healthy and lasting relationship.

At this time, SLAs are encouraged to expand their social network, while more deeply connecting to current and new friends. By the end of Stage 9, the emerging SLA has permanently become courageously, but safely, vulnerable, resilient, emotionally connected, and a self-loving friend and/or lover. This is when the 1 + 1 = 2 Relationship Math equation finally makes the most sense.

STAGE 10: BECOMING SELF-LOVE ABUNDANT

Once at Stage 10, the newly transformed SLA will have created a personal and relational identity infused with strength, empowerment, and, of course, self-love. One taste of self-love and they will acquire a lifelong appetite for it. The SLA will never again subject themselves to the bitter poison their former pathological narcissists fed them. They will protect their newfound emotional freedom and self-love at all costs. When being suffocated, the SLA will fight back with every ounce of energy they can muster to guard against compromising their newly discovered self-love.

Just as the attachment trauma was the rock-solid SLDD, SLA is the beautiful mansion where one permanently resides. With the resolution of attachment trauma and core shame, the SLA is more capable of experiencing existential peace, which goes hand-in-hand with deeper and more meaningful spiritual experiences. This is when psychotherapy/treatment is no longer necessary and the Codependency Cure has been achieved.

SLDD recovery is a frightening and even risky proposition, as the path to SLA—the Codependency Cure—is strewn with obstacles and painful experiences. The difficulty of the first five stages is sure to make the faint of heart run for the hills, but if the recovering SLD perseveres, the payoff will be beyond compare.

THE TEN SELF-LOVE ABUNDANCE PROMISES

1. The identification and understanding of SLDD's root causes.
2. The resolution of long-buried attachment trauma.
3. The neutralization of septic levels of core shame.
4. The eradication of pathological loneliness, SLDD's insidious withdrawal symptom.
5. An ability to sustain SLDD Addiction recovery.
6. The end of the need to self-medicate vis-à-vis the Human Magnet Syndrome.
7. The shifting of attraction or chemistry patterns towards self-loving individuals.
8. The emergence of a reflexive repulsion response when in the company of pathological narcissists.
9. The emergence of existential peace—the ability to feel whole and happy just because you are yourself.
10. The permanent transformation to SLA and the permanent disappearance of SLDD.

Reflections

- What is the single biggest obstacle that keeps you most connected to SLDD?

- Write a paragraph or more about your future self for each of the SLA Pyramid levels.

Chapter Thirteen

YOUR LIFE BEGINS NOW

This book has fulfilled its purpose if the container in which your Self-Love Deficit Disorder (SLDD) denial, that had been hermetically sealed, has now been cracked open. It has succeeded if you better comprehend the inner workings of SLDD and its addictive compulsion to run away from loneliness and core shame, while running toward a dangerous source of comfort. And, if you are now aware of how and why your inner human magnet tethers you to pathological narcissists —who once seemed familiar and safe, but later siphoned off your emotional life source—I have achieved my mission to educate and protect.

I am sure this book has exposed some enlightening, but shocking, truths that have more than likely caused a great deal of sadness, anger, regret, and anxiety. It would be completely justifiable if you are not ready to absorb them. Learning about the ravages of SLDD, with its deep-seated nature and the uphill battle that will be required to overcome it, may have triggered a sense of insecurity or even despair. Unfortunately, there is no other way to begin your recovery.

Despite the absence of shortcuts, rest assured there is most definitely hope. The emotional ledge on which you precariously teeter will soon transform into a stable, albeit shaky, foundation, upon which your developing Self-Love Abundance (SLA) will rest. I don't blame you if you are wary of my pronouncement, or if you simply don't trust it. It is, without a doubt, a scary proposition.

THE FAKE PHOTO ON THE MIRROR TRICK

Your narcissist's perception of you has always been skewed to their liking or, even worse, to their need. If they recognize and verbally affirm your beauty, they will more than likely claim it as another of their own well-deserved and highly coveted trophies. Your "claimed" beauty became their prized compliment-inducing possession that, at best, would make them temporarily happy with themselves.

It is time you become aware of the gaslighter's primary tricks of the trade. This has been used to turn you against yourself, all the while keeping you under their thumb. They knew if you saw your true and natural inner beauty, the resulting self-esteem and self-love would foil their diabolical plans to achieve control over you. Little did you know that, early in your relationship, they swapped out your psychological mirror with one that had a "fake photo" glued to it.

It is the sad truth that the pathetic and unlovable person in the mirror, who you have always identified with, *was never even you!* The image you have mistakenly, but understandably, believed was the real you had been doctored to reflect only the narcissist's implanted narrative. It is time for you to hear the truth, and please hear it clearly: the person you always hoped you were *actually exists!* The reflection you see, which you regularly look at with disgust, disappointment, and shame is not, and never was, you! In fact, it isn't even a real reflection at all.

The gaslighter's insatiable need to be the most beautiful person in your world has resulted in their calculated decision to commandeer your "mirrors." They have always been threatened by your inner and outer beauty because it is in direct opposition to the despicable image of themselves their personality-disordered mind conveniently removed from their conscious mind. Hence, they gaslit you into accepting the shamefully ugly photo version of you in place of your mirror's honest and accurate reflection. Through the despicable fake photo on the mirror trick, they have effectively contorted your face into unflattering proportions or reduced it to a collection of hard-to-look-at imperfections.

An important step toward SLA requires you to metaphorically throw away that hijacked, broken mirror and invest in one that accurately reflects your perfectly imperfect, beautiful self. It might take time to recognize the excellence in what you see; take as much as you need—and more. Anything as good as Self-Love Abundance is worth the difficult healing and recovery work, and the time necessary to reach it.

I want you to step up to your nearest mirror. Once in front of it, recite the following statements:

- The reflection I see is 100% true; it is all me.
- I will allow myself to see what my true reflection is and withhold any judgment of it.
- I verify and accept this imperfect reflection as my true (and accurate) self.
- If my mirror should reflect a not-good-enough or shameful image, I will reject it, walk away, and shake the narcissist's gaslit photo out of my head.
- When I am ready, I will return to my mirror and absorb the reflection—without judgment.
- I will allow myself to gaze upon unrecognized and unappreciated perfection and, maybe for the first time, see the person I always was, but was never allowed to see.
- I will allow myself to consider I am, and always was, beautiful.
- I will learn to love myself, as I need it more than anything.

DROP THE BATON!

We must end the global blight of Self-Love Deficit Disorder, if not for ourselves, then for our children and their children's children. You, as a husband or wife, sister or brother, friend, or, for that matter, simply as a concerned member of mankind, should consider joining my crusade of stamping out this crippling disorder and becoming a part of the worldwide self-loving fraternity.

I beseech you to let go of your codependency baton, hang up your running cleats, and confidently and gracefully walk away from your family's long line of winning, but losing, track stars. The price you will pay if you stay on your family's team will come at too high of a cost. Please trust me on this. I know.

The path to the Codependency Cure and Self-Love Abundance is a rocky one, to be sure. It will be strewn with obstacles over which you will likely trip. You will probably fall, get hurt, and not want to get up again. It is neither a short nor an easy road to travel, but as I am sure you have heard many times before, *it is not the journey, but the destination.* As noted, expect to make a one-to-two-year commitment to complete the journey. This might seem like a long time. However, if you consider the combination of the dysfunctional forces responsible for your SLDD, and the percentage of your life you have already been encumbered by it, you will see how patience and perseverance will get you where you need to be—sooner than you can imagine. And the payoff will be more than you could conceive.

Be prepared. Something as good as SLA is going to ruffle some feathers. The bird that learns to fly again, after having its wings clipped, will compel its captor to want to return it to its cage. If you resist their efforts to force you back inside the cage, they will likely double down on methods that originally worked to bring you into compliance. And try they will. The math is simple: there will be an equal ratio between your attempts to escape and their countermeasures to re-clip your wings. Remember that. This will be the fight of a lifetime; it will not be easy, and there will be painful, but surmountable, consequences.

As each component of your gaslit self is dismantled, you will reacquaint yourself with your real self and others-narrative. Despite not always being happy or positive, they will no longer point downward to the shameful abyss where SLDD resides, but rather in the direction of the sky, where your self-loving future can be found.

What would you say if I told you that you always held all the winning cards in your hand, but never knew it? Now that narcissists are no longer choreographing your reality, you can finally be what you were always meant to be.

Often, the toughest journeys are the ones that have the biggest payoffs. Although my dad taught me little about self-love, every so often he accidentally passed on tidbits of wisdom. He used to say, "there is no such thing as a free lunch." Regarding your fight for SLA, he was spot on. This "lunch" will be expensive, but believe me when I tell you it will be worth all the time and energy you "spend" on it.

MY SURGEON GENERAL'S WARNING

If I were the Surgeon General of the U.S., I would post the following warning where everyone could see it. Unlike warnings posted on cigarette packs and bottles of wine, this one would warn about the potential dangers of what will happen if you don't do something to rectify your current SLDD, as well as warn you of the pain that will occur when you do. Knowledge is power, and power is paramount for the uphill battle to get the monkey off your back and join the community of self-loving people.

SURGEON GENERAL WARNING:
Ceasing one's Codependency/Self-Love Deficit Disorder will result in abnormally high rates of conflict, disapproval and heartbreak. Other risks include rejection and abandonment as well as a loss of so-called loving, supportive and loyal friends and loved ones. Anticipate at least six-months of debilitating core shame, self-doubt and pathological loneliness.

THE WILL TO SURVIVE

When my wife and I recently visited Alaska, one of our stopping points on a bus tour was a section of the Alaskan Tundra. In the area where we stood, a group of trees were malformed, crooked and not very tall. Our tour guide explained that the fact they existed at all was a miracle of nature. He went on to say that, for eight months of the year, a 15-foot pile of dense snow completely covers these trees. The tour guide assured us that, like clockwork, these trees bounce back every incredibly short summer. I was awed by how evolution and these trees partnered up to create a winning survival strategy.

In that moment, my mind's eye conjured up a panoramic view of a completely white and barren landscape. I reflected on the tremendous physical strain the compacted snow had on these fragile trees. I was fascinated by the idea that they could survive, year after year, on only a little bit of sunshine and warmth. My mind wandered to the human version of surviving in such a tundra. This is when I drew a parallel between these trees and the lives of many recovering SLDs with whom I have worked. Despite no apparent way out of their misery, with very little sustenance and against all odds, both the Alaskan trees and these SLDs never stop trying to survive the harsh "elements."

Many of my clients, and perhaps you, have simply had enough of being buried underneath a proverbial 15-foot mountain of snow. Now is as good a time as any to get out your shovel and start digging your way to the surface. Begin your much-deserved and perpetually delayed plans of moving upward where the sun and warmth will help you grow into the person of your dreams.

THE TAPESTRY I CALL MY LIFE

Writing this book required me to step back and inspect the tapestry in which my life's story is woven. Despite the tears, snags, and frayed edges, I am proud to report it is beautiful. I have come to realize its beauty is determined not by size, color, pattern, textile, or the way it was fashioned. Instead, the sum of its parts and the history behind it make it a treasured work of art. Like it or not, all my life's events, from the debilitating shame of my second divorce to the miraculous joy of the birth of my only son, Benjamin, were meticulously intertwined. The tapestry will always be a living, breathing representation of where I come from, what I became, and where I wish to go. From this cherished piece of historical art—

my life—I was able to extract the lessons contained in this book. But I didn't do it alone.

MY CODEPENDENT GUARDIAN ANGELS

The events that created my tapestry were neither haphazard nor coincidental. Rather, they were fastidiously organized and facilitated by a conspiring group of *codependent guardian angels*—namely, my mom, Mikki Rosenberg, her father, Grandpa Chuck, and my Dad's mother, Grandma Molly. I believe all three found solace and a sense of divine purpose by arranging the dominoes of my life, so when they did fall, they would move me in the direction in which I most needed to go.

These sweet angels never experienced the joy and freedom of self-love abundance; they took their attachment trauma, core shame, and loneliness to their graves. I sincerely believe they have been assigned "heavenly" duties to spread the self-love gospel though the earthbound emissaries they influence and guide. Because I am one, I consider myself the most fortunate person in the world.

I cannot count how many times an insight, discovery, or random life-changing thought appeared to come out of nowhere. Because of my sensitivity and openness to spiritual phenomena, I recognize these are messages from my lead guardian angel, my mom, saying she is proud of me, and I am not alone. Thanks to the heavens and the undying flame that has refused to be snuffed out, I have come to realize the dream I've had since I was a young man. I am hopeful my miracle can also be yours.

Thank you, Mom, Grandpa Chuck, and Grandma Molly.

Reflections

- What is the single most important reason you need to "drop the baton"?

- What will be the family repercussions when you drop it?

- Do you have any experiences with unexplainable phenomena, such as a guardian angel?

ABOUT THE AUTHOR

ROSS ROSENBERG is the owner of Clinical Care Consultants, a multi-location Chicago-area-based counseling center, and the Self-Love Recovery Institute, a self-help training and professional development company. He has been a psychotherapist for almost 30 years and is considered an international expert on narcissism, codependency, trauma, and sex addiction. His YouTube channel, which  has garnered 7.1 million views/70,000 subscribers (at the time of this writing), has resulted in global recognition of his work.

Ross's first edition of *The Human Magnet Syndrome: Why We Love People Who Hurt Us*, sold over 50,000 copies and is considered a staple in most codependency treatment and recovery circles.

Ross is an internationally renowned seminar leader and has made presentations in 29 U.S. states, Amsterdam, and London. He's been regularly featured on national TV and radio shows, and blogs/writes for prominent online publications.

GLOSSARY OF TERMS

AA: Alcoholics Anonymous

ASPD: Antisocial Personality Disorder

BPD: Borderline Personality Disorder

CODA: Codependents Anonymous

COS: Continuum of Self

CSV: Continuum of Self Values

HMS: Human Magnet Syndrome

LO: Limerent Object

LRC: Love, Respect, and Care

NAS: Narcissistic Abuse Syndrome

NPD: Narcissistic Personality Disorder

OCD: Obsessive-Compulsive Disorder

ODA: Observe, Don't Absorb

ORO: Others-Relationship Orientation

RCC: Relationship Compatibility Continuum

RCT: Relationship Compatibility Theory

RO: Relationship Orientations

SLA: Self-Love Abundance

SLD: Self-Love Deficient

SLDD: Self-Love Deficit Disorder

SLR: Self-Love Recovery

SRO: Self-Relationship Orientation

BIBLIOGRAPHY

Ainsworth, M. D. S. (1973). "The Development of Infant-Mother Attachment." In B. Cardwell & H. Ricciuti (Eds.), *Review of Child Development Research* (Vol. 3, pp. 1-94). Chicago: University of Chicago Press.

Al-Alem, L., and Omar, H. A. (2008). "Borderline Personality Disorder: An Overview of History, Diagnosis and Treatment in Adolescents." Pharmacology and Nutritional Sciences Faculty Publications.

American Psychiatric Association. (2013). *Diagnostic and Statistical Manual of Mental Disorders* (5th ed.). Arlington, VA: Author.

American Psychiatric Association (2000). *Diagnostic and Statistical Manual of Mental Disorders DSM-IV (text review)*. Washington, DC: Author.

Anthenelli, R. M., Smith, T.L., Irwin, M.R., and Schuckit, M.A. (1994). "A Comparative Study of Criteria for Subgrouping Alcoholics: The Primary/ Secondary Diagnostic Scheme versus Variations of the Type 1/Type 2 Criteria." *American Journal of Psychiatry*, 151(10), 1468-1474.

Author Unknown. (2017). "All About Attachment." *Psychology Today* Website: https://www.psychologytoday.com/basics/attachment

Author Unknown. (2010). "The Pew Charitable Trust's Research & Analysis: The Impact of the September 2008 Economic Collapse." Philadelphia, PA: Pew Charitable Trust.

Beattie, M. (1986). *Codependent No More: How to Stop Controlling Others and Start Caring for Yourself* (2nd ed.). Center City, MN: Hazelden.

Belden, R. (1990). *Iron Man Family Outing: Poems about Transition into a More Conscious Manhood.* Austin, TX: Author.

Berk, M., Grosjean, B., and Warnick, H. (2009). "Beyond Threats: Risk Factors or Suicide Completion in Borderline Personality Disorder." *Current Psychiatry*, 8(5): 32–41.

Boeree, C. (2006). "Personality Theories: Erik Erikson 1902–1994." Retrieved from: http://webspace.ship.edu/cgboer/erikson.html

Bowlby, J. (1969, 1983). *Attachment: Attachment and Loss, Vol. 1* (1-2 ed.). New York, NY: Basic Books.

Cadoret, R. J., Troughton, E., and Widmer, R. (1984). "Clinical Differences between Antisocial and Primary Alcoholics." *Comprehensive Psychiatry*, 25: 1–8.

Clark, J. and Stoffel, V.C. (1992). "Assessment of Codependency Behavior in Two Health Student Groups." *American Journal of Occupational Therapy,* 46(9): 821–828.

Co-Dependents Anonymous (2010). "Patterns and Characteristics of Codependence." Retrieved from: http://coda.org/index.cfm/newcomers/patterns-and-characteristics-of-codependence/

Colović N, Leković D, Gotić M. (2016). "Treatment by Bloodletting In The Past And Present." *Srpski Arhiv Za Celokupno Lekarstvo.* 2016, Mar–Apr: 144(3-4): 240–8.

Davis, A. and Appel, T. (2010). "Bloodletting Instruments in the National Museum of History and Technology." *Smithsonian Studies in History and Technology*; no. 41

Dougherty, M. (2017). "Why are We Getting Taller as a Species?" *Scientific American*.

Elwood J. M., Little, J., and Elwood, J. H. (1992). *Epidemiology and Control of Neural Tube Defects*. New York, NY: Oxford University Press.

Erikson, E. H. (1950). *Childhood and Society*. New York, NY: Norton.

Fazel, S., and Danesh, J. (2002). "Serious Mental Disorder in 23,000 Prisoners: A Systematic Review of 62 Surveys." *The Lancet*, 359: 545–550.

Friel, J., and Friel L., (1986). *Adult Children Secrets of Dysfunctional Families: The Secrets of Dysfunctional Families*. Deerfield Beach, FL: HCI.

Greenstone, G. (2010). "The History of Bloodletting." *British Columbia Medical Journal*. Vol. 52, No. 1, January–February 2010, p.12–14, Premise.

Hare, R. D. (1996). Psychopathy: A Clinical Construct Whose Time Has Come. *Criminal Justice & Behavior*, 23(1): 25–54.

Hare, R. D. (1993). *Without Conscience: The Disturbing World of Psychopaths among Us*. New York, NY: Pocket Books.

Harlow, H. F. (1962). "Development of Affection in Primates." In E. L. Bliss (Ed.), *Roots of Behavior* (pp. 157-166). New York, NY: HarperCollins.

Hazan, C., and Shaver, P. (1987). "Romantic Love Conceptualized as an Attachment Process." *Journal of Personality and Social Psychology*, 52(3): 511–524.

Insel, T. (2010). *What's in a Name? The Outlook for Borderline Personality Disorder*. National Institute of Mental Health. Retrieved from: nimh.nih.gov/about/directors/thomas-insel/blog/2010/

Johnson, S. (2012). *Therapist's Guide to Pediatric Affect and Behavior Regulation (Practical Resources for the Mental Health Professional)*. Academic Press.

Kelley, D., and Kelley, T. (2006). *Alcoholic Relationship Survival Guide: What to Do When You Don't Know What to Do*. Port Charlotte, FL: Kelley Training Systems.

Kellogg, T., and Harrison-Davis, M. (1983). *Broken Toys, Broken Dreams: Understanding and Healing Boundaries, Codependence, Compulsion and Family Relationships*. New York, NY: Bratt Publishing.

Kernberg, O. (1984). *Severe Personality Disorders*. New Haven, CT: Yale University Press.

Keys, D. (2012). *Narcissists Exposed—75 Things Narcissists Don't Want You to Know*. Washington, DC: Light's House Publishing.

Kreisman, J., and Straus, H. (2010). *I Hate You—Don't Leave Me: Understanding the Borderline Personality*. New York, NY: Perigree Trade.

Kulkarni, J. (2015). "Borderline Personality Disorder is a Hurtful Label for Real Suffering—Time We Changed It." Retrieved from: https://theconversation.com/borderline-personality-disorder-is-a-hurtful-label-for-real-suffering-time-we-changed-it-41760

Laign, J. (1989). *A Patient Poll. Focus on the Family and Chemical Dependency*, p.16.

Lasch, C. (1991). *The Culture of Narcissism: American life in an Age of Diminishing Expectations* (Rev. ed.) New York, NY: W.W. Norton & Company.

Layton, J. (2017). "How Brainwashing Works." https://science.howstuffworks.com/life/inside-the-mind/human-brain/brainwashing1.htm

Lenzenweger, M., Lane, M., Loranger, A., and Kessler, R. (2007). "DSM-IV Personality Disorders in the National Comorbidity Survey Replication." *Biological Psychiatry*, 62(6): 553–64.

Lewis, C. E., Cloninger, C. R., and Pais, J. (1983). "Alcoholism, Antisocial Personality and Drug Use in a Criminal Population." *Alcohol and Alcoholism*, 18: 53–60.

Lifton, R. (1963). *Thought Reform and the Psychology of Totalism*. New York, NY: W.W. Norton & Co.

Linehan, M. (1993). *Cognitive-Behavioral Treatment of Borderline Personality Disorder*. New York, NY: Guilford Press.

Lydon, J. E., Jamieson, D. W., and Zanna, M. P. (1988). "Interpersonal Similarity and the Social and Intellectual Dimensions of First Impressions." *Social Cognition*, 6(4): 269–286.

Maccoby, M. (2004). *Narcissistic Leaders: The Incredible Pros, the Inevitable Cons*. Watertown, MA: Harvard Business Review.

Malmquist, C.A. (2006). *Homicide: A Psychiatric Perspective*. Washington, DC: American Psychiatric Publishing, Inc.

Marsh, E., and Wolfe, D. (2008). *Abnormal Child Psychology* (4th ed.). Independence, KY: Wadsworth Publishing.

Maslow, A. (1966). *The Psychology of Science: A Reconnaissance*. New York, NY: Harper & Row.

Miller, A. (1979). *The Drama of the Gifted Child: The Search for the True Self*. New York, NY: Basic Books.

Mosely, M. (2012). "Why is There Only One Human Species?" BBC. http://www.bbc.com/news/science-environment-13874671

National Alliance of Mental Illness (NAMI). (2017). *Borderline Personality Disorder*. Retrieved from: https://www.nami.org/Learn-More/Mental-Health-Conditions/Borderline-Personality-Disorder

Nordqvist, C. (2012, February 24). "What is Borderline Personality Disorder (BPD)?" Retrieved from: http://www.medicalnewstoday.com/articles/9670.php (on March 14, 2012)

Oliver, D. (2004-2012). "Antisocial Personality Disorder (APD)?" Retrieved from: http://www.bipolarcentral.com/other illnesses/apd.php (on December 10, 2012)

Orwell, G. (1949). *1984*. New York, NY: Penguin.

Payson, E. (2002). *The Wizard of Oz and Other Narcissists*. Royal Oak, MI: Julian Day Publications.

Perry, S. (2003). *Loving in Flow: How the Happiest Couples Get and Stay that Way*. Naperville, IL: Sourcebooks, Inc.

Porr, V. (2001). "How Advocacy is Bringing Borderline Personality Disorder into the Light: Advocacy Issues." Retrieved from: http://www.tara4bpd.org/how-advocacy-is-bringing-borderline-personality-disorder-into-the-light/ (on December 4, 2012)

Prabhakar, K. (2006). *Proceedings of the Third AIMS International Conference on Management: An Analytical Study on Assessing Human Competencies Based on Tests*. January 1–4, 2006. Ahmedabad: Indian Institute of Management.

Riggio, O., et al. (2015). "Management of Hepatic Encephalopathy as an Inpatient." *Clinical Liver Disease Journal*, 5(3): 79–82.

Schulze, L., et al. (2013). "Gray Matter Abnormalities in Patients with Narcissistic Personality Disorder." *Journal of Psychiatric Research*. Retrieved from: http://dx.doi.org/10.1016/j.jpsychires.2013.05.017

Science Learning Hub. (2009). "Light and Telescopes." http://www.sciencelearn.org.nz/resources/1625-light-and-telescopes

Shearer, E., and Gottfried, J. (2017). *News Use Across Social Media Platforms 2017*. Pew Research Website: http://www.journalism.org/2017/09/07/news-use-across-social-media-platforms-2017/

Shepherd, T. and Linn, D. (2014). *Behavior and Classroom Management in the Multicultural Classroom: Proactive, Active, and Reactive Strategies.* Thousand Oaks, CA: Sage Publications.

Singleton, N., Meltzer, H., and Gatward, R. (1998). Office of National Statistics Survey of Psychiatric Morbidity.

Substance Abuse and Mental Health Services Administration. (2011). "Report to Congress on Borderline Personality Disorder." HHS Publication No: SMA11-4644.

Tennov, D. (1999). *Love and Limerence.* Lanham, MD: Scarborough House.

Tottenham, N., et al. (2010). "Prolonged Institutional Rearing is Associated with Atypically Large Amygdala Volume and Difficulties in Emotion Regulation." *Developmental Science*, 3(1): 46–61.

Watts, A. L., et al. (2013). "The Double-Edged Sword of Grandiose Narcissism: Implications for Successful and Unsuccessful Leadership Among U.S. Presidents." *Psychological Science*, 24(12): 2379–2389.

Weller, C. (2014). "What's the Difference Between a Sociopath and a Psychopath? (Not Much, But One Might Kill You)." Retrieved from: http://www.medicaldaily.com/whats-difference-between-sociopath-and-psychopath-not-much-one-might-kill-you-270694

Wingfield, N., and Wakabayashi, D. (2017). "What Worries? Big Tech Companies Post Glowing Quarterly Profits." *The New York Times.*

Wolven, K., (2015). "Grandiose and Vulnerable Narcissism: Where Do the Emotional Differences Lie?" Psychology Theses. Aiken, SC: University of South Carolina.

World Health Organization. (1992). *ICD-10 Classification of Mental and Behavioral Disorders: Clinical Descriptions and Diagnostic Guidelines.* Geneva, Switzerland: Author.

Wrosch, A. (1992). "Undue Influence, Involuntary Servitude and Brainwashing: A More Consistent, Interests-cased Approach" Retrieved from: http://digitalcommons.lmu.edu/llr/vol25/iss2/4

Morgan James
Speakers Group

www.TheMorganJamesSpeakersGroup.com

We connect Morgan James published
authors with live and online events
and audiences who will benefit
from their expertise.

CPSIA information can be obtained
at www.ICGtesting.com
Printed in the USA
BVHW071238060519
547457BV00009B/1296/P